D0554582

Harris, Trudier
From mammies to militants

DATE DUE

OEMCO

From Mammies to Militants

Domestics in Black American Literature

From Mammies to Militants

Domestics in Black American Literature

TRUDIER HARRIS

TEMPLE UNIVERSITY PRESS
Philadelphia

Temple University Press, Philadelphia 19122
© 1982 by Temple University. All rights reserved
Published 1982
Printed in the United States of America

Library of Congress Cataloging in Publication Data

Harris, Trudier.
    From mammies to militants.

    Bibliography: p.
    1. American fiction—Afro-American authors—
History and criticism.   2. American fiction—20th
century—History and criticism.   3. Domestics in
literature.   4. Afro-Americans in literature.
5. Women in literature.   I. Title.
PS374.N4H3   1982   813'.009'896073   82-10567
ISBN 0-87722-279-7

For Unareed Harris
and
in Memory of
Terrell Harris, Sr.

ACKNOWLEDGMENTS

I am grateful to many of my colleagues throughout the country who have encouraged me in the completion of this project. Some have written letters of recommendation for grants; others have read portions or all of this manuscript; and still others have simply been there with wagonloads of moral support. Thanks especially to the following persons, each of whom knows the unique value of the laurels bestowed: Martha Reid of Moravian College; Thadious M. Davis, J. Lee Greene, and Louis Rubin, Jr., of the University of North Carolina at Chapel Hill; Frances A. Grimes, formerly of Hampton Institute; Lynn Z. Bloom of the College of William and Mary; Elizabeth Rauh Bethel of Lander College; R. Baxter Miller of the University of Tennessee at Knoxville; and Nathan I. Huggins of Harvard University.

I am especially grateful to Anna Harris McCarthy for helping with the interviewing process and for reading this manuscript many, many times during the summer of 1981.

Two grants from the University Research Council at North Carolina in 1980 and in 1981 aided in my completion of this project, as did a Junior Faculty Development Award during the summer of 1981. Appointment to the Mary Ingraham Bunting Institute at Radcliffe/ Harvard as a Faculty Fellow during 1981–82, with funding from the Carnegie Corporation, gave me the time and space to produce the final version of this manuscript. While I am indebted to all, the ideas reflected in this volume are my own.

CONTENTS

PREFACE

The writers treated in this volume are linked by their portrayals of black women who work as domestics. The terms domestic and maid are used interchangeably throughout this study and do not include all servants or all slaves. Both terms here refer to those black women who leave their homes and families to go to work for white women and their families, and who have responsibility for the practical operation of the white household, including cooking, washing, ironing, cleaning, and child-rearing duties. These domestics can be live-in servants, which means they have small, inconspicuous, sparsely furnished rooms in the homes of the families for whom they work; or they can be day workers, which means they perform most of the household chores for the white women but return home to their own families at the end of the day.[1] Workers in this second category may work for several families, two or three days of the week, or they might work for one family for one or two days a week for an extended period of time stretching into years.[2] Other day workers may go to the same family almost every day of the week and have the same general responsibilities as the live-in workers. The terms also refer to the slave women who worked in the "big houses" as cooks and mammies.

The image of the black woman as domestic is one that more than thirty black writers treat, among them authors as well known as

Charles Waddell Chesnutt, Paul Laurence Dunbar, Mari Evans, Rudolph Fisher, Lorraine Hansberry, Langston Hughes, Kristin Hunter, William Melvin Kelley, John O. Killens, Paule Marshall, Toni Morrison, Ann Petry, Ted Shine, Alice Walker, John A. Williams, Margaret Walker, Douglas Turner Ward, and Richard Wright, and authors as little known as Lorenz Graham and Barbara Woods.

This study considers the position of the domestic in literature by combining folkloristic, sociological, historical, and psychological analyses with the literary ones. Power relationships inherent in the concept of place, that Blacks are always inferior to whites, provide the initial focus in which I view the interactions between black women and their adoptive white families. How does the black woman operate in the white woman's house? How is she made to compromise her own culture to work in another? Does the white world make any concessions at all to who she is? How is her character shaped by prolonged and intimate contact with the white world? Does she take her work, and all its implications, back home with her? Can she, fully, "go home"?

I am also interested in the influence of geography on the portrayal of the black domestic. Do maids pictured in southern settings behave differently from those pictured in northern settings? If so, can the portrayal be related to the background of the writer, or to something inherent in the conception of the particular character? Can mask-wearing or role-playing be relevant, or the myth of the North as a freer environment? Perhaps the tradition of paternalism as a carry-over from slavery produced a unique kind of domestic in the South (or perhaps not). During the Great Migration, many black women came (or were lured) to the North to fill jobs as domestics, bringing the southern cultural and sociological heritage with them: did they respond in new ways to their new and mythic environment? In most instances, the literature reflects a substantial change in the pattern of behavior, a change which probably has geography as its basis. A consideration of how black writers, in their portrayal of character, are shaped by their respective regions will be relevant to answering these questions.

To judge how the truth of history and folklore informs the truth of literature, I have interviewed several black women who are now working or have worked in the homes of whites. Since early 1979, I have talked with black women in Williamsburg, Virginia, in Tusca-loosa, Alabama, and in Chapel Hill, North Carolina, about their jobs as domestics. Results of those interviews have been incorporated into my study. Because the women who work as domestics are usually a part of a group most clearly identified as the black folk community, I assumed that they might circulate specific, formulaic tales about their employers, that they might, as an occupational group, venerate maids as legendary among them as John Henry among steel-driving men. I also thought they might reveal standard, formulaic ways in which their white mistresses tested their honesty or other qualities. Such tales in the folk community could, if they had parallels in the literature, reflect the process by which folk culture influences the shaping of literature, and particularly how black writers have used these sources.

A survey of black women in literature written by black Americans reveals that their paradigmatic effort is to hold on to an essence of self against forces that would stereotype them, force them to conform, or dehumanize them. William Wells Brown's Clotel (1853) is hardly allowed to realize that she has a self; her primary objective is to be a case for the abolition of slavery. Charles Waddell Chesnutt's Rena Walden (1900) is torn among too many selves, while Nella Larsen's Helga Crane (1928) is a chameleon adjusting to other people's conceptions of what it should mean to be a black woman. Zora Neale Hurston's Janie (1937) must combat stereotypes based on age in order to achieve for herself the life she wants, and Toni Morrison's Sula (1974) destroys when self-expression is denied to her. Black women of all classes and stations in the literature thus find themselves fighting just to be. This is especially true of the black women depicted as domestics.

This discussion is limited to detailed studies of eleven works in black American literature in which maids appear as prominent characters. I have selected these works because they show the black women in the homes of whites, interacting with them, or because discussion of the black woman's work as a maid is what provides the central dramatic focus in the work. For example, Charles Waddell Chesnutt's *The Marrow of Tradition* (1901) is treated because Mammy Jane is pictured in the Carteret home taking care of the little white boy, while Lorenz Graham's *South Town* (1958), in which the black woman's work in the white woman's house provides a central incident, is not treated, because the scene is referred to instead of being dramatized within the novel. On the one hand, Douglas Turner Ward's *Happy Ending* (1964) is treated because the discussion of what has happened in the home of the white couple for whom Ellie and Vi work as laundress and maid is *the* substance of the play; on the other hand, Lorraine Hansberry's *A Raisin in the Sun* is not treated because Ruth's and Mama Lena Younger's domestic jobs are mentioned as part of the family's financial plight, but they do not comprise the central dramatic action of the play. Even with these qualifications, however, spatial limitations have still necessitated the exclusion of several works which demand more extensive study from critics of black American literature.[3]

The issue of stereotypes is central to my study. Are maids in the literature presented as individuals or as types? Have the authors manipulated popular stereotypes of maids to make certain points or have they made an effort to create three-dimensional characters and treat them realistically? Most of the black writers who have created maids have had specific, more than artistic, goals in mind for their creations. These goals were frequently dictated by the time periods in which the authors wrote as well as by their degree of commitment to changing the social and political conditions of Blacks in America. One writer might have designed his works to suggest a direction for the economic or social advancement of black people; another might have designed hers to spark political consciousness and black awareness among Blacks. Such obvious goal orientation meant the writers were not as free in their artistic creations as they could have been if they had made the creation of art their primary objective. Chesnutt, for example, was determined to help pave the way for Blacks contemporary with him to gain "recognition and equality" and to level the caste system in America. Born in 1858 and raised in part among the black population of North Carolina, Chesnutt knew first hand the segment of the population from which he drew the characterization of Mammy Jane. He had seen the superstitiousness of Blacks in North Carolina and had complained about it, and he despised the servile "family retainers" who found their way all too often into the popular fiction of his day. A model of successes Blacks could sometimes achieve if they were talented and aggressive, Chesnutt did not suffer those lightly who, like his Mammy Jane, did not take advantage of clear opportunity.

Only minimal changes occurred in the social status of black people between the time of Mammy Jane's portrayal and the portrayal of Mildred in the 1950's. An immediate ancestor of the domestics presented in the works in the 1960's, Mildred is aggressive and self-asserting. During the fifties, in the atmosphere that permitted and developed from the Montgomery bus boycott, Alice Childress's Mildred could challenge all the old limits in her confrontations with her white employers. Like Chesnutt, Childress was conscious of presenting a character whose function went directly beyond the literature. If other domestics could not be as courageous as Mildred in forcing their employers to change, they could at least take heart from Mildred's adventures.

The sometimes fantastic nature of the incidents Mildred recounts gave way to some equally fantastic occurrences in the works of playwrights and other writers from the 1960's and 1970's. Yet there was enough probability in what Mildred presented to cause reflection beyond the initial incredulity. No less is that true of characters in works such as *Happy Ending* and *Contribution*. These works, and others contemporary with them, were clearly designed to encourage Blacks to do something about their powerless conditions, politely if possible, violently if necessary. Messages more urgent than those presented by Mildred or that to be derived from Mammy Jane took primary importance over characters. John A. Williams, Douglas Turner Ward, Barbara Woods, Ted Shine, and Ed Bullins are all community-oriented in their works, and their domestics are all thus manipulated in the interest of political statements they want to make. The intensity of the political statement in each work affects the degree of realistic portraiture. Mrs. Grace Love's facade in Shine's *Contribution*, for example, might be probable, but Bullins's Mamie Lee King is more for audience identification than a "true," realistic portrait of what a maid in her position would have done.

The commitment of these writers to bettering conditions for black people in this country transcends their particular social backgrounds as well as their geographical origins. Their sharing of artistic goals in treating southern and northern maids does not reflect a similar

geographical distinction which leads from the writers to the characters they created. Alice Childress, for example, was born in South
Carolina and spent time there before moving to New York. Yet
Mildred stretches even the northern mold to its limits. Douglas
Turner Ward, born in Louisiana, adopts the mask of the true southern maids to his characters in Harlem only to undercut that mask and
their southernness. John A. Williams, in addition to dealing with
questions of class and status, is intent on reflecting his own biography, the fact that his mother worked as a maid; therefore, what he has
to say about maids is informed by those experiences and an indi-
vidualized, painful response to the type of the domestic. William
Melvin Kelley, in satirizing middle-class urban white America, uses
his maid as a fixture, an expected accompaniment to the status
towards which he levels his criticisms; geography does not clearly
dictate to him. Ann Petry, who realized that her novel would be
considered a "problem novel," wanted nevertheless to identify those
forces both within and outside the black community which were and
are responsible for its stagnation and its possible destruction; the
characterization of her maid cannot therefore be attributed solely to
her northernness.

In determining their goals as writers in the specific portrayals of
the black domestics presented here, the majority of the black writers
studied recognize bonds which tie them to the black community at
large. They therefore respond to what they see as specific needs in
that community. By maintaining close connections, indeed a spiritual affinity, to the popular and folk communities in which they share
a heritage, they illustrate, through their portrayals of black domestics, that the line between art and politics is ever a fine one.

From Mammies to Militants

Domestics in Black American Literature

CHAPTER ONE

ON MAIDS:
Historical Background and General Characteristics

"Domestic workers have done a awful lot of good things in this country besides clean up peoples' houses," says Alice Childress's Mildred in *Like One of the Family . . . Conversations from a Domestic's Life* (1956). "We've taken care of our brothers and fathers and husbands when the factory gates and office desks and pretty near everything else was closed to them; we've helped many a neighbor, doin' everything from helpin' to clothe their children to buryin' the dead. . . . And it's a rare thing for anybody to find a colored family in this land that can't trace a domestic worker somewhere in their history. . . ."[1] This astute observation underscores the importance of the domestic to black history as well as to black American literature, yet the black domestics who have gone quietly about their lives, supporting their families and buttressing a culture, have been considered too common for unusual notice in the histories and too merely elements of background or local color for treatment in literary criticism. Nonetheless, the central position black domestics have occupied in black life, as Mildred maintains, is one which demands more than passing notice. And Childress's memorable Mildred is a witness that the image of the black woman as domestic deserves consideration, along with other, more discussed images, in the criticism of literary portrayals of the black experience in America.

Whether victims of sexual exploitation during slavery, or tragic

mulattoes who tried to escape their blackness by passing, or extremely dark-skinned black women who suffered inter- and intra-
racial prejudice, or matriarchs, or welfare recipients, or the new
super black women of the 1960's, black women have been treated as
types. Maya Angelou summarizes the easy evaluations and categori-
zations of black women in America thus: "Called Matriarch, Emascu-
lator and Hot Momma. Sometimes Sister, Pretty Baby, Auntie,
Mammy and Girl. Called Unwed Mother, Welfare Recipient and
Inner City Consumer. The Black American Woman has had to admit
that while nobody knew the troubles she saw, everybody, his brother
and his dog, felt qualified to explain her, even to herself."[2] Angelou's
comment writes the labels under those historical and sociological
cubbyholes into which living black women have been shoved, cubbyholes into which they have also been thrust in literature and in
criticism. The categories, whether raw slander or shoddy attempts at
truth, leave little room—as Angelou recognizes—for realistic indi-
vidualistic treatment of black women. Once the slots have been
determined, more expansive concepts of character are inevitably
ignored. And surprisingly, one of the roles in which the black female
character may be displayed in significant complexity—that of domestic, maid, or worker in the white woman's house—is often missing
from listings of types.

But its integral place in black American experience suggests that
the role or image of the black woman as domestic is the basic
historical conception from which other images and stereotypes have
grown. Dependency on service pans, the name for leftover food
domestic workers were given to take home to their families, foreshadows the dependency of welfare, for certainly that paternalistic
phenomenon influenced social expectations. Sexual exploitation of
the maid by the employer's husband, which is a direct extension of
slavery, perhaps contributed its share to the stereotyped images of
the black woman as hot momma or unwed mother. And the parallels
continue. Thus an understanding of the relationship between mistress and maid explains, in part, other images of black women in the
popular imagination as well as in literature.

The image of the maid is certainly one with which the majority of
black women can identify and empathize, and it is one with which
many Blacks have personal ties. A large percentage of Blacks in the

current generation who are doctors of philosophy or medical doctors or lawyers—or writers—are so because black women in their pasts scrubbed floors or washed or cooked for whites. Some have worked at such jobs themselves: Childress, for example, may be described as a domestic turned playwright, actress, and novelist, having worked as a maid before her successful theatrical performances and before her writing successes. In her quickness to point out that she had worked as a maid because that was the only work available to her, Childress may be contrasted with Zora Neale Hurston, who, in her declining years, worked as a maid on Rivo Island in Miami, Florida. Hurston maintained, in one explanation, that she was gathering material to begin a national magazine "for and by domestics" when the fact was, as Robert Hemenway points out in his biography of her, she was desperate for money and had turned to the one job which had always been available to black women.[3] Suggestively, then—in spite of the different ways they accounted for the fact—both Hurston and Childress, successful black authors, knew first-hand what the domestic's life was like. Childress incorporated her own experiences with information she received from domestics around the country in the mistress/maid relationships she describes in *Like One of the Family*.[4] Other black women I have interviewed in the past two years, women who are public school teachers and university professors, tell of having worked as maids during their college years in the 1950's or 1960's, when they saw the jobs as media by which they could pay for essentials such as tuition or obtain the extra spending money that scholarships did not offer. They recognized that the combination of paternalism and appreciation with which the white women would view them would be, under the circumstances, more useful than not.

Some of the college girls who worked as maids discovered that a husband's interest in the "sweet young thing" who had entered his home could also be used to advantage. They maneuvered around advances when they could, either by making sure that the man's wife was at home when they went to work or by leaving quickly if she were not. But their commitment was to education, not to their jobs or their mistresses. If a husband's attraction subsidized that commitment, there was no reason for complaint: thus it came about that the goal in many instances came to be to exploit the man's sexual interest without actually ending up in bed. If playful promises could net an extra ten or twenty dollars for the black coed of those days, that was certainly a solid addition to her college finances. This particular pattern of mutual exploitation is also depicted in the literature. In Alice Walker's *Meridian* (1976), the title character works for a slightly perverted bachelor professor in order to supplement her meagre student's income. She takes advantage of the professor's sexual interest in her and, since he is beyond the age of any real sexual capacity, feels relatively safe in allowing herself to be caught when he chases her around his office. In exchange for being caught, she gets raisins, Fig Newtons, Cokes, tuna, mints, Baby Ruths, and dime-store combs to take back to her room to share with her roommate. She also gets typing paper and enough money to buy a *good* (her emphasis) tennis racket.[5] "The truth was, her scholarship did not cover all her school expenses and her other needs, too. The truth *was* she depended on the extras Mr. Raymonds gave her. Every Coke, every cookie, every can of deviled ham, every tennis racket that he gave her meant one less that she had to buy" (p. 107). The professor is black, but the literary scene depicted evokes comparison to historical college girl/maid–master relationships.

Not only have black college women worked as domestics during their college years, both in life and in literature; both in life and literature they have often found that that was the only work available to them once they were out of college. Just as Fenton Johnson's scarlet woman in "The Scarlet Woman" (1916) finds herself with a college ("white girl's") education and nothing to do with it, so historically did many Blacks discover that they had to readjust their expectations of what they could do after they had attended college. Three such cases are presented by David Katzman in *Seven Days A Week: Women and Domestic Service in Industrializing America*.[6] Toni Morrison's First Corinthians in *Song of Solomon* (1977) is another good example from the literature: Corinthians spends three years in college, with a junior year in France ("Bryn Mawr in 1940. France in 1939"),[7] only to discover that work she had imagined was available to her was not. "Her education had taught her how to be an enlightened mother and wife, able to contribute to the civilization—or in her case, the civilizing—of her community. And if marriage was not achieved, there were alternative roles: teacher, librarian, or . . . well, something intelligent and public-spirited" (pp.

188–189). When, after years of waiting, no such marriage or job emerges, she goes to work as a maid. Her family, and especially her mother, are unaware of the work she does. She deliberately exaggerates her position. She tells her mother that she is Michael-Mary Graham's "amanuensis," a "rickety Latin word," Morrison says, which made the work "sound intricate, demanding, and totally in keeping with her education" (p. 188). When she looks for work, Corinthians finds that she has no skills, for "Bryn Mawr had done what a four-year dose of liberal education was designed to do: unfit her for eighty percent of the useful work of the world. . . . After graduation she returned to a work world in which colored girls, regardless of their background, were in demand for one and only one kind of work" (p. 190). Corinthians started work as a maid in 1961, approximately twenty-one years after she had graduated from college. Morrison comments on her attitude toward her work and toward her fellow workers:

> She avoided the other maids on the street, and those whom she saw regularly on the bus assumed that she had some higher household position than theirs since she came to work in high-heeled shoes and only a woman who didn't have to be on her feet all day could stand the pressure of heels on the long ride home. Corinthians was careful; she carried no shopping bag of shoes, aprons, or uniforms. Instead she had a book. A small gray book on which *Contes de Daudet* was printed in gold lettering on its cover. Once she was inside Miss Graham's house she changed into her uniform (which was a discreet blue anyway, not white) and put on a pair of loafers before she dropped to her knees with the pail of soapy water (pp. 190–191).

Attitude is the most obvious thing that separates Corinthians from the black women who may have dropped out of school after the second grade. Corinthians is careful never to convey to her employer that she has a college education. And such care is, ironically, unnecessary, for the woman is more interested in having a maid than in knowing that maid's personal history.

Obviously, then, literature grows out of life; and obviously, too, knowledge about black domestics is so pervasive in black life and culture that Blacks who read such literary works automatically bring to them information with which they can offer immediate responses. The exchange approximates that which occurs between a folk story-teller and his audience; readers of tales of domestics, like the listeners in the folk audience, can respond with appreciation, dismay, skepticism, or agreement which stems from their own knowledge of the drama/tale that is unfolding before them. There is a reflective, complementary relationship between the world represented by history and folklore, and that of novels and dramas. The fact of that relationship is its own justification.

Because domestic work has been the job most consistently available to black women in this country, the history of black women is in part the history of the development of the domestic's job. David Katzman treats that development, pointing out that, prior to the early twentieth century, black domestics were concentrated in the South. In other parts of the country, white immigrant live-in workers provided the normal domestic service. By the 1920's, Katzman maintains, technological advances had limited severely the need for live-in workers and restrictions on immigration had limited immigrant access to the United States.[8] World War I had made it possible for women to pursue varying kinds of jobs. More women enrolled in colleges in search of opportunities to lead lives more expansive than those they would have had otherwise, as wives and mothers—or domestic servants. The drudgery of housework, therefore, was abandoned for more profitable and stimulating work by a large percentage of those free to do so. In percentages, black women formed the largest group who did not benefit by these changes. They migrated North and moved into the domestic positions once held by German and Irish immigrants.

This blackening of the domestic work force in the East, the North, and the West seemed conspicuous because such jobs were now taken into statistical account. They were clearly identified as jobs for which one received at least minimum compensation. The actual fact of black women's involvement in domestic work, as Katzman recognizes, did not blossom suddenly forth in the twentieth century. The majority of black women who worked had been domestics from the days of slavery. According to Elizabeth Almquist, options for black women after slavery were as clear as they were limited. "Nearly all black women who were not involved in farming became domestic workers.

They cooked, cleaned, and tended children in the same households where they had formerly worked as slaves. Black women had virtually no options other than domestic service in either the South or the North."[9] The trend continued into the twentieth century, with fifty-seven percent of black women being "unskilled laborers, service workers, or private household workers" in 1910.[10] Custom and informal arrangements where old clothes or food sufficed instead of or in addition to wages was a generally accepted pattern in the South, one which extended to other parts of the country as black women moved there to work.[11] As black women moved North around the turn of the century, they formed, Katzman declares, an "urban servant population" and succeeded "in shifting domestic work from a live-in to a live-out occupation." On southern soil prior to the twentieth century, however, " 'domestic servant' was synonymous with 'black woman.' "

What black women were able to do was determined in large part by what black men were able to do. Ray Marshall points out in *The Negro Worker* that:

> the main occupations open to Negroes after Reconstruction were those which were regarded as 'Negro' jobs (which were, by definition, hot, dirty, or otherwise disagreeable), those for which they were trained as slaves, or occupations which served the Negro communities. Racial job patterns had a strong caste element about them. Slavery and color marked the Negro as an inferior person; therefore, whites considered it improper for Negroes to compete directly with them for the better jobs. It was especially unthinkable that Negroes should hold supervisory positions over whites.[12]

Custom thus combined with law and other factors to ensure the low employment status of Blacks. "The lack of education and training prevented entrance to the professions for both black men and women, and much industrial employment was for men only. Therefore black women had little choice but to accept private household work. The treatment of male workers in both the North and South meant that most black women had to work and this in turn created a never-ending supply of women for domestic employment. Consequently employers could treat black maids and cooks however they wished."[13] And they wished to keep wages low, to keep maids isolated in the individual white homes so they would be less tempted to try to bring any union-inspired structure into the employer/employee relationship. While a maid may have addressed her employer as Mrs. White, and was expected to know and keep her place, that was as much formality as was allowed into the relationship.

The informal relationship which existed between mistress and maid, which made working hours irregular and wages discretionary, meant that many black women who worked as domestics would never be recognized by statisticians as having jobs, a fact which highlighted the inconsistencies in the working relationship. On the one hand, an arrangement by which a woman might one day spend three hours on a week's wash or two hours cooking dinner is not comparable to the exploitative live-in arrangement Katzman describes as commonly having been the lot of immigrant domestics.[14] On the other hand, emotional stress and financial exploitation might have been comparable. To whom could the black woman complain if she were forced to leave her children alone for two hours to cook dinner for a white woman, or if she received fifty cents instead of a promised two dollars for the work she did? Since control of time, wages, and work was solely in the hands of the white woman, black women were essentially alone in the hiring and firing process. They did not have an immigration office to place them or a church or relatives as sponsors. As Gerda Lerner points out in *Black Women in White America*, black maids have had few unions—all of them of short longevity—and no lobbying groups. She comments that "domestic workers have been one of the most difficult groups of workers to organize." She attributes this to "the individual nature of the work, the isolation of the workers from one another, their low economic and social status and the intense competition among them. . . ." Still, "there have," Lerner continues, "been various attempts made at organizing domestic workers. In 1920, there were ten locals of domestic workers in Southern cities affiliated with the Hotel and Restaurant Employees Union, AFL. In 1936, a domestic Workers' Union started by seven women in Washington, D.C., had over a hundred members one year later and had succeeded in raising the prevailing wage from $3 to $10 a week. . . . The most ambitious organizing effort was that headed by Dora Jones, the black executive secretary of the Domestic Workers' Union, which was founded in 1934 and was affiliated with the Building Service Union, Local 149, in New York City. Five years later the organization had 350 members, 75 percent of them black women."[15] Union wages were certainly an improvement, but even they did not vary substantially, at the lower end of the scale, from wages received in the deep South by non-union domestic workers. Women with whom I talked in Tuscaloosa, Alabama, recalled receiving $2.50 a week during the thirties.[16]

Competition created by widespread poverty and a dogged determination to survive encouraged many black women in the South to walk the streets of white neighborhoods in hopes of finding work. Attacks from dogs or insults from whites were only two of the possible consequences of such daring. A potential worker could quickly discover that she had encroached upon territory already staked out by another woman like herself, and she could suffer verbal abuse for being "underhanded." But seeking domestic jobs, especially in the 1930's, was particularly dehumanizing for women in the North. The misery of it was captured in an article entitled "The Bronx Slave Market":

> Any corner in the congested sections of New York City's Bronx is fertile soil for mushroom "slave marts.". . . As early as 8 a.m. they come; as late as 1 p.m. they remain. Rain or shine, cold or hot, you will find them there—Negro women, old and young—sometimes bedraggled, sometimes neatly dressed—but with the invariable paper bundle [containing a uniform], waiting expectantly for Bronx housewives to buy their strength and energy for an hour, two hours, or even for a day at the munificent rate of fifteen, twenty, twenty-five, or, if luck be with them, thirty cents an hour. If not the wives themselves, maybe their husbands, their sons, or their brothers, under the subterfuge of work, offer worldly-wise girls higher bids for their time. . . . Fortunate, indeed, is she who gets the full hourly rate promised. Often, her day's slavery is rewarded with a single dollar bill or whatever her unscrupulous employer pleases to pay. More often, the clock is set back for an hour or more. Too often she is sent away without any pay at all.[17]

Such experiences teach any black woman who goes to work as a maid to a white family that to them her role is more important than she is: she should cook, clean, take care of the children—and be invisible or self-effacing, especially when guests arrive but generally as well. Katzman comments on this last expectation:

> One peculiar and most degrading aspect of domestic service was the requisite of invisibility. The ideal servant as servant (as opposed to servant as a status symbol for the employer) would be invisible and silent, responsive to demands but deaf to gossip, household chatter, and conflicts, attentive to the needs of mistress and master but blind to their faults, sensitive to the moods and whims of those around them but undemanding of family warmth, love, or security. Only blacks could be invisible people in white homes. It was even common for whites to discuss the inferiority of blacks in front of their black servants.[18]

The family may also discuss its most troubling affairs and assume that the entity which serves dinner is unthinking, incapable of communicating family secrets beyond the dining room walls. To them, a maid in her role of invisibility is certainly not someone who would make trouble, who would upset the status quo. And to a large extent they are right. Maids, historically, have not been a source of disturbance as far as race relations or employer/employee relations are concerned. This historical lack of organized agitation is also reflected in the literature in which black writers portray black live-in workers and day workers, each of whom finds herself alone in her efforts to find and keep her jobs in the homes of whites.

Preconceived notions about their place and function usually force maids to conform, in reality or through dissembling, to the cubbyholes that have been predetermined for them. Just as cleaning and cooking are expected, so too is a certain physical appearance. The maid is expected, for example, as was First Corinthians, to wear a uniform, which, aside from its practical functions, symbolically negates individuality. When the black woman takes off the clothes in which she has ridden the train or bus to her job and puts on that uniform, she becomes THE MAID, not somebody's mother or sister or wife. Her primary function is to serve the needs of the family which has thus defined her. Although she may make minor changes in the definition from one family to the next, basic expectations remain essentially the same.[19]

Uniforms are less worn by maids today, but at one time they, or some other depersonalizing dress, were standard.[20] A maid was required to look as if she were subservient to the white family, and especially to the white mistress, in both dress and demeanor. As Maggie Holmes, a domestic whom Studs Terkel interviewed, pointed out: "You can't go to work dressed like they do, 'cause they think you're not working—like you should get dirty, at least. They don't say what kind of uniform, just say uniform. This is in case anybody come in, the black be workin'. They don't want you walkin' around dressed up, lookin' like them. They asks you sometimes, 'Don't you have somethin' else to put on?' "[21] First Corinthians was able to wear heels and a dress to work because the woman she worked for was a pretentious, eccentric poet; Corinthians' dress and uppity manners "gave her house the foreign air she liked to affect, for she was the core, the very heartbeat, of the city's literary world" (p. 191). Other maids from the literature, however, quietly acquiesced to the submerging of their personalities in the uniform. Consider the attitude of Carrie Johnson, in Marian Minus's "Girl, Colored" (1940), a maid who understands perfectly the position of the domestic and does not attempt to romanticize that position: ". . . Carrie gave her attention to the neat brown paper bundle in her lap. . . . It held her stiffly starched white work dress, a pair of comfortable shoes. . . ."[22]

No maid could expect to keep a job if she appeared for it in her Sunday-go-to-meeting dress or if she arrived for an interview with luscious curls, lipstick, and beautifully manicured nails. The message conveyed by that personal fastidiousness would be that the black woman was stepping out of her predetermined place. It would also raise stereotypical questions about motives. Why should such a good-looking black woman seek a job as a maid? Might she just want to get into a position to engage in hanky-panky with the white master and thereby acquire a lover who might assist her financially?

Any black woman who works as a maid, therefore, probably understands the social, psychological, and historical forces which shape a reaction to her. She understands how she must maneuver in the home of the white family in order to salvage what portion of dignity she can, to resist depersonalization and dehumanization, and to exert a small amount of control within her confined space. To survive with dignity, she must learn that, although they may be constrained, her responses need not be pedestrian. Many maids in the literature boringly acquiesce to the whites, but several others realize that caged birds can do more than fly a straight path back and forth across their cages.

In moving from her home to that of the white woman, the black woman connects two racially and spatially distinct worlds in one direction—she goes into the white world. And here begin the complex ironies of consideration, as Alice Childress playfully but seriously suggests, as "one of the family." Of the many elements which govern the black domestic's interaction with the white world, space—with its implications both physical and cultural—is perhaps the foremost. The black woman is presumably at home in her own environment; but when she enters the white woman's kitchen, she moves into a culture which is at least apart from her own, if not alien or openly hostile. Black town and white town, as portrayed by James Baldwin and Jean Toomer, have metaphorical connotations as well as physical dimensions. When the black woman goes into the white world, she initiates compromise: when she immerses herself in the white culture, she loses the psychological security derived from familiar surroundings and must make adjustments accordingly.

Once the black woman leaves the black community, she will encounter cultural differences which suggest that she can no longer be completely, comfortably, at home. She must make some kind of change in the way she acts, which amounts to a compromise of some sort. Even if she "loves the white folks to death," the possibility is that she is different in her affection from that she shows when she is at home in her own community. The change or compromise can therefore be an intensification or exaggeration of traits or emotions that are already inherent in her basic personality, or it can mean adoption of modes of behavior totally different from what is usual with her. Whether the black woman is at one with the white world or opposed to it, a form of compromise, either positive or negative from her point of view, is at the heart of the change she makes.

Moving from black town to white town might be but a matter of blocks or a long bus ride, but in either case the spatial dividing line is apparent. Studs Terkel makes the fact of the two "towns" vivid in his discussion of black domestic workers in Chicago. His informant notes that most of her jobs were " 'way out in the suburbs. You get a bus and you ride till you get a subway. After you gets to Howard [a boundary line], you gets the El. If you get to the end of the line and there's no bus, they pick you up.' . . . A commonly observed phenomenon: during the early evening hour, trains, crowded, predominantly by young white men carrying attaché cases, pass trains headed in the opposite direction, crowded, predominantly by middle-aged black women carrying brown paper bags. Neither group, it appears, glances at the other."[23] A parallel division is apparent within the home of the white woman for whom the black woman works. The most comfortable realm of the latter's existence is the kitchen; it becomes the black town, the nigger room, of the white house. The black woman cleans the living room or the dining room or the bedroom or the bathroom and retires to the kitchen. She sits in the kitchen when she has time for sitting and there requests that she go to other parts of the house come to her. There the black woman must meet and greet anyone who comes looking for her, as in Kelley's *dem* (1964). There relatives must come to visit wife or mother, as in Toni Morrison's *The Bluest Eye* (1970) or John A. Williams's "Son in the Afternoon" (1962). Certainly the kitchen is the "natural" place for the domestic to be, for surely cooking is a major and time-consuming duty. But the kitchen is also the one room in the house where the white woman can give up spatial ownership without compromising herself. Kitchens have connotations of hard work and meniality— sweat, grime, broken fingernails, and other things from which the mistress wishes to dissociate herself. Passing *that particular* space on to the domestic is a royal decree of her subservience and inferiority.

Since work *must* be done, making the kitchen the nigger room is not the ultimate compromise for the white woman. After all, she, her husband, or her children can psychologically reclaim the territory at any moment. When the white woman enters the kitchen and the black woman is present, physical space is dominated by psychological space. The black woman must grovel in her own "house," or at least recognize that she cannot set the rules even there. *Backstairs at the White House*, which was run as a television mini-series in 1979, vividly illustrated this point. Liberal Mrs. Roosevelt wanted Maggie Rogers, first maid at the White House, to supervise personally the preparation of food for Mrs. Chiang. In a scene in the kitchen, Mrs.

Roosevelt requests that Maggie sit while they plan menus together. The viewer can see in Maggie's hesitant movements the history of a tradition of place. Black domestics do not sit in the presence of white women, and especially not the First Lady—even in the kitchen. Although Maggie is coaxed eventually into sitting, the scene nevertheless illustrates much about traditional roles, place, and reclaiming of space by the white mistress when that becomes necessary.[24]

The concept of physical space—and its attendant psychological implications—has as its basis the broad concept of place for all Blacks. Place can refer to status, to physical location, or to both. Status encompasses the sense of place slaves very quickly learned was expected of them; status and physical location include the sense of place the sharecropper landlord consigned to his black tenants, as well as the sense of place the Blacks on southern buses were taught was theirs. Place in any context espouses the hierarchy of masters and slaves, owners and owned, privileged and non-privileged. As an inheritor of this unpleasant tradition, the black woman who works as a domestic, and who knows her place as the whites define it, either the physical location of the kitchen or the status of inferiority, can make one of several choices. She can wear a mask, or she can repress herself and her culture completely, or she can suffer the neuroses and practical penalties that result from the inability to mask or to suppress the self.

Mask-wearing as a mode of survival among Blacks is as old as slavery in this country. A slave who did not tell whites that slavery was enjoyable, Frederick Douglass warned, might find himself sold down the river into the harsh plantations of Alabama or Louisiana. And we have seen how black women in college used masks to their advantage in their temporary jobs as domestics. The professional black domestic, just as she has her heritage of an externally defined sense of place, also has the historical mechanism for dealing with that definition. She can bow and scrape and say "yes-um" until eternity if she separates the circumstances of her existence in the white woman's house from her conception of herself. If she maintains her cultural reference and believes in that reality, then the impositions that are made upon her will have less of a traumatic effect. She must manipulate a mask carefully and consciously, separating the illusion she creates from reality, or she might be overwhelmed by the loss of a cultural identity. The two domestics in Douglas Turner Ward's

Happy Ending (1964) are perfect examples of black women who know precisely who and what they are, and who can work as maids without significant psychological damage to themselves. They are in control of their masks. Any compromise effected as a result of their work as domestics is distinctly to their advantage, whether in the accumulation of material goods or in pleasure derived from the power of successful trickery.

To lose cultural identity, however, or to suppress the self, is another possible compromise. This can happen to the domestic who loses all sense of a black self and adopts the culture into which she moves, the one who concludes that white is indeed right and that it is correct to oppress Blacks. She may seek to emulate the white world's pursuit of the American Dream and suffer an attendant corruption of her own values, as Lutie Johnson does in *The Street* (1946), or she may judge her own family by the standards of the whites, as Granny Huggs does in *God Bless the Child* (1964). Or, the identification with whites may be intense escapism, as it is with Pauline Breedlove in *The Bluest Eye* (1970). Because she does not have pretty things at home to delight in arranging, Pauline takes exquisite pleasure in tending the possessions of her white employer. Because she sees only ugliness and dirt at home, she revels in the primness and cleanliness of the white house in which she works. Her work for whites becomes an elaborate form of self-hatred; she attempts to escape herself and her culture by identifying with those who hate her and her kind.

Other domestics cannot identify with those who exploit their labor and demean them; nor can they wear the mask successfully. The form of compromise they must effect is ultimately more destructive than either of the other two. The domestic in this last instance becomes a perennial fence walker, an inhabitant in a psychological and cultural vacuum. She cannot identify with whites because her own history is constantly before her. She cannot wear the mask because anger prevents emotional control of it. Still, she needs a job. Psychological frustration is her only constant; she can end by beating her children or, though basically non-violent, killing those for whom she works. Perhaps Barbara Woods's Rosa in "The Final Supper" (1970) would best exemplify these women.

A domestic may, then, cope with spatial and psychological limitations and conflicts in a number of ways. How she compromises determines, in part, how she interacts, on a daily basis, with the whites with whom she comes into contact—how she reacts, for example, to some of the stereotypes Angelou notes. Richard Wright's "Man of All Work," Carl, goes to work as maid to a white family when his wife becomes ill; dressed as a woman, he is subjected to numerous sexual advances from the family's drunken husband and father. Because Carl has a clear notion of what he wants out of the job, however, he is able to make adjustments and, at least for a time, evade the advances without alienating his white employer.

Since the white mistress controls wages, the black woman must maneuver between defiance and self-preserving acquiescence. In one scene in *The Bluest Eye* (1970), Pauline Breedlove is told that she will receive her wages only if she leaves her drunken husband. If Pauline refuses to comply, no money will change hands, which is perhaps the state of affairs the mistress prefers. Traditionally, real wages are usually meagre; supplemental wages, in the form of food and cast-off clothing, are more plentiful. The useless items, such as decorative bowls, that Granny Huggs brings home in *God Bless the Child* (1964) serve to illustrate the point. And Maggie brought home so much duck in *Backstairs at the White House* that her family balked at eating it. The incongruity of living in a tiny walk-up apartment, barely able to pay rent or installments on a refrigerator, and eating duck, is grossly absurd. Nonetheless, such handouts, or "service pans," are considered additional benefits of the job.[25] These "benefits" are partly designed to discourage petitions for wage increases. After all, the black woman who works for the white family should be pleased with the privilege of working for them, the white woman's thoughts probably run. To request more money is to be ungrateful and uppity. It means stepping out of place, trying to be more white and equal. Surely niggers don't need *that* much money to live on. Besides, they're probably stealing everything they can escape with comfortably anyway.

The stereotyped notion that black domestics will steal is pervasive among white mistresses. Many are the tales, for example, of black domestics whose honesty has been tested by the white mistress who leaves bills and coins where the black woman must clean. One woman identified a common pattern: "I had them put money down and pretend they can't find it and have me look for it. I worked for one, she had dropped ten dollars on the floor, and I was sweepin' and

I'm glad I seen it, because if I had put that sweeper on it, she coulda said I got it. I had to push the couch back and the ten dollars was there. Oh, I had 'em, when you go to dust, they put something . . . to test you."[26] Inherent in the action of the mistress is her belief that the maid will steal. Alice Childress treats this stereotyped idea in her conversation, "The Pocketbook Game," which appears in *Like One of the Family* (1956). Mildred is talking with her friend Marge, who is also a domestic; she tells of watching Mrs. E, her white employer, clutching her purse the entire time Mildred is cleaning. Sensitive to the implication of light-handedness, she gets an opportunity to turn the tables when Mrs. E asks her to get the super to fix a kitchen faucet. Mildred goes into the hallway, stands for a few minutes, and does the following:

> . . . I rushed back to the door and knocked on it as hard and frantic as I could. She flung open the door sayin', "What's the matter? Did you see the super?" . . . "No," I says, gaspin' hard for breath, "I was almost downstairs when I remembered . . . *I left my pocketbook!*"
>
> With that I dashed in, grabbed my purse and then went down to get the super! Later, when I was leavin' she says real timid-like, "Mildred, I hope that you don't think I distrust you because . . ." I cut her off real quick. . . . "That's all right, Mrs. E. . . , I understand. 'Cause if I paid anybody as little as you pay me, I'd hold my pocketbook too!" (p. 27).

In her relationship to the white woman, Mildred has been able to score a moral victory over Mrs. E., who exploits labor done by Blacks without consideration for black human beings. Mildred, in confronting the stereotype that Blacks will inevitably steal if tempted, has also been able to negate another stereotype—that of the intellectually dull, naturally submissive black domestic who cannot perceive or fails to resent the insulting insinuations of her white employer.

When the mistress suspects or accuses the black woman of theft, it reveals more about her than she is aware. An accusation of theft from the white mistress presupposes her awareness of some injustice in the relationship between maid and employer. Only by putting herself in the place of the maid (if only momentarily) can the white woman really feel that unfairness and injustice and, therefore, gauge the potential for stealing that might result. "If I were paid so poorly for that much work," the white employer essentially says, unconsciously, "I would retaliate by taking enough to close the gap between actual compensation and real work." Recognizing how guilty she would be, were their relationship reversed, the white mistress projects wrongdoing onto the maid.

Certainly, too, the maid recognizes the injustices. She does not necessarily act (steal), however, to correct that wrong. The things she could appropriate, even if she were inclined to do so, such as a pie or a few dollars or a hand-me-down dress, cannot possibly compensate for the physical deterioration of the body—specifically for the bad backs and feet, and varicose veins—that will inevitably result from a maid's hard work. Nor can it possibly alleviate the psychological stress of working with someone who considers her less than fully human.

The mistress, of course, never verbalizes these recognitions and neither does the maid. In fact, what is left unstated between them forms the basis of the ethical code that governs the relationships between Blacks and whites, especially in the South. What happens between mistress and maid conforms to rules as strict as those defined by Richard Wright in "The Ethics of Living Jim Crow," rules established by Southern tradition and sanctified by custom and law. The mistress does not expect the maid to be demanding, but the maid expects that of the mistress. The mistress expects the maid to accept all hand-me-downs and service pans; the maid knows she is expected to accept these things and does so. The mistress thinks the maid will steal; the maid knows that and is therefore very careful to leave bills and coins precisely where she finds them. The mistress expects the maid to be a good mammy simply because, she believes, it's in her blood; the maid knows she is expected to give expert care to the mistress's children and neglects her own in order to be the ideal servant. The mistress believes that, however motherly her maid, a lascivious black wench lurks just beneath her bland exterior. The maid knows the mistress thinks she is a hot momma and tries to be reassuringly invisible and self-effacing. That some of these notions contradict others does not affect mistress or maid, although the maid may certainly see some points of irony: "When they say about the neighborhood we live in is dirty, why do they ask me to come and clean their house? We, the people in the slums, the same nasty women they have come to their house in the suburbs every day. If these women are so filthy, why you want them to clean for you? They don't go and clean for us. We go and clean for them."[27] Such contradictions are the way things are. The pattern was handed down from slavery and the majority of mistresses and maids are not inclined to alter it. But there have been a few iconoclasts, in art as in life. Between 1901 and 1977, some literary maids broke the mold shaped by southern attitudes and managed to bring new life to the worn portrayal of the domestic.

CHAPTER TWO

ON SOUTHERN
AND NORTHERN MAIDS:
Geography, Mammies,
and Militants

In the progression from mammies to militants, three stages must be considered. The political or apolitical position the maid finds herself in and the attitudes she holds toward her job and toward herself grow in part out of the knowledge that she is on either northern or southern ground, North and South having meant very different things to Blacks historically, in respect to freedom and confinement. Thus true southern maids epitomize mammyism; transitional or moderate figures wear masks evoking the true southern maid; and militants wear southern masks only to bring about violence or never wear them—instead confronting exploitation directly.

Maids who are described as being truly southern are, then, those who generally acquiesce in the paternalistic and place-defined relationship between mistress and maid as it has been shaped by the attitudes and traditions of southern society. Whether on northern or southern soil, they generally make few, if any, claims of dignity and self-worth within the established employer/employee relationship. They are more likely than the others to be "ideal servants," the mammy figures traditionally identified with southern plantation households. These women usually compromise everything of themselves and of their connections to the black community in order to exist in the white world.

Transitional maids, or the moderates in the progression from mammies to militants, are those black women who realize that straightforward political action, such as demanding fair wages, striking against their employers, or asserting their blackness on their jobs, is unavailable to them yet refuse to merge their personalities completely with those of the white women for whom they work. The transitional maids, therefore, are the ones who will readily adopt masks, rebelling covertly like Brer Rabbit against the world which would dehumanize them. They may take food for their families, but their subversive actions are generally small and contained; they are never overtly militant. On southern soil they are seemingly just as acquiescent as the true southern maid; but whether on northern or southern soil they recognize an amount of suffering and deprivation within the black community that the true southern maid fails to see, and they are able to see the white community as partially responsible for such suffering. Though economic necessity teaches them to curb their yearning to rebel overtly, these women, not mammies and not yet militants, identify more with the black world than with the white.

The militants, usually northern maids pictured in northern settings, carry with them the almost mythical belief that the North is a freer place for black people. That faith encourages them to talk back, to be defiant in reaction to the sixteen-hour days their mistresses may want to squeeze into eight, to assert themselves whenever possible. They refuse to stay in the kitchen; they refuse to be silent; they refuse to recognize the power of any external force to shape their identities and redefine their cultural values. They will resort to violence when necessary to preserve their senses of self and the communities of which they are a part. Their ultimate act of violation against the place to which they have been confined and the injustices they have suffered is to return to the South and encourage violence there. Northern, militant maids are like true southern maids only in skin color.

The true southern maid is the mammy whose ineffective compromise in the home of the white mistress causes her to identify completely with the status quo; she believes within her heart in the rightness of the established order of which she is a part. She has lost her black cultural identity (*if* she ever had one) and all sense of spiritual identification with black people. She would believe in the adage: "If you're black, stay back; if you're brown, stick around; if you're white, you're right."

Southern maid Mammy Jane, in Charles Waddell Chesnutt's *The Marrow of Tradition* (1901), is proud to identify herself and her family with the white family for whom she works, and she is as conservative as they. She becomes very upset, for example, when younger black people in her town try to improve their conditions by getting educations: a "new issue" Negro, she believes, is much more uppity than her God or her wise white folks ever intended.[1] Such a true southern maid does not recognize cultural and historical supports which could be available to her. Even if she leaves the South, moves to the North, and works for a white woman there, as does Pauline Breedlove, in Toni Morrison's *The Bluest Eye* (1970), her perceptions remain essentially ahistorical and acultural.[2] Born in Alabama and stunted by the poisons of that soil, Pauline carries southern reflexes north with her. Her training in the mammy tradition, like Kristin Hunter's Granny Huggs's, in *God Bless the Child* (1964), had been so strong that its assumptions have become second nature to her. These women's identities are so meshed with whites and white culture that they cannot change; nor do they have the level of *consciousness* which would even remotely suggest that change might be desirable. Moving north means only a change of location for them; they have none of the respect for their black skins or identity with other Blacks which would cause them to have a change of mind about the work they do. They have difficulty envisioning a world other than one of white masters and black servants, white power and black submissiveness, white expectations and black fulfillment of expectations.

They are just as hesitant to step out of expectations as Richard Wright himself was—as Bigger Thomas, the invisible man, and many other male as well as female characters are. They therefore share with them a sad kinship. Thus, on northern soil, Wright acted in many instances as he "knew" from his southern experiences would be "appropriate." When he arrived in Chicago and started work, he responded to the need to take a day off the way he would have in the South: he lied. He told his white employer that there was a death in his family when he really wanted the day to have an interview for another job.[3] Wright knew that if he had been on southern soil and asked for a day off, he would have been considered an uppity nigger or a lazy one. In order to accomplish his true purpose, he knew he would have had to lie to southern whites and indeed, under the rigid Southern caste structure, would have been expected to if he wanted to keep his job. He was able to genuflect in both instances, however, without granting superiority to those to whom he genuflected. Still, if Wright, with his forceful will and sure identity, could offer such preconditioned responses, even more so can the less strong, less racially secure Bigger Thomas, Pauline Breedlove, and Granny Huggs.

Bigger Thomas, in Wright's *Native Son* (1940), born and raised through his formative years in the South, carries with him to the North a lack of security in identity and culture and a conditioning which has him at its mercy, and therefore at the mercy of whites. Although his father had been "killed in a riot . . . in the South,"[4] what that incident could have meant to Bigger has never reached a level of consciousness with him. Prosecuting attorney Buckley, in his tirades against Bigger at his trial for the murder of a white girl, speaks more truth than he knows when he says that Bigger is "just a scared colored boy from Mississippi" (p. 288). His move north has not given him the freedom it was to give so many Blacks in reality—or the militant black maids in literature. Although he commits violence, it happens without premeditation, which is not the case with the militant maids. Bigger, like the southern mammies on northern soil, is almost incapacitated by what he brings to that environment. He is suspended in the psychic limitations shaped by his southern experiences. In that, he is both a victim and a perpetrator, both innocent and guilty. Circumstances shape him, but he consents to the shaping; he is certainly not responsible for the conditions under which he was reared in the South and his education to the tenth grade has not been liberating, but he is, at some level, responsible for the extent to which he has allowed himself to be shaped by them. Bigger, like Pauline Breedlove and Granny Huggs, cannot escape the mental bars that have been constructed by their southern experiences.

The sense of their place, both in terms of location and status, that Pauline and Granny feel can also be seen in Bigger Thomas, the invisible man, and other characters in the literature. When Bigger enters the gate at the Dalton household, he waits for someone "to challenge him" (p. 46). His awareness of being in a white neighborhood and hence out of place physically reverberates in his mind. Upon his arrival in New York, the invisible man finds himself crushed against a huge white woman in the subway. Southern history tells him that that situation is dangerous to him just as it tells a true southern maid that sitting in the living room having tea with her white mistress is forbidden to her. He makes a hasty exit from the subway and resolves to walk the rest of his way, no matter how far his destination. His actions show that his mind is still just as far down South as Granny Huggs's and Pauline Breedlove's are. The soil on which he lives has changed, but his conditioned reactions to whites have not. In spite of his three years of college, he automatically responds to taboo with flight—just as Pauline responds with grinning pleasure when her white employer praises her pies, or Granny goes dutifully to hold her dying employer's hand even though her own daughter has just had a heart attack.

Both the invisible man and Bigger Thomas, interestingly, share with both Granny Huggs and Pauline Breedlove the severing of ties with the traditional black folk culture of the South. Bigger Thomas rejects the balm of black religion, is unaware of the blues even when he's living them, cannot control his mask, and is uncertain in the badman role he sometimes assumes. The invisible man searches throughout the novel for a racial and cultural identity. He moves from thinking of pork chops and grits as being negative reflections of a southern background to declaring that one must be confident in whatever one likes. He moves from thinking he can use chitterlings to humiliate his college president to believing that to be ashamed of what one is is to deny the essence of one's identity. Nor does Granny Huggs recognize a southern black heritage in which she has a share; she knows her place only in relation to whites. Pauline, also like the invisible man, tries to escape what she believes is negative in her southern background; she copies images from the movies and tries to alter her southern accent. She joins Bigger Thomas in using movies as an escape from the reality of her existence. Her immersion in religion later in the novel is more a detachment from rather than a true understanding of the function of religion in black southern life. She joins a church which "frowns" on shouting; such emotional displays are especially typical of black churches in the South. Territorial determinants, though, assert themselves with all of these characters. What they deny in actions, they make up in subconscious thoughts and responses to the northern environment. And those unconscious responses come in part from their refusal to see anything intrinsically positive and healthy in their own cultures. They have refused to accept the perception of reality passed down in black folk culture. To refuse to accept that reality, as Ellison has pointed out,[5] is to be set adrift from one's black self. And if one has no basis for trusting one's own perception of reality, external stimuli can mold one's personality into almost any shape. What Bigger Thomas, the invisible man, and the mammies of literature demonstrate about reflex actions of southern-bred Blacks on northern soil is also shown in the confused reaction of Ruth Bowman to white men in James Baldwin's "Come Out the Wilderness"; in the reluctance of Claude Brown's mother to complain to her landlord about broken windows and leaky window casings, in his *Manchild in the Promised Land*; and in King Solomon Gillis's submission, in Rudolph Fisher's "The City of Refuge," to the "cullud policemens" who arrest him.[6] There is an obvious gap between who they are or could be and how they persist in perceiving themselves; they consistently view themselves as amorphous personalities which take on the traits required in particular situations. They continue to believe that black is somehow not as good as white—even when conspicuous contrary evidence exists. Their condition may be compared to that of the dog in a popular folk story in which a boy takes his dog out for a walk and ties its leash to a pole while he joins a group of children playing. The dog wants to play, but sits quietly even after the rope has come untied—having a miserable time. Upon his return, the boy pats his pet on the head for being a good dog.[7] The invisible man, Pauline Breedlove, Bigger Thomas, Granny Huggs, King Solomon Gillis, Ruth Bowman, Mrs. Brown—all are tied by the invisible leashes of their southern upbringings. They cannot recognize freedom when it is extended to them because they think they are tied to restrictions, to subservience, and to self-denial, all of which amount to negation. The maids who partake of this literary heritage share a response to their mistresses and job situations which is fearful, self-denying, and acquiescent. Whether in Birmingham, Meridian, Harlem, or Detroit, the southernness in their actions will insure that they will continue to be mammies.

Maids in the literature who may be classified as transitional figures, or moderates, in the progression from mammies to militants, may also live on southern or northern soil, and they may seem to be as acquiescent as the true southern maids. But their southernness is performance, a mask used to their advantage. These women, unlike Pauline Breedlove and Granny Huggs, have a clear understanding of their culture and history and of their places in both. Their apparent belief in the status quo is a deception. With a heightened consciousness of themselves, they have the common sense to recognize the territorial imperatives which restrict them. Apparently submissive, quiet, and unassuming, they can also be ideal servants. Whenever an opportunity presents itself, however, they counteract the negation of their humanity.

These women are tricksters in the white women's houses, clandestinely using their cultural heritages to their advantage. Tricksters in black history and folklore can be human or animal, either John the Slave or Brer Rabbit. The trickster's weapon is indirection, as, wearing his mask, he soothes his larger, more powerful adversaries into a false sense of his harmlessness, then takes destructive advantage of their trust. Trickster tales in black history generally suggest the position of the slave and the newly freed Black. The exploits of Brer Rabbit provided vicarious transcendence for a black community which was powerless against cruel masters and later against the Black Codes. Tales of Brer Rabbit, then, represent symbolic wish fulfillment and a desire for escape from the master/slave environment, or at least a desire to minimize the powerlessness of Blacks in relation to whites.

The moderate maids of literature have their folklore father in the usually non-violent John the Slave. John understands the plantation and its operation just as the moderate maid understands the white household and its operation; he knows that the goods of the world have not been distributed equally between master and slave. He understands too that it is suicidal for him to call ole Marse a cheat to his face or to imply in any way that ole Marse is unfair. Through his actions, though, John tries to close the gap in material goods which exists between master and slave. By wearing the mask of the "good nigger," the one who has the master's every interest at heart, John manages to get more food for his family, to get whiskey for his "aches and fevers," and to reduce the amount of work he is expected to do. John knows he can never hit his master, for that would mean being lynched at worst and being sold down the river at best. And to think of leading a rebellion is beyond him. The circumstances of his condition are too overwhelming for John to control to any earthshaking extent—but in small ways he asserts his humanity and privately celebrates his little triumphs over ole Marse. He continues to be viewed with favor by his master.[8]

Like folklore's John, the mask-wearing moderate maids of literature may object to the way things are, but they realize that power is divided too unequally for them to initiate open confrontation with their mistresses. They use quiet indirection to sabotage the mistress's work schedules and to appropriate what they can for their families. They turn stereotypes to their advantage. Since the mistress probably believes that Blacks are lazy, as well as shiftless, careless, and light-handed, these maids may take an unusual amount of time to iron—"lazily"—in order to avoid getting on to other work unfairly imposed. They may handle silver "carelessly" so that they will not be asked to clean it again. They, like John, must understand the mistress perfectly in order to know what her limitations are and the extent to which her patience can be stretched. Thus Verta Mae Grosnover records in *Thursdays and Every Other Sunday Off* (1972) that "a laundress in Baltimore . . . would work a week behind [schedule] so that her child could wear the clothes of the young mistress to school."[9] Two maids I interviewed in Tuscaloosa, Alabama, had other ways of getting the upper hand. One, Mrs. Sarah Brown, recalled her annoyance when one white women unreasonably demanded a fresh cup of coffee.

> She was kind of nasty. She was the person that wanted you to clean up the house and go out the back door, come in the back door, go out the back door. And one day I carried her up a cup of coffee, and she told me to carry it back because some had wasted in the saucer and my finger mighta been in it. So, I carried it back for her, but I carried the same cup of coffee right back. I just poured the coffee out the saucer over in the cup. I won't tell you what else I did [but I] put it back in the cup and carried it right back to her.[10]

I was left to assume that Mrs. Brown had performed a dirty trick with the coffee, adding either spit sugar or finger sugar. The other informant, Mrs. Burton, resorted to tricks in an effort to combat the excessive amount of work she was assigned. She would arrive at work and find a list of things to do: "If she was gonna leave there in the morning and stay all day, she'd make sure you didn't rest. She'd have a sheet of paper. I'd do some of it, then I'd tend to the baby (jolly laughter)." When the white woman came home and found many things undone, Mrs. Burton would simply say that the baby had demanded all of her attention.[11] Since the employer had made taking care of the baby the maid's primary duty, she couldn't really fault her for not completing all of her tasks. Her roaring laughter reflected Mrs. Burton's appreciation of her trick and the pleasure she took in retelling the story.

Self-preservation—with a tinge of humor and transcendence—is primary with such women. In a world which would exploit their labor and deny their humanity, they experience no guilt or regret for their tricking actions. In an immoral, or sometimes amoral, world, they likewise set aside morality. Just as Blacks historically have seen no incongruity in going to root doctors on Friday and shouting and praying in a Christian church on Sunday, they find no incongruity in responding in a less than Christian fashion to the white world while otherwise adhering to Christian behavior.

The moderate maid on southern soil is well represented by Richard Wright's Carl in "Man of All Work." In his role as black maid, Carl knows that he must create the illusion of the ideal servant behind the mask he wears. He must convince the Fairchilds that what they see is reality, that he is indeed no more than he seems to be; he must control the inquisitiveness of the family's little girl, ward off the sexual advances of the father, and soothe the fears of the mother. And all of this must be done while he cooks, cleans, and entertains the child. Because Carl knows he is in a world where tightrope-walking is the norm, he does it as gracefully as can be expected. He illustrates how a maid can exist in the home of the whites for whom she works without sharing their values and without letting them exploit her and, most importantly, without alienating them.

On northern territory, the transitional maids, the moderates, are represented by Lutie Johnson in Ann Petry's *The Street* (1946) and Opal Simmons in William Melvin Kelley's *dem* (1964). Both of these women are ideal servants—but primarily because they know how to wear masks and keep their true feelings to themselves. Recognizing that they must work, they are nevertheless aware of a world beyond the one in which they do so. They are ultimately able to keep a part of themselves immune to the values they encounter on their jobs, though Lutie's enlightenment is clearer once she leaves her job, and to find worth in the black communities of which they feel themselves part. And, unlike Pauline Breedlove and Granny Huggs, they are able to see those communities as they are: they do not reject the black world because they do not believe it compares favorably with the white one, as a Mammy Jane would do. Still, however militant their thoughts, these transitional figures act always moderately, indirectly.

Human tricksters, perhaps because they obviously live in the real world, seldom resort to violence. Brer Rabbit, by contrast, is more often than not amoral, brutal, and violent. He *may* be content to trick purely by pulling the wool over his opponent's eyes, but he usually delights in adding physical abuse to deception. He wishes to make it clear to the fox, the lion, or the bear that he is superior to each. He tricks the fox into fishing without a hook and having his tail frozen off (this is one incident); he talks Brer Bear into being ridden like a horse and spurred accordingly; he cons the alligator family into the center of a field which he then sets on fire, thereby burning their smooth white skins into crinkly brown ones; and he coaxes all of the animals into granting him his freedom in the famous tarbaby story.[12] In at least one version of a Brer Rabbit tale, he wields a shotgun, openly and aggressively confronting the guests at a party to which he has not been invited; he eats as much as he wants, rapes a guest, and defecates on the floor.[13] Unsatisfied with making himself equal to his enemies, he delights in flaunting the power he trickily acquires over them. In such actions he takes on the badman role of the amoral Staggolee, who has a "tombstone disposition and a graveyard mind." Staggolee courts danger—openly, sassily, aggressively.[14]

If the mask-wearing moderate maids resemble John, the more active northern maids are the Brer Rabbits and the Staggolees. At their various stages of development, they illustrate increasing degrees of militancy. For all of them, territory is a symbolic reality; the North means freedom and sassiness, the antithesis of confinement and self-denial. It suggests no need for the same kind of mask that the moderates wear. For the northern maid, then, indirection gives way to direct confrontation. If the mistress leaves a note for the maid specifying the day's work, the maid is likely to leave one in return if she considers the work excessive. If the mistress demands Saturday work, the maid is likely to refuse or complain. She is aware of her history and culture and makes no pretense about who she is or what she thinks. She insists on recognition of her humanity.

In her directness, Mildred in Alice Childress's *Like One of the Family* (1956) is *the* northern maid—a drastic departure from the mammies and the moderates. A New Yorker, Mildred considers freedom in the North a reality. She has the audacity to reprimand white mistresses for not raising their children properly; she sits in the living room and chats with white visitors from Alabama; and she criticizes her white employers for not being sufficiently conscious of the Civil Rights movement. Mildred is a character who recreates in her description of her mere presence in white women's houses the intimidation she implies they must have felt. She violates both spatial and psychological limitations. If work is not to her liking, she makes that known. If she thinks her working relationship with the mistress could be improved by a little heart-to-heart talk with the mistress, then she initiates that. She is a generous and hard worker, but she refuses to be taken advantage of. Her identities as a black woman and as a black maid are complete and healthy. She therefore moves in and out of the white world with graceful detachment, with wit and humor, and with a style reminiscent of a less-than-violent badman hero.

Mildred is at the beginning of the militant type which will progress to committing violence in the literature of the 1960's and early 1970's. Mildred talks back to her employers and gives them directions for minding their own business, but she is never antagonistically aggressive toward them; that is, she never does anything that would cause them physical harm or prolonged emotional disturbance. Her militancy is in her confronting them, openly and directly. The character in John A. Williams's "Son in the Afternoon" (1962) goes a step beyond Mildred in that he is obsessed with the emotional destructiveness of the white world which had taken his mother, a maid, away from him since he was a child. He rejects Mildred's humane setting of limits because he does not believe that whites deserve that kind of consideration. He is intent upon raping their minds. The two maids in Douglas Turner Ward's *Happy Ending* (1964), wearing the non-violent mask of the militant Brer Rabbit, do more than appropriate items for survival; they steal egregiously from their employers as an act of revolution. Ward's characters, like Mildred, do not intend to do physical harm to their employers, but like the "Son" they intend to leave them as violated as they possibly can—not mentally in their case, but financially. Their own exploitative natures show how far they have moved beyond the Lutie Johnsons of the world. They have no consciences and thus experience no regret or remorse for what they do. The amorality they share with Brer Rabbit defines them as militants. And yet, Ellie and Vi, Ward's maids, are still not in the ultimate stage of domestic militancy because they refuse to confront their employers both openly and violently, and they refuse to destroy the basis on which the mistress/maid relationship has been established.

Direct confrontation, overt physical violence, and ultimate denial of the power of the white world to control Blacks are the traits of the final stage in the progression of domestics from mammies to militants. Maids in this category wear masks, like Brer Rabbit at his most militant, only to cover violent, destructive intentions: they are without mercy and without guilt. Characters in Barbara Woods's "The Final Supper" (1970), Ted Shine's *Contribution* (1968), and Ed Bullins's *The Gentleman Caller* (1969) all see murdering their white employers as the only way to change their intolerable situations as domestics. Woods's character poisons her master's family and slits his throat; Shine's domestic poisons two of her masters and their relatives; and Bullins's seemingly acquiescent southern maid blasts her mistress with a shotgun. Both Shine's and Bullins's characters kill, and they survive to kill again if that act should prove necessary. They are militants who use their revolutionary activity to benefit all black people.

Interestingly, Shine's play is set on southern territory and yet represents the ultimate in maid militancy. If militancy can come to the South and redefine the limits within that territory, then perhaps there is hope for the freeing of minds like Pauline Breedlove's and Granny Huggs's. If the maids most identified with whites—that is, those in the South and the northern mammies who were bred in the South—can break their chains, then perhaps there can be universal reform. Shine, then, as do Bullins and Woods, uses his maid as a political tool. Psychologically, their black women who work as domestics are centuries removed from the mammies.

CHAPTER THREE

THE MAID AS SOUTHERN
AND NORTHERN MAMMY

The literary and historical image of the domestic as mammy is one easily recognized and much maligned, a type which invariably tends toward stereotype. As repulsive as outside observers may judge the role to have been, black women who found themselves in it were privileged indeed within the plantation households in which the type was established. Mammies who had established reputations for responsibility and reliability, who were mature and experienced, usually did less work than other slaves. According to Jessie Parkhurst, the mammy was primarily in charge of child-rearing, sometimes assisting with household tasks when the children in her care had grown large enough to help care for themselves. She was versatile enough to fill "any gap that occurred in the southern household," able to move from child-rearing to cooking to ordering supplies. Generally, she was "next to the mistress in authority" and bossed "everyone and everything in the household."[1] If she did not live in the big house, she lived nearby; she dressed well, was not usually punished or sold, and could cultivate an intimacy with the master that none of the other slaves dared. "She was considered self-respecting, independent, loyal, forward, gentle, captious, affectionate, true, strong, just, warm-hearted, compassionate-hearted, fearless, popular, brave, good, pious, quick-witted, capable, thrifty, proud, regal, courageous, superior, skilful, tender, queenly, dignified, neat, quick, tender, competent, possessed with a temper, trustworthy, faithful, patient, tyrannical, sensible, discreet, efficient, careful, harsh, devoted, truthful, neither apish nor servile."[2] That may have been the type, but it quickly degenerated into stereotype. Mammy's self-respect was lost in groveling before and fawning upon her mistress, master, and young white charges. Her loyalty became self-effacement and her affection anticipated the exaggeration of the minstrel tradition. Her piety and patience worked more often than not in favor of the whites, and her tyranny was most ruthless when it was exercised over other Blacks. Devoted she was, but in contrast to what Parkhurst asserts, she also believed in aping white manners, and, if she was not servile, she certainly believed herself inferior to those for whom she worked. They honored her by singling her out from the black masses, and she repaid them with lifetime devotion.

Features inherent in the job made it necessary for the black mammy to deny her own family in order to rear generation after generation of whites who would, ironically, grow up to oppress Blacks yet further. And because she consented to this denial, the popular stereotyping intensified—particularly when black women persisted in voluntary engagement in such roles after slavery. Images formed from years of habit could not be easily uprooted from the minds of these black women; to them, whites were the models for everything good and right, while black was ugly and undesirable. Such women were utterly without progressive political consciousness.

The three characters classified as mammies in this chapter— Mammy Jane in Chesnutt's *The Marrow of Tradition* (1901), Lourinda "Granny" Huggs in Hunter's *God Bless the Child* (1964), and Pauline Breedlove in Morrison's *The Bluest Eye* (1970)—follow this pattern, totally identifying with whites and white culture and negating blackness and black culture. They hold whites up as models for moral and social emulation, and they refuse to believe that there is anything in the black world that can remotely compare with the cleanliness, the purity, the goodness they see in the white world.

Charles Waddell Chesnutt's *The Marrow of Tradition* (1901) is set in Wellington (Wilmington), North Carolina, in the late 1890's, at its climax featuring racial rioting such as occurred in Wilmington in

1898; and, as one of its several subplots, it offers a portrait of a black southern nursemaid who is only a few years and a few psychological steps removed from slavery. Mammy Jane is an aging "family retainer" whose connections to the Merkell/Carteret family extend over three generations. Having reared the present Mrs. Carteret and her mother, Mammy Jane refuses to allow anyone else to rear the long-awaited Carteret baby, whose birth is imminent at the opening of the novel. The son born to Olivia and Major Carteret is nearly the same age as the son born to Janet and Adam Miller, Janet being the long-ignored "colored" sister of Olivia Carteret and Miller a black doctor. In order to save their son's life, white Olivia is eventually forced to acknowledge kinship to black Janet and the white-supremacist Major is forced to humble himself before the black doctor.

Ironies, coincidences, and the fantastic all characterize the novel; its melodrama is suggested even by the very short plot summary above. In its presentation of the black nursemaid, however, *The Marrow of Tradition* is realistic fiction. Mammy Jane is very much the epitome of the true southern maid, the mammy as she has been herein defined. Most critics writing about *The Marrow of Tradition* simply ignore Mammy Jane's place in the novel or dismiss her role as functional, like those of several stereotyped, minor characters in the novel.[3] However, the fact that Chesnutt decided that such a character as Mammy Jane should exist in his novel, that the social and political climate with which he was concerned dictated her presence, demands a more than cursory consideration of her role. William L. Andrews's point on the conception of character in the novel is relevant here. ". . . Chesnutt conceives of characters and scenes in *The Marrow of Tradition* primarily as demonstration vehicles for general social truths about the New South."[4] Certainly Mammy Jane is a type, and certainly Chesnutt recognized her as such,[5] but what she says and how she acts in that role reflect the historical pattern of many black women after Emancipation, women who found themselves without identities beyond those of the white families for whom they had spent most of their lives working. To the extent that Mammy Jane reflects a truth which goes deeper than the type, her role is important. To the extent that she illustrates a major obstacle to the movement toward self-assertion for many of her contemporaries, her role is equally important.

Mammy Jane enters the novel with a curtsy, and she bows and scrapes her way to her death. She is exemplary in her subservience and unfalteringly believes in her "place." She knows that God has put her on earth to serve quality white folks; she can envision nothing beyond that. Her attitude comes out in the first scene in which Major Carteret enters a room where she is waiting:

> Mammy Jane hobbled to her feet and bobbed a curtsy. She was never lacking in respect to white people of proper quality; but Major Carteret, the quintessence of aristocracy, called out all her reserves of deference. The major was always kind and considerate to these old family retainers, brought up in the feudal atmosphere now so rapidly passing away. Mammy Jane loved Mrs. Carteret; toward the major she entertained a feeling bordering upon awe.[6]

When a young, newly educated black nurse is hired to substitute for Mammy Jane when she suffers from rheumatism, the old woman is appalled by what she considers the girl's lack of respect. The girl ignores the advice Mammy Jane gives and obviously has little patience with the old black woman's adoration of the young white child. "Dese yer young niggers ain' got de manners dey wuz bawned wid!" Mammy Jane exclaims in response to the girl's attitude. And later, when Major Carteret maintains that Jane's attitude toward place and education is correct, she responds:

> Dat's w'at I tells dese young niggers . . . w'en I hears 'em gwine on wid deir foolishniss; but dey don' min' me. Dey 'lows dey knows mo' d'n I does, 'ca'se dey be'n l'arnt ter look in a book. But, pshuh! my ole mist'ess showed me mo' d'n dem niggers 'll l'arn in a thousan' years! I's fetch' my gran'son Jerry up ter be 'umble, an' keep in 'is place. An' I tells dese other niggers dat ef dey'd do de same, an' not crowd de w'ite folks, dey'd git ernuff ter eat, an' live out deir days in peace an' comfo't. But dey don' min' me—dey don' min' me! (pp. 43–44)

Of Janet Miller's riding in a buggy she says, "Well, well! Fo'ty yeahs ago who'd 'a' ever expected ter see a nigger gal ridin' in her own buggy? My, my! but I don' know,—I don' know! It don' look right, an' it ain' gwine ter las!—you can't make me b'lieve!" (p. 106) Mammy Jane's prediction that things will not "last" is correct, for the riot changes a lot, yet she is too weak of mind and spirit to try to view the inevitable changes in any but a negative light.

In making his a "story of Southern life" (p. 42), Chesnutt has his Mammy Jane mirror many attitudes held by whites during reconstruction days, the most vocalized of which is the opposition to any change from the pre-war status of the Negro. Major Carteret, archsupporter of white supremacy and editor of the local whitesupremacist newspaper, the *Morning Chronicle*, and his cohorts, General Belmont and Captain McBane, are the chief spokesmen for a nostalgic ideal of Blacks' keeping their subservient place. Staunchly devoted to the concept of "no nigger domination," they work fiercely to reverse the political gains Blacks have made, General Belmont verbalizing what he sees as a distressing trend:

> Things are in an awful condition! A negro justice of the peace has opened an office on Market Street, and only yesterday summoned a white man to appear before him. Negro lawyers get most of the business in the criminal court. Last evening a group of young white ladies, going quietly along the street arm-in-arm, were forced off the sidewalk by a crowd of negro girls. Coming down the street just now, I saw a spectacle of social equality and negro domination that made my blood boil with indignation,—a white and a black convict, chained together, crossing the city in charge of a negro officer! We cannot stand that sort of thing, Carteret,—it is the last straw! Something must be done, and that quickly! (p. 33)

General Belmont could very easily be echoing Mammy Jane, and we can further see their agreement in his appreciation of Jerry. "Jerry now," says Belmont, "is a very good negro. He's not one of your new negroes, who think themselves as good as white men, and want to run the government. Jerry knows his place,—he is respectful, humble, obedient, and content with the face and place assigned to him by nature" (p. 87). Jerry identifies thoroughly with "quality" white folks; when he wishes he were white so he could enjoy the kinds of privileges whites have (p. 36), the wish is grounded in compliment and appreciation, not rebellion. Jerry is indeed content with his role.

Mammy Jane, like General Belmont, Captain McBane, and Major Carteret, would like to conserve black/white relationships as they were before the war. The major makes his point clear at a dinner early in the novel: "No doubt the negro is capable of a certain doglike fidelity,—I make the comparison in a kindly sense,—a certain personal devotion which is admirable in itself, and fits him eminently for a servile career" (p. 24). Mammy Jane gets along well with the major because his description fits her precisely. The major continues his theme in an editorial he writes a few pages later in the novel; it concerns "the unfitness of the negro to participate in government,—an unfitness due to his limited education, his lack of experience, his criminal tendencies, and more especially to his hopeless mental and physical inferiority to the white race" (p. 31). It is a divinely ordained inferiority, the major believes, then, that makes Mammy Jane's role in life the ideal one for the Negro.

The major believes generally that Blacks should go in and come out of back doors. In one instance, place as physical location is literalized into place as status. "It was traditional in Wellington that no colored person had ever entered the front door of the Carteret residence, and that the luckless individual who once presented himself there upon alleged business and resented being ordered to the back door had been unceremoniously thrown over the piazza railing into a rather thorny clump of rosebushes below" (p. 68). The fellow's punishment had been slight, to say the least, for even emergencies do not relax the customary rule of the house. Major Carteret feels strongly enough about it to refuse, at first, to allow Dr. Miller to enter through the front door to attend his young son, and even the black woman who comes to tell the Carterets of their Aunt Polly's death comes in through the back door though she has to go around the house to do it (p. 175). Having lost personal property as a result of the war, Major Carteret and others like him are intense in upholding whatever is left that clearly defines them as different from those they judge to be unequal to them. For Major Carteret, then, the passing of such distinctions is tantamount to the final dissolution of culture as he knows it. He will not accept the change passively, as the last words of the following lamentation for the passing of "old times" make clear:

> The old times have vanished, the old ties have been ruptured. The old relations of dependence and loyal obedience on the part of the colored people, the responsibility of protection and kindness upon that of the whites, have passed away forever. The young negroes

are too self-assertive. Education is spoiling them, Jane; they have been badly taught. They are not content with their station in life. Some time they will overstep the mark. The white people are patient, but there is a limit to their endurance (p. 43).

Here is a quintessential expression of place and conservatism.*

It is perhaps appropriate to the novel's period that the major shares his ideas with Mammy Jane more often than his ethereal, ineffective wife does so, as she probably would in later works; still, Mammy Jane's role in relation to her mistress is important. Olivia Carteret shares her husband's fidelity to the status quo. She has no fancy words of justification to offer because women-folks are expected just to do, but she shows in her actions that she does believe in the social distance between herself and Mammy Jane and the paradoxically even greater gulf between herself and Janet Miller. As one character points out, blood is thicker than water unless it runs into unapproved channels; then it is the thinnest of substances. Olivia therefore ignores Janet as best she can, and Mammy Jane feels justification in the distinctions she draws and in that neglect. Janet may have acquired many things, by black standards, but she still is not in either of the other women's eyes the white woman's equal. Mammy Jane is as annoyed as Olivia when Janet intrudes herself into Mrs. Carteret's presence by driving on the same street or by passing by the Carteret home.

The nature of the relationship between Mammy Jane and Olivia Carteret is clearest, however, when Mammy Jane is taking care of Theodore Felix, "Dodie," the Carteret baby. Olivia trusts the old servant implicitly, for Mammy Jane has cared for both her and her mother; she accepts it as the natural order of things that black Mammy Jane's life has been devoted to rearing white children. Mammy Jane has, therefore, proprietary rights to the Carteret house and baby, and when she returns from a brief absence and asks how the substitute nurse has worked out, Olivia maintains: "She does fairly well, Mammy Jane, but I could hardly expect her to love the

---

*It underscores the pathetic inability to accept change, and it hints at the fear whites have of Blacks, which will later contribute to the tragic violence of the riot.

baby as you do. There's no one like you, Mammy Jane" (p. 41). There
is certainly no one like her in her devotion to the child. Noting, for
example, that the baby has a slight mole on its neck, just at the point
at which a hangman's noose would take hold, Mammy Jane decides
that in spite of the child's white heritage, which will surely protect it,
she —it—still needs the help of the black conjure woman. She goes to
the woman, gets a charm, and buries it in the yard of the Carteret
house. She buries, turns, and reburies the charm when little Dodie is
about to have an operation; and, after the baby almost falls from a
window, she attaches what she considers to be a more potent charm
to the child's very crib. Olivia, touched, refuses to remove it. Her
devotion to the Carteret family and baby gives Mammy Jane license
within the household that is peculiarly the mammy's. She can voice
opinions that other Blacks would not be able to voice; she can talk
with the white doctor Price about Carteret family secrets; and she is
allowed to be familiar, to an extent, with Olivia and Major Carteret.

Mammy Jane's place is wherever the white folks want and need
her to be, either for work or for show. The christening of the Carteret
baby is an opportunity for show: "Upon this special occasion Mammy
Jane had been provided with a seat downstairs among the white
people, to her own intense satisfaction, and to the secret envy of a
small colored attendance in the gallery, to whom she was ostenta-
tiously pointed out by her grandson Jerry, porter at the Morning
Chronicle office, who sat among them in the front row" (p. 12). Pride
in identification with whites exudes from Mammy Jane for most of the
novel. Her compromise in the white world is one which does not
allow for an appreciation of her own culture or of her own history
without the mediating influence of the whites around her. Thus folk
culture for Mammy Jane is not a thing of intrinsic value, a source of
truth, identity, and the reality Ellison noted, but a medium for
protecting the status quo that the whites hold on to so strongly, a
source of reinforcements of the status of the white folks she dearly
loves: thus she turns to the root doctor to make sure little Dodie
Carteret will live and thrive and grow up to oppress more Blacks.
Sharing the stereotyped images that whites have of Blacks, and
sometimes going beyond those, she does not realize that she herself
is a stereotype. For example, when the Carteret baby is taken to a

window to see a mockingbird and nearly falls out of the window when
Janet Miller is driving by, Olivia blames the incident on Janet. So too
does Mammy Jane:

> Mammy Jane entertained a theory of her own about the accident,
> by which the blame was placed, in another way, exactly where
> Mrs. Carteret had laid it. Julia's daughter, Janet, had been looking
> intently toward the window just before little Dodie had sprung
> from Clara's arms. Might she not have cast the evil eye upon the
> baby, and sought thereby to draw him out of the window? One
> would not ordinarily expect so young a woman to possess such a
> power, but she might have acquired it, for this very purpose, from
> some more experienced person. By the same reasoning, the mock-
> ingbird might have been a familiar of the witch, and the two might
> have conspired to lure the infant to destruction. Whether this
> were so or not, the transaction at least wore a peculiar look. There
> was no use telling Mis 'Livy about it, for she didn't believe, or
> pretended not to believe, in witchcraft and conjuration. But one
> could not be too careful. The child was certainly born to be
> exposed to great dangers—the mole behind the left ear was an
> unfailing sign—and no precaution should be omitted to counteract
> its baleful influence (pp. 107–108).[7]

Mammy Jane's immersion in the folk culture, like many historical
mammies', Chesnutt suggests, makes her an ignorant anachronism in
a world which struggles to move forward, a world which is held back
in its progress by those like her and the whites who share their views.
One might excuse Mammy Jane's actions by saying that she is simply
a product of the times, one who is offered no alternative lifestyle. But
many Blacks in the novel do not hold the same views that Mammy
Jane does. From Dr. Miller and the nurse of the younger generation
to ole Sam who explains to Miller that whites have refused to allow
him to attend the scheduled operation on Dodie, there are Blacks
who see a reality beyond the place assigned by whites.[8] They do not
avoid whites, but they do not defer to them, and they certainly do not
work roots to aid them; they also advocate improving the lot of Blacks
through the education that Mammy Jane sees as a decided mistake, a

hindrance for Blacks. Mammy Jane's position, then, is partly custom, habit, and tradition, and partly choice.[9] She is not completely blameless in her subservience; in fact, her zeal is a volunteer's.

Ironically, the adoration Mammy Jane has given to the whites cannot ultimately protect her from their wrath against all Blacks. She is killed in the rioting that Major Carteret has initiated with inflammatory editorials in his newspaper. Although both Olivia and Major Carteret had maintained that they would protect Mammy Jane against all possible dangers, and insist that she is somehow special, they cannot control the white-fired bullet that takes her life even as she is on her way to their home to seek that promised protection. She is merely another Black to the angry white men who have declared war on all persons of color. But even imminent death does not alter Mammy Jane's perceptions of what is happening around her—or her identity with the white world. As Dr. Miller lifts her head into a more comfortable position there on the street, her final cry is: "Comin', missis, comin'!" (p. 296) Insisting that her death was an accident, that no white man in town would willfully shoot poor Jane, Major Carteret fails to realize that he himself has killed her. His unconscious but absolute hatred of all Blacks, his belief that they should not move beyond a predetermined place, his campaign against "nigger domination" are all responsible for Jane's death. Try as he might to compartmentalize the good niggers and the bad niggers, they are finally all treated the same. Mammy Jane has, therefore, through her own identification with the whites, been an instrument in her own destruction. That is the consequence for the true southern domestic, the mammy, who cannot effect a healthy compromise when she goes to work for whites.

Mammy Jane's actions, paradoxically, at once reinforce and give the lie to the myth of the strength of black women. She is strong—fanatical even—in her devotion to and work for whites. Simultaneously, she is weak in identity derived either from pride or from culture or race. The price she pays for being the ideal servant is to become a black-faced puppet; sadly, she worships the controllers of her strings. She cannot envision change because she can see nothing wrong with her present condition. Total absorption in where she is and total identification with the people for whom she works make her the quintessential southern domestic. Her upbringing on southern soil, amid paternalistic traditions of black self-denial and dependency, has made Mammy Jane, if not tragic, at least pathetic.

Mammy Jane's situation may be pathetic, but that of Mrs. Lourinda Baxter "Granny" Huggs in *God Bless the Child* (1964) is absurd. Like Mammy Jane, Granny is a family retainer with four decades of service to a single family, the Liveseys—Grandmother Helen, Mother Emilie, and little Miss Iris—who mirror her own family exactly. (Apparently Granny is about the same age as Miss Helen; her daughter Regina "Queenie" Fleming could be Miss Emilie's age; and Miss Iris and Granny's granddaughter Rosalie "Rosie" Fleming are exactly the same age.) Granny does everything for the Liveseys, from rearing three generations of their children to buying and cooking their food to cleaning their house and ordering its furniture. Although the story takes place in the North, Granny has moved with the family from Virginia. She is truly southern in her adherence to the paternalistic order decreeing that there shall be white masters and black servants, to the sense of place expected of her. Indeed, Granny's move to the North is merely geographical change; in her attitude toward the whites for whom she works, she makes it clear that the story might just as well have taken place in Mississippi or Alabama. The city into which Granny and her white folks had moved many years ago is not named, but its character is obvious from the activities which go on there. Its highly visible black numbers runners, winos, and gangsters all confirm for Granny that her identification with the genteel, quality white folks is correct and that she should instill that identification in her family. Like many mammies historically, she judges her family by standards and values she encounters in the white world. Her granddaughter Rosie, seven at the opening of the novel, dies shortly after she is twenty-one, having been driven by her internalization of the materialistic values Granny worships to work too obsessively, too ruinously hard, to obtain material things.

Throughout the novel, Granny's attitude is one of detachment from Blacks generally, from her family, and ultimately even from the granddaughter who works so desperately to please her. That detachment, that aura of lady-like superiority, has been shaped in imitation of what Granny believes she sees among whites. Her connection to

the Liveseys allows her to consider herself infinitely better than
other Blacks, and her light skin intensifies that superior feeling.
Barely willing to tolerate her brown-skinned granddaughter and
falling just short of being a tragic mulatto herself, she is color-struck
and thoroughly conscious of a division between lighter- and darker-
skinned Blacks. "Down Home," she says, "we were always the
lightest. That's how come we were house servants, not field servants.
My mother was mixed. She was a gypsy creole. Her name was Tamir,
and she used to play on a funny kind of round-shaped guitar. . . . She
had wavy black hair so long she could sit on it. . . . She spoke three
languages, French and Indian and Gypsy."[10] When Rosie asks why
Granny is so light and she is so dark, Granny speaks with the
positiveness of the mammies who advised their white charges to find
suitable marriage partners and were bitterly disappointed if they
didn't. "Because . . . that no 'count father of yours was black as coal
tar. I tried to bring this girl [Queenie] up right, and then she ran off
and got married without thinkin' about improvin' the race" (p. 19).
Handicapped by a color for which she is not responsible, Rosie works
ever more diligently to please Granny and thus atone for what seems
to be an unforgivable sin. She gains Granny's affection, fleetingly,
only when she comes close to approximating the formal social graces
Granny values above all else. But she cannot earn Granny's lasting
affection, for Granny is cut apart from everyone black, and she
probably confronts herself only through a medium comparable to the
plastic used to cover furniture.

Granny's adventures in the Livesey household suggest that she
out-herods Herod, that she is more white in attitude than the whites
for whom she works. Although Granny rides the bus to work, she
impatiently insists that the chauffeur drive her home on occasions.
The fact that she wants a ride is not relevant here; her attitude toward
the chauffeur is. She considers him "field help" (p. 7), thereby
showing the ingrained distinction she makes between those worthy
of consideration and those not. Indeed, many mammies were leaders
in suggesting whom one should socialize with and whom not. She
perhaps takes more pleasure in playing the big woman with local
merchants than Miss Helen does. The salespeople who originally
thought her an "ignorant old colored woman" quickly learned the
power of her signature in buying for the Liveseys and quickly learned

to bow and scrape to her: "they would never find out that she did not know how to write anything but her name" (p. 5). Her lack of education does not detract from Granny's exalted evaluation of herself, or from her belief that she is a model for emulation in conduct and other Blacks are no-good "trashy niggers" (p. 21).

When the novel opens, Granny is a live-in worker to the Liveseys. In her absence, Rosie begins to romanticize the life Granny has across town. Even at seven years old, Rosie believes her grandmother should not be a resident of the roach-infested apartment in which she and Queenie live. It is all right, Rosie believes, for her mother and herself to smell the toilets and burnt hair and cooking greens of their apartment building, but her grandmother "was different. Granny did not live here; she lived across town in a white palace with marble stairs and crystal fountains, and when she came to be with them on her Thursdays and every-other-weekends, she was company" (p. 15). And Granny forever acts like company. Seldom does she descend from her papier-mâché pedestal to experience the reality of black life of which she is a part.

Thus she ignores the roaches which irreverently traipse over the broken china she brings home from the Liveseys. She brings out elegant candles when the ever-failing electrical system fails once again. She refuses to see the unpainted walls and falling plaster in the apartment where her daughter and granddaughter live. She does not care that Rosie does not go to school as long as she knows the difference between real and imitation silk. She does not care that Queenie could still be happily married if she, her mother, had not insisted that the husband was too black and that he had married Queenie only because of her pregnancy. She does not care that Rosie does not respect Queenie, or even see how she has contributed to that lack of respect. But most importantly, she has no sense of the confused lives she creates around her. Having destroyed Queenie's marriage, she prefers the gangster Tommy Tucker as a suitor to the granddaughter she will drive to her death, scorning the gentle and sturdy Larnie Bell. Once again Granny fails to distinguish between imitation silk and the real thing. Granny believes in show, in appearance, in form rather than in substance. In one brief scene, the conniving Tucker appeals to her gullible southern gentility, and she is ready to throw Rosie into his irresponsible arms (pp. 96–97). The novel is essentially one of suspense: we wait to see how far Rosie will go to please her grandmother before she either kills herself or sees beneath her grandmother's facade. It is also a tale of the destructive effects the mammy role has on the mammy's family. For all the good Granny may believe she contributes to the Liveseys, there is countervailing destruction in the Fleming household. What she does to her family stems from her being a live-in worker for the Liveseys; all of her responses to the world have been shaped by what she encounters in the world of the Liveseys.

It is clear early in the novel that Granny has succeeded very well in setting up the Livesey world as preferable to that of the Huggses and the Flemings. When Rosie plays hooky from school at age seven, one of her pastimes is not merely imitation of grown-ups but imitation of the Liveseys (or at least of their world as she romantically conceives of it). She dresses in her mother's new red dress, applies lipstick and jewelry, and looks at herself in the mirror:

> The vision in the mirror was not Rosie Fleming. It was Missiris, Madam Queen in the house where Granny worked, Princess in all the fairy tales Rosie was just learning to read. Missiris wore long red skirts and lots of red beads and bangles and silk scarves and clinking earrings. Missiris was spoiled rotten because she had a sweet mother named Missemilie and a beautiful grandmother called Misshelen. Missiris had her meals brought up to her on silver trays, and she had a magic carpet that flew her out the window. Zoom! And when Madam Queen Princess Missiris walked down the street and swished her skirts everyone stepped out of her way. Swish! Rosie stamped her feet and the crowds made way for her. Crowds of frightened roaches, scurrying under the bedroom linoleum. Swish! (pp. 12–13).

The reality of these roaches is what Granny ignores throughout the novel, and it is what Rosie will try to overcome. The vision of beauty, cleanliness, the absence of roaches, drives her to her destruction. While the ambition in itself is certainly not unadmirable, its fanatical pursuit is. And perhaps Rosie gives new meaning even to the fanatical.

In the third-floor walk-up where Granny expresses her attitude of silk and china, the seven-year-old Rosie plays the game of squashing roaches. She attacks an army of them before she eats breakfast:

> The counter was three feet high and eighteen inches deep. Rosie could just reach the back of it by standing on tiptoe. She raised both hands and came down on the marching column . . . killing four in one smash. Another quick smash caught two more babies at the end of the rapidly retreating column. From the corner of her eye she saw the giant granddaddy of them all scurry from the ceiling and rush down the wall. She rocked on tiptoe, waiting, gathering strength.
>
> Now he was within reach. Her palm came down on him just as he was about to dart inside the cupboard.
>
> "Got the bastard," she said.
>
> She opened a drawer, ignoring the sudden flurry of movement inside, and took out a pencil and the notebook that said:
>
> "Rosalie Fleming.
>
> My Book."
>
> She wrote the date and, beside it, the number 10, then carefully put book and pencil away. Seven babies and a big one who was worth three points. Not a bad morning. Rosie decided to stay home from school and kill roaches all day (p. 11).

Into this world of roaches, sleeping on cots, and never having enough money, Granny brings a concentrated detachment derived from having none of these worries. Into life, she brings the *form* of living, a show to be put on to impress others, for life itself is simply too graphically unpleasant for her. She arrives a few hours later, and the following scene occurs when she asks what she, her daughter, and her granddaughter are having for dinner:

> "Chinese food on the table," Mom said, pointing, and pouring herself another drink. "Help yourself."
>
> Granny touched the cardboard carton with one reluctant fingertip. "It's cold."
>
> "Well, I ain' movin'," Mom said, "Let your precious grandchild do some work for a change."
>
> "Rosalie," Granny chirped in her best peacemaking voice, "you

run set the table while I heat this up a little bit. Get out the flowered tablecloth and put water in some glasses. And get the blue Chinese platter Miss Helen gave me," she added. "Nobody but field hands eat out of cardboard boxes."

After a long search, Rosie found three plates in the cupboard that weren't cracked. She killed two roaches when she went back for glasses.

"What's all that racket?" Granny called.

"I'm just setting the table, Granny," Rosie answered. She always hoped Granny didn't know about the roaches.

"That's a good grandchild. Now look in the top of my bag and see if you can find some little lemon dessert pies" (pp. 16–17).

Little lemon dessert pies are just as incongruous in this environment as Maggie's duck was in *Backstairs at the White House*. Granny remains interested in the surface of things, not the depths that are the substance of life. Focus on the order of the Livesey household will not allow her to see beyond the superficial disorder in her daughter's apartment to the deeper disorder reflected in Rosie's and Queenie's attitudes toward each other as well as in the physical clutter of the apartment.

Rosie's desire that her grandmother not see the roaches is matched only by the grandmother's refusal to see what she does not wish to, and by the energy with which she forces forms of etiquette on her daughter and granddaughter. To accompany her flowered table-cloth and Chinese platter, Granny regales Rosie during dinner with tales of the extravagant birthday party Missiris will have the following day. Rosie's expressions of "Gosh!", "No foolin', Granny?", and "Great day in the morning!" (pp. 17, 18) evince her willingness to believe in the possibilities of that world beyond her roach scoreboard, and she is as willing to abide by Granny's admonitions about dress and behavior as Granny is to offer them.

On the Sunday morning that Granny prepares Rosie's eighteenth birthday breakfast, she insists that Rosie make herself presentable. She orders Rosie to take off her pajamas and "put on something respectable. . . . And don't be fiddling around in front of that mirror neither. Just wash your face and comb that disgraceful head and come on" (p. 64). There is no thought that on one's birthday, at least, one might be liberated from some of the normal, expected formalities.

Not in Granny's mind. She insists on dressing up and using a white linen table cloth and candles. All of this, which might be tolerable if born of love, is not: Granny's own artwork, which turns inward to herself, is all that matters to her. (We will see the same self-absorption in Morrison's Pauline Breedlove.) She is more interested in showing that she knows what is appropriate than in why it should fit one setting as opposed to another. And the manners that are the trademark of the mammy are all important to her, whether they are displayed by a snake or a gentleman.[11] Rosie is slightly surprised when Tommy Tucker, the numbers runner, is able to win Granny over by being complimentary and congenial. "For the first time in her life, she doubted Granny's judgment. Couldn't she see past people's manners to what they were like inside? Or didn't she care, as long as the outside was charming?" (p. 99). Rosie is over eighteen when she asks these questions, and her grandmother's influence is too strong to be neutralized. Rosie will continue to believe in the biggest, most glittering things as those most worthy of possessing.

Granny uses the many occasions when she brings things home from the Liveseys to teach Rosie lessons about quality, another extension of her mammy manners from the white household to the black. She brings china, sterling silver, crystal beads, a rainbow-colored bowl, crystal stemware, and bracelets, among other things, which she has usually helped to select, and she insists that Rosie develop the correct attitude toward those rarities. She even explains some of the circumstances under which she has acquired some of the things. In the case of the rainbow bowl, she had convinced Miss Emilie that there was a crack in it so she could bring it to Rosie. The stratagem was unnecessary, for Miss Emilie responded "It's not worth anything, Lourinda, it's just in the way. Why don't you take it on home?" (p. 20). When Rosie questions its value, Granny says: "Child, them people got so much money that they forgets it as soon as they spends it. It might be worth a thousand million dollars" (p. 20). That answer satisfies Rosie, and she assumes she has something of value. In the following few minutes, however, she and Queenie fight over the bowl and break it. Rosie keeps some of the pieces in her pocket during a school day, cutting her fingers in self-imposed penance for her part in the destruction of the bowl. Though the value of the bowl may have been questionable, and Granny's willingness to excuse its castoff status certainly is, Rosie nevertheless treasures it, even in pieces, as a tangible symbol of the romantic white world. The bowl had made "home an ugly place" after she had seen the apartment through its rainbow colors (p. 32).

When Rosie quits school at seventeen, three months before graduation, she explains to her friend Dolly: "I want things. I want things so bad I'd kill myself to get 'em" (p. 59). Although she does not intend the statement as prophecy, it comes true; before that culmination, however, Rosie does acquire things. She starts work as a salesgirl in a department store, then immediately begins a night job as a waitress. She buys extravagant presents for Granny and Queenie in addition to taking over the expenses of the apartment once Queenie becomes ill. She is sensitive to Granny's complaints about inferior quality and overextends herself in trying to buy the best. She buys slippers for Granny which cost $39.50, and for that fleeting moment, the old woman is pleased: ". . . she examined them slowly and critically, picking at the little seams where the soles joined the uppers, poking at the lining with her fingernails, sniffing the leather of the soles and, finally, rubbing her fingers over the surface of the fur. 'Real Persian,' she said at last. 'Real well made, too. For these days' " (p. 175). But Granny's satisfaction is episodic, and each new episode must top the previous one: she always manages to suggest that Rosie has fallen just short of ultimately pleasing. Slips, silk dresses, fabulous shoes—Rosie spends to alleviate the depression of the bills she acquires by spending. So the cycle goes.

She gets into trouble with numbers runners and gangsters in her bid to get Granny a house for her seventieth birthday. Miss Helen having died without remembering Granny in her will, Granny has moved in with Rosie and Queenie—still taking everything as if it were her just due. Rosie feels pressured to make up to her grandmother for the fact that Granny has been cut off penniless from the job in which she has served with such dedication for so many years. She tries to give Granny the kind of elegance she has imagined her being exposed to in her forty years with the Liveseys. Rosie acquires the house shortly after she turns twenty-one, and she again overextends herself by furnishing its ten rooms and basement in the most lavish manner. She wants to make sure that Granny feels like a queen in *this* house—a house which had belonged to Miss Birdie Rice, a friend of Miss Helen's who was so rich that even Miss Helen had looked up to her. It's doubly delicious that Granny should have something that even her special, quality white folks were jealous of (pp. 184–185). However, Granny's sense of accomplishment is still within limits she has imposed upon herself, as is apparent to Rosie's friend Dolly when she is being shown through the house:

> Granny led the way up the dark curving staircase. "This here is the original wood," she said. "Over fifty years old. You feel these stair treads? Solid. Not a creak anywhere." It would take Dolly many more years of knowing Rosie to understand all the reasons why she had wanted to own this particular house, but now, hearing the pride in the old lady's voice, she knew the main one. Granny would never have lived as mistress in Miss Helen's house . . . but she was convinced this one was even better. It was the perfect compromise, satisfying both her urge to grandeur and her deeply ingrained sense of place (p. 215).

The last symbolic present Rosie buys for her grandmother is a punch bowl to replace one Granny had loved at Miss Helen's house. It was used, she said, at Miss Emilie's wedding. "I was the only one they could trust to handle it. It must have weighed pret' near thirty pounds, but I always polished it and put it away by myself. . . . I almost got to thinkin' that bowl belonged to me, 'cause I was the only one took care of it. You could look in it and see rainbows. I used to hold it up to the light and see 'em all the time. I always called it my Rainbow Bowl" (p. 221). The bowl had been sold after Miss Helen's death. It is perhaps because Granny's romanticization of the bowl reminds Rosie of the rainbow bowl she had broken that she orders a new one which costs seventeen hundred and fifty dollars. Rosie buys it at the lowest point of her financial credibility—and it, along with the house and all the furnishings, will be sold after her funeral.

During all the buying, Granny saunters along, detachedly ignoring her granddaughter's declining health, continuing to serve the Liveseys before anything or anyone else. During Miss Helen's illness, Queenie has a heart attack and needs twenty-four hour attention for two weeks once she is brought home from the hospital. Granny declines to care for her daughter, preferring instead to attend Miss Helen and to leave Rosie with bills for a nurse in addition to the four-hundred-dollar hospital bill. In that scene, the usually unruffled

Granny has one of her rare emotional outbursts, one that almost approaches anger:

> "I mean," Rosie explained, "you'll have to take off a couple weeks from work so you can look after Mom."
> "Oh, I couldn't do that, Rosie," Granny said innocently. "My folks need me."
> "Ain't we your folks?" Rosie asked sharply, then bit her tongue. She heaved a deep sigh. "Granny, how's Mom gonna get her meals 'n her medicine? She can't get up for two more weeks yet."
> "Oh, I spect she'll be up before then," Granny answered. "The doctor sent her home, didn't he?"
> "He said she has to stay in bed. She's still sick, Granny." She made a helpless gesture to Larnie for aid.
> "A minute ago, she couldn't get her breath," he said.
> An irritable harshness replaced the usual lilt of Granny's voice. "Don't talk to me about sickness. That's all I've heard for three months. Nurses and doctors. Needles and medicine. Temperatures and pills." She sat down on the edge of the bed with sudden heaviness. "I been with Miss Helen forty-five years, Rosie, and the last couple weeks, she don't even know me. Not one sign of recognition. But I keep right on doin' for her, 'cause I know she wouldn't want nobody else to do it. Taking her temperature, taking her her trays, feeding her, nursing her around the clock."
> Her head drooped alarmingly. "It's thankless work, Rosie. It wears me out. I don't feel so strong myself these days."
> "I know, Granny." Rosie was full of remorse. "I'm sorry."
> "It's a terrible thing, watching somebody you love die, when you been with her all your life, and you know it means your own time's comin' soon" (p. 142).

The mammy's first loyalty is to her white folks, and Granny fits the pattern superbly. Biological ties weaken in the face of tradition and custom. Thus Granny shifts the focus of concern and gets her way: she frightens Rosie into giving in and hiring nurses for Queenie, and thereby drives her further into debt. Granny feels no guilt about the debt or about her neglect of her own family. Her claims of frailty and overwork are just that—claims. As Queenie points out, Granny will outlive both her daughter and her granddaughter. She will watch both of them die without considering either death "a terrible thing."

Granny will never care enough about her family to allow them to live by any other standards than those she thinks appropriate for Miss Helen and her family. Since they cannot be Miss Emilie and Miss Iris, Queenie and Rosie will never be good enough for Granny. As Queenie correctly points out to her daughter: "You ain't gonna be good enough till you turn white" (p. 227). Since Rosie obviously cannot do that, her grandmother's affection is forever lost to her. Rosie will never be "all pink and gold peach-face and long bobbing Shirley Temple curls" (p. 25) like the doll Granny brings home for her. No little black girl will ever be able to live up to the standard of beauty that Granny Huggs has embraced.

Unfailingly, Granny manages to wrap a glowing aura of fantasy about each of the worlds around her. She says early in the novel: "If they's things you don't like and you can't do nothin' about them, you just best pretend they ain't there" (p. 67). Since the preferred lifestyle she offers her family cannot ultimately be realized, she finally moves beyond them altogether, into a state where even the little contact they had with her is no longer possible. Upon Queenie's death, she is detached enough to throw Larnie out of the house a few minutes after she announces the death to Rosie; then she goes to remind Rosie not to get her eyes all red from crying (pp. 244–245). When Rosie dies, she shows absolutely no emotion, but she does have a word for the recently widowed Larnie: "Now mind, I want nothing but lilies and carnations for this funeral. Don't be ordering none of them cheap little roses" (p. 279). These are the very last words of the novel. In the land beyond her mind and behind her consciousness, Granny has remained true to her image of herself and the world.

The extent to which Granny ignores reality can be most consummately illustrated by a conversation she has with Larnie when they at last realize that Rosie is incurably ill. Rosie's debts are so extensive that the house and goods will have to be sold to pay them, yet Granny refuses to accept that. She clings to fantasy because in the world in which she has spent a lifetime as a mammy she has never witnessed the kind of financial worries confronting her own family:

Granny said, "Did you tell her?"

Larnie said, "No. No sense in that now."

"It's a mercy," Granny said. "Long as she don't know, it don't seem true."

"It's true all right," Larnie said. "We gonna lose this house and everything in it, and even then we won't be finished payin' all she owes."

Granny said, "Hush, boy, she might hear you. She won't never let it happen."

Larnie said, "She can't not let anything happen, not now. Time to stop believing in fairy tales."

Granny sounded like she was going to cry. She sounded like that a lot of times, but she never did. "No use talkin' to a crude person like you. You've no idea what a refined person has to go through" (p. 274).

Granny refuses to believe that Rosie can't solve the problems, or that she will die. "Doctors don't know everything," she says to Larnie. "Neither do you" (p. 274). Granny is like a showperson in a menagerie who insists upon her fanciful vision of reality in spite of poverty, roaches, sickness, and death. Yet she rules passively, quietly. And she is more venomous than the black widow spider, for it is not for the sake of storing food to nurture her offspring that she kills; rather, she gluttonously kills her offspring in order to keep feeding some image she has of herself. It is amazing that someone so small and seemingly acquiescent can be so destructive. In the end she perhaps views herself as a martyr, a saint whose elect status has been denied by those too ignorant to see by her lights.

By the time the scene below takes place, the sick, exhausted Rosie is already beyond recovering her physical or mental health. She has aborted Larnie's baby and her lungs are in rags. Granny sends her upstairs to find "a little something I brought home," a present.

Rosie ran breathlessly up both flights of stairs. Two minutes later she descended slowly with a wad of yellowed tissue paper.

"That's the last thing I have of Miss Helen's, Rosalie," Granny told her. "When I was leavin', Miss Emilie sneaked it in my hand. She said she didn't want me to think they'd ever forget me."

"I'll treasure it, Granny," Rosie promised without much conviction. It was an old cameo in a tarnished setting, probably brass.

She turned it over in her hand. The clasp on the back was broken. She wanted badly to believe that it was priceless treasure, but she could not prevent her knowing eyes from assessing it as worthless, cast-off junk.

To conceal her crying, Rosie hugged the old lady tightly, until she felt a stiffening and sensed that Granny was repelled by so much display of emotion. A horribly humorous thought crossed her mind then. Probably all the things Granny had ever brought home were junk (p. 262).

The blinders thus come off in time only for Rosie to see clearly what her past has been, and that she has not escaped it at all. The roach-infested apartment has been traded in on a termite *and* roach-infested antiquated mansion worth much less money, energy, and hope than she has put into it. The delusions she suffers on her deathbed are the clearest visions she has. She lies watching as a roach crawls down her bedpost. She screams for her dead mother, then cries out for Larnie:

But there was no answer.

She turned back and contemplated her old friend.

"You sure followed me a long way," she remarked as he skittered into a crack in the baseboard. "How come you like colored people so much, anyway?"

She added, with increased emphasis, "Well, maybe you like me, but I sure don't like you." Rosie crouched and carefully explored the crack with her fingers. "There better not be no more," she mumbled.

There weren't any more roaches. But there was something worse: the dry empty husk of an egg. And her shuddering hand came away with a coating of fine brown powder.

"Termites!"

Rosie flew downstairs to check the rest of her house for signs of decay, and found them everywhere she looked. Streaks on the wall, scars on the furniture, a long crack down the face of the marble mantel that resembled the west coast of Africa.

The question was: were they new, or had they been there all the time? Had her living room shrunk overnight to its present crowded proportions, or had it always been less grand than her magnifying imagination made it seem? One thing was clear: she had fought and clawed her way to the place where she wanted to be, only to see it crumble into the same ruins she had left behind. . . . The question was: had she bought a palace . . . or just an old, drafty, run-down, rotting house? (p. 276).

She runs through the house looking for more decay and for more roaches in the kitchen; she finds more than enough. It leads her into a frenzy of throwing dishes from cabinets, crying, and smashing roaches with both hands. The hopeless battle and the fact that she is ill and out of bed, fast getting a chill that she does not need, force her to ask the question: *"Did rich white people have roaches too?"* (p. 277) The admission of that possibility completes her mental breakdown; she dashes out in her nightgown and into a bar:

> The crowd in Benny's was startled to see something small and dark and swift dart through it then like a demented arrow. It was a thin girl in a soaked nightgown; apparently drunk, for she was screaming and gesturing wildly. She seemed to be demanding service at the bar. Refused, she began to smash things, knocking a dozen glasses to the floor with one sweep of her hand (p. 278).

Thrown out of the bar, Rosie dies. Rosie dies and Queenie dies, but what Granny represents, even when seemingly aged and frail, lingers on when forces which appear to be stronger are dead. How can the attitudes which perpetuate self-destruction in black communities be killed? How can addiction to standards of beauty and lifestyles inappropriate to the black community be rooted out of the community? Perhaps Hunter sees no viable answer.

Though a true southern maid, Granny does appropriate a few things from the Liveseys; she essentially tricks Miss Emilie out of the rainbow bowl for Rosie, and she steals a Shirley Temple doll for her. But she does not steal out of any heightened sense of awareness, or out of any political sense of injustice; she does it pathetically because it seems to be the thing to do to get closer to the whiteness she so adores and the white ways she so much admires. Her trickery is misdirected, and her consciousness is in a state of cultural lag. Her case illustrates the extent to which immersion in the white culture can have a detrimental effect upon the black domestic who is incapable of compromising effectively—and upon her family. In the extent to which Granny allows her job as maid to destroy natural bonds of affection, the extent to which she lacks political and social consciousness, and the extent to which she is unaware of the implications of northern territory, she anticipates Morrison's Pauline Breedlove, who is also a southern mammy in northern territory.

Toni Morrison's *The Bluest Eye* (1970) is the story of the influences on young black girls growing up in the early 1940's. It offers positive and negative role models and values, and presents, embodied in the maid Pauline Breedlove, one of the most destructive forces which shapes the lifeview of black girls in a world where they are taught that black beauty is not the model for their emulation. Set in Lorain, Ohio, the novel recounts the story of two black families, the Breedloves and the MacTeers, contrasting nine-year-old Claudia MacTeer, her ten-year-old sister Frieda, and their parents with Pecola and Sammy Breedlove and their parents, Cholly and Pauline. Although Claudia has a narrative voice, her point of view alternating with the omniscient voice of Morrison, the story is more about the Breedloves, particularly Pecola, than about the MacTeers. The MacTeers, lavish with love if not with luxuries, manage to give their daughters healthy world views, and the girls manage to have healthy responses to their blackness. On the other hand, eleven-year-old Pecola, who has been baptized in the Shirley Temple cult of beauty, wishes for blue eyes as a manifest sign that she has escaped her blackness and the ugliness she sees it. Instead of nurturing in her daughter a positive image of herself, Pauline Breedlove rejects Pecola because she lacks, in her eyes, the beauty and virtue of the white children in the world where Pauline works as maid. Claudia and Frieda watch over this negation of life as Pecola is rejected by children at school, beaten by her mother, raped and impregnated by her drunken father, and finally driven insane as a result of those successive shocks. Pecola Breedlove and Rosie Fleming are sisters in more than one metaphorical sense.

Like Mammy Jane, Pauline Breedlove identifies completely with the white world and takes excessive, self-deprecating pride in child-rearing, cooking, and cleaning for it. She rejoices in the perfect little family of which she is a part in the white house and of which she can never envision the parallel in the black world. The irony of her notion of family is apparent in the omniscient sections of the novel, where Morrison uses the children's reader about Dick, Jane, Mother, Father, their fine suburban house, their dog, and their cat to show that middle class white family structures and values in the United States are grossly antithetical to the black experience. Poverty is omnipresent for the Breedloves, and their house is a cast-off hand-me-down store-front shamble. Father is a drunk and Mother is a maid; Dick runs away from home, Jane inadvertently poisons the dog, and the cat is almost killed. Pauline fails to see the folly of expecting her family to be like the storybook white family, and she lacks both the knowledge and the instinct to nurture her children into healthy adults. Hollywood movies represent her vision of the best of all possible worlds, one to which she escapes as often as she can. Clark Gable and Jean Harlow are a happy contrast to the few clothes and two rooms she must live in. Children born to a parent with such distorted, unrealistic values can only miraculously develop strong conceptions of themselves.

Pauline, like Mammy Jane and Granny Huggs and all other true southern mammies, is apolitical. She never suspects that her family may live in an abandoned store front because her husband has been driven to drink as a result of the pressures he has faced on his job. She never considers that the lacks she sees so vividly in her own family may in some way be related to the place to which the Fishers (her current employers) and those like them have assigned all Blacks in the United States, or considers that they might be related to the psychologically destructive self-images foisted upon Blacks; instead, she blames her children for not being beautiful, bright, and adorable and her husband for not being able to find and hold a job. She cannot conceive that her husband's drinking habits might not be totally his fault or that she should judge her children by a standard of beauty that has not been formed by and for American whites.

Pauline Breedlove, then, left the South physically, but in her actions and attitudes toward the whites for whom she works, she is still very much a southern mammy. Born in Alabama, she was "the ninth of eleven children" in a family which "lived on a ridge of red Alabama clay seven miles from the nearest road."[12] A nail puncture through her foot when she was two saved her, Morrison says, from "total anonymity." She used the slight deformity which resulted to explain many things: why she had no nickname, why there were no jokes or stories about her, why nobody teased her. "Her general feeling of separateness and unworthiness she blamed on her foot" (p. 88). She had only four years of schooling, and she apparently experienced little that was unusual or exciting as a child. She "cultivated quiet and private pleasures," Morrison says. "She liked, most of all, to arrange things. To line things up in rows—jars on shelves at canning, peach pits on the step, sticks, stones, leaves. . . . Whatever portable plurality she found, she organized into neat lines, according to their size, shape, or gradations of color. Just as she would never align a pine needle with the leaf of a cottonwood tree, she would never put the jars of tomatoes next to the green beans" (pp. 88–89). She missed, Morrison maintains, "paints and crayons."

Pauline's family moved to Kentucky when she was an adolescent, and there, as the oldest girl at home, once her mother returned to work, she:

> took over the care of the house. She kept the fence in repair, pulling the pointed stakes erect, securing them with bits of wire, collected eggs, swept, cooked, washed, and minded the two younger children—a pair of twins called Chicken and Pie, who were still in school. She was not only good at housekeeping, *she enjoyed it*. After her parents left for work and the other children were at school or in mines, the house was quiet. The stillness and isolation both calmed and energized her. She could arrange and clean without interruption until two o'clock, when Chicken and Pie came home (pp. 89–90, emphasis mine).

She passively acquiesced in whatever happened to her. When her order was disturbed, she quietly restored it after the disturbance: Morrison reports that "when by some accident somebody scattered her rows, they always stopped to retrieve them for her, and she was never angry, for it gave her a chance to rearrange them again" (pp. 88–89).

All this foreshadows what Pauline will do once she gets to Lorain. Still lacking the paints and crayons and still undistinguished, she will resort to making maid work into art work, a perverse creativity which will separate her further and further from her family. Her love and near-reverence for household work and for the arrangement of things will intensify in Ohio.

Pauline arrives in Ohio to discover that the world created for her by Cholly, the long-awaited, knightly "Presence" for whom she has hoped, is not without loneliness and "vacant places." Cholly goes off to work, and she follows her old pattern of cleaning things. Unfortunately, the two have only two rooms and it doesn't take very long to clean them. Pauline is both idle and totally dependent upon Cholly; she stagnates at home while he works or goes drinking with new friends. Pauline is further set apart because she cannot reach out of her southernness to touch the northern Blacks around her. She "felt uncomfortable with the few black women she met. They were amused by her because she did not straighten her hair. When she tried to make up her face as they did, it came off rather badly. Their goading glances and private snickers at her way of talking (saying 'chil'ren') and dressing developed in her a desire for new clothes" (p. 94); the desire for clothes leads to quarrels with Cholly about money. Pauline decides to go to work, at first by the day. The money she makes helps with the clothes, but more and more she and Cholly fight over money, and they soon destroy the hopefulness with which their marriage had begun. Pauline quickly retreats into the solace of constant cleaning: "After several months of doing day work, she took a steady job in the home of a family of slender means and nervous, pretentious ways" (p. 94). She loses a tooth, has two children whom she rejects at some level of consciousness because she believes they are ugly, and begins to see Cholly as a mere sinful burden she will carry for many years. Apart from her absences from domestic work during the births of her children, her return to it is permanent.

Pauline Breedlove, in the homes of the white women for whom she works, becomes another example of the maid who cannot effect an acceptable compromise between the kind of work she does and the person she is. She maintains her subservience and is presumably thankful for the jobs she has. As her husband grows in drunkenness and her children in ugliness, as her husband's sporadic work habits force her to assume the dominant position of breadwinner, she relies increasingly on the white house for identity. Morrison comments:

It was her good fortune to find a permanent job in the home of a well-to-do family whose members were affectionate, appreciative, and generous. She looked at their houses, smelled their linen, touched their silk draperies, and loved all of it. . . . She became what is known as an ideal servant, for such a role filled practically all of her needs. When she bathed the little Fisher girl, it was in a porcelain tub with silvery taps running infinite quantities of hot, clear water. She dried her in fluffy white towels and put her in cuddly night clothes. Then she brushed the yellow hair, enjoying the roll and slip of it between her fingers. No zinc tub, no buckets of stove-heated water, no flaky, stiff, grayish towels washed in a kitchen sink, dried in a dusty backyard, no tangled black puffs of rough wool to comb. Soon she stopped trying to keep her own house. The things she could afford to buy did not last, had no beauty or style, and were absorbed by the dingy storefront. More and more she neglected her house, her children, her man—they were like the afterthoughts one has just before sleep, the early-morning and late-evening edges of her day, the dark edges that made the daily life with the Fishers lighter, more delicate, more lovely. Here she could arrange things, clean things, line things up in neat rows. . . . All the meaningfulness of her life was in her work (pp. 100–101, 102).

Pauline, a "queen" in the Fisher household, "reign[s] over" the bounty there, especially in the kitchen. Pauline Breedlove, who has never had a nickname (a sign of lack of affection from family and kin, she believes), is christened "Polly" (p. 101) by the Fishers, and she gets exquisite pleasure from the attention. She in turn protects the Fishers' home against "invasion" by her own family.

Her desire so to protect it indicates how ineffectively Pauline has compromised. She has suppressed self completely and because her goals are not obvious or long range, in that she is not using the whites to support kids in college or something comparable, she runs the risk of becoming a possession. Any white mistress might say, "That's my Mary," as a measure of appreciation, but when her employer says, "That's our Polly," Pauline beams. She is truly "theirs." She denies love to her own children, Pecola and Sammy, and adores the little white girl for whose family she works; her actions show that distortion or perversion of parental affection can be one of the major consequences of ineffective compromise. Pauline becomes a glorified mammy because she sees that as the crowning achievement of an

undistinguished existence. Therefore, when Pecola and her friends
Claudia and Frieda come to the kitchen to see her, they must wait
patiently and immobilely while Pauline gathers wash. When the
black children, in typical childish fashion, explore the kitchen and
Pecola spills a "deep-dish berry cobbler," Pauline becomes the sol-
dier defending the white outpost against what she views as unscrupu-
lous enemies:

> In one gallop she was on Pecola, and with the back of her hand
> knocked her to the floor. Pecola slid in the pie juice, one leg
> folding under her. Mrs. Breedlove yanked her up by the arm,
> slapped her again, and in a voice thin with anger, abused Pecola
> directly and Frieda and me [Claudia] by implication.
> "Crazy fool . . . my floor, mess . . . look what you . . . work . . .
> get on out . . . now that . . . crazy . . . my floor, my floor . . . my
> floor." . . .
> The little girl in pink started to cry. Mrs. Breedlove turned to
> her. "Hush, baby, hush. Come here. Oh, Lord, look at your dress.
> Don't cry no more. Polly will change it." She went to the sink and
> turned tap water on a fresh towel. Over her shoulder she spit out
> words to us like rotten pieces of apple. "Pick up that wash and get
> on out of here, so I can get this mess cleaned up" (pp. 86–87).

Pecola suffers painful burns from the hot pie, but her mother ignores
her. In rushing to comfort "the little pink-and-yellow girl" and abus-
ing her own child, Pauline continues the slave tradition of an adult
Black making the welfare of a white child his or her primary concern.
The vehemence with which she screams at the black children to get
out of "my" kitchen epitomizes both the vehemence of her attempt to
reject biological kinship with her own child and the vehemence of her
rejection of cultural kinship with anything black; she "banishes the
three black girls from Paradise."[13] Black is ugly and bad; white is the
model for the good and the beautiful.

We can only sense in Pecola's quiet departure a portion of what
Wright actually says he felt when he and his brother were in the
kitchen of a white woman for whom his mother worked. That which
Wright received there may have been tolerable, but that which was
denied to him made the greater impression:

I got occasional scraps of bread and meat; but many times I regretted having come, for my nostrils would be assailed with the scent of food that did not belong to me and which I was forbidden to eat. Toward evening my mother would take the hot dishes into the dining room where the white people were seated, and I would stand as near as the dining-room door as possible to get a quick glimpse of the white faces gathered around the loaded table, eating, laughing, talking. If the white people left anything, my brother and I would eat well; but if they did not, we would have our usual bread and tea.[14]

Although Wright's mother does not go to the lengths that Pauline Breedlove does in protecting the sanctity of white property and food, she must nevertheless, by the very nature of her work, set constricting boundaries on what Wright and his brother may and may not do in "her" kitchen. Pauline Breedlove draws the boundary lines in such a way as to cast out her child from cleanliness, beauty and good food and to encircle herself with those things; she is completely an appendage to the white world.

Pauline's consequent ownership by her white mistresses enables the women to interfere in the intimate areas of her life. One white woman, for example, is able to demand that she leave the drunken Cholly Breedlove if she is to continue to work for her; when Cholly shows up drunk and Pauline follows him away from her job, the white woman refuses to allow her to return unless she has left him. She also refuses to pay Pauline the eleven dollars she owes her:

> She didn't understand that all I needed from her was my eleven dollars to pay the gas man so I could cook. She couldn't get that one thing through her thick head. "Are you going to leave him, Pauline?" she kept on saying. I thought she'd give me my money if I said I would, so I said "Yes, ma'am." "All right," she said. "You leave him, and then come back to work, and we'll let bygones be bygones." "Can I have my money today?" I said. "No" she said. "Only when you leave him. I'm only thinking of you and your future. What good is he, Pauline, what good is he to you?" (p. 96)

While Pauline realizes that "*it didn't seem none too bright for a black woman to leave a black man for a white woman*" (p. 95), the intimacy she herself has cultivated allows the woman to be as presumptuous as she desires. Pauline has put herself in the position to have her life directed just as easily as a child might have its life directed. And indeed, Pauline is essentially an impressionable child, one whose identity may be shaped and determined by the whites. Since control of wages is one of the most important components of the maid/ mistress relationship, Pauline has especially compromised herself; she does not get the eleven dollars. This disappointment, however, does not cause Pauline to reverse her identification with whites.

Whatever is sustaining or spiritually uplifting, Pauline finds in Jesus and the white folks (especially the Fishers), never in her own family and home. Her sense of self-worth comes from playing the role of THE MAID. She is titillated with appreciation when Mr. Fisher says; "I would rather sell her blueberry cobblers than real estate," or when she overhears Mrs. Fisher saying, "We'll never let her go. We could never find anybody like Polly. She will *not* leave the kitchen until everything is in order. Really, she is the ideal servant" (p. 101). And just as she kept a world of orderliness, privately, when she was a child, so now does she keep the joy she gets from the Fishers to herself. "Here she found beauty, order, cleanliness, and praise. . . . Pauline kept this order, this beauty, for herself, a private world, and never introduced it into her storefront, or to her children" (pp. 101–102).

The storefront is where the Breedloves live, the shocking contrast to the primness of the Fisher house. Morrison describes the corner house that Pauline will never make into a home as an abandoned store which "foisted" itself on the passerby. The store had in turn been a pizza parlor, a bakery, and a base of gypsy operations, and was now but a box of "peeling gray":

> The plan of the living quarters was as unimaginative as a first-generation Greek landlord could contrive it to be. The large "store" area was partitioned into two rooms by beaverboard planks that did not reach to the ceiling. There was a living room, which the family called the front room, and the bedroom, where all the living was done. In the front room were two sofas, an upright piano, and a tiny artificial Christmas tree which had been there, decorated and dust-laden, for two years. The bedroom had three

beds: a narrow iron bed for Sammy, fourteen years old, another for Pecola, eleven years old, and a double bed for Cholly and Mrs. Breedlove. In the center of the bedroom, for the even distribution of heat, stood a coal stove. Trunks, chairs, a small end table, and a cardboard "wardrobe" closet were placed around the walls. The kitchen was in the back of this apartment, a separate room. There were no bath facilities. Only a toilet bowl, inaccessible to the eye, if not the ear, of the tenants.

There is nothing more to say about the furnishings. They were anything but describable, having been conceived, manufactured, shipped, and sold in various states of thoughtlessness, greed, and indifference (p. 31).

Pauline has no desire to improve the place; she has, in fact, given up on its possibilities for change.

This background at "home" heightens her delight in housecleaning elsewhere, and it highlights the perversion of the artistry she works. Her creativity does not exist apart from her fanatical carrying out of her job. She trades family, culture, and heritage to become an anachronistic mammy, and she recognizes no life beyond that identity. She is incapable of putting into accurate perspective the historical and social forces which cause her to be where she is, for she lacks powers of introspection. She willingly exists in a world someone else has defined for her and, through her consent, is guilty of exhibiting the traits which illustrate that her role is more important than she is.

Pauline keeps white cleanliness and beauty for herself, but forces upon her family the respectability that constitutes her idea of white Christianity:

She came into her own with the women who had despised her, by being more moral than they; she avenged herself on Cholly by forcing him to indulge in the weaknesses she despised. She joined a church where shouting was frowned upon, served on Stewardess Board No. 3, and became a member of Ladies Circle No. 1. At prayer meeting she moaned and sighed over Cholly's ways, and hoped God would help her keep the children from the sins of the father. She stopped saying 'chil'ren' and said 'childring' instead. She let another tooth fall, and was outraged by painted ladies who thought only of clothes and men. Holding Cholly as a model of sin and failure, she bore him like a crown of thorns, and her children like a cross (p. 100).

She marries Jesus as she had the white folks, pushing the romantic relationship she has had with Cholly into the background and blanketing herself in the respectability of the church. She initially misses the gentleness with which she and Cholly had once made love, then consoles herself. *"But I don't care 'bout it no more. My Maker will take care of me. I know He will. I know He will. Besides, it don't make no difference about this old earth. There is sure to be a glory"* (p. 104). The knock-down, drag-out fights she has with Cholly do not seem to clash with either her understanding of religion or her image of Christian wifeliness.

Pauline fails as a mother not only by analogy to *Dick and Jane* but by any definition of motherhood. She has bent her children "toward respectability, and in so doing taught them fear: fear of being clumsy, fear of being like their father, fear of not being loved by God, fear of madness like Cholly's mother's. Into her son she beat a loud desire to run away [which he had done twenty-seven times by the age of fourteen], and into her daughter she beat a fear of growing up, fear of other people, fear of life" (p. 102). In their ugliness, their poverty, in short, their non-whiteness, they win Pauline's tolerance—and she accepts a responsibility to give them the mere subsistencies of life— but they cannot win her love. She distances herself from them to the point of insisting that they refer to her as "Mrs. Breedlove," saving, as we have seen, all her love, affection, gentleness, and warmth for the Fishers and others like them. She kowtows to the whites and, through her religion, wields cruel power over her own family: just as she humbles herself before white women in their power, remembering always her place, her children are expected to humble themselves before the power of the church and accept the lowly place in her world that she has assigned to them. Under the guise of bringing them up as Christians, she has shaped them, in part, as she was shaped in the South—to be hesitant about living, to be generally unaggressive, to be apologetic for being alive.

Both Jacqueline de Weever and Barbara Christian talk about inversion in *The Bluest Eye*, about how expected roles are therein negated.[15] Its fathers are not like those in *Dick and Jane*; they do not inspire love and respect in their children. Mothers are not warm and smiling. There are enough stunted adults in the novel to ensure that children like Pecola will never develop healthy conceptions of what they as adults might be. Instead, Pecola, like Gwendolyn Brooks's Little Lincoln West, grows "uglily upward."[16] Pauline can only succeed in transferring her own warped vision and self-hatred to her daughter—a legacy uncannily destructive.

The substance of the legacy she passes on prevents Pauline from separating her identity from the whites long enough for her to wear a mask on her job. She would never think of appropriating any goods from the homes of whites for whom she works; the praise she gets from Mr. and Mrs. Fisher perhaps, to her, takes the place of several dollars pay (the salary they pay her is not mentioned). She cannot conceive of unfairness in the domestic arrangements of which she is a part; she has every confidence that the whites will appreciate her great abilities as a domestic and will reward her justly and fairly. She is undoubtedly good at what she does, but she is equally undoubtedly overworked and giving much more than she is receiving. Her satisfaction with the status quo in itself betrays her as a mammy. Although she is in the North, that mythic place of symbolic if not real freedom, she has absorbed the white world's vision of her place and proper subservience as thoroughly as had the South's Mammy Jane.

CHAPTER FOUR

AN ANOMALY IN
SOUTHERN TERRITORY

Richard Wright's "Man of All Work" (1961) is a classic study of the stereotyped attitudes that surround the black domestic who goes to work in the white world. Specifically, it deals with sexual exploitation of the black maid, but it also touches upon black/white relationships in general: upon white men's response to black women, upon the taboo on white women as sex objects for black men, upon the mutual exploitation of the races.[1] It further raises questions about the over-protection of black men by black women; in their efforts to keep black men from being emasculated by forces outside the home, the women sometimes create situations where the men are emasculated in their relationships with them. The story finally comments on whites in their roles as parents.

Although the story may be classified as an anomaly because it has a male character who plays the role of a female, it still has features which tie it more closely to the traits identified with southern maids instead of with northern ones. In fact, much suggests that the setting has purposely been given an exaggerated, almost mythical southern-ness. It does not bear the name of any southern city, but it is as comparable to Savannah or Macon or Mobile as Paule Marshall's Bourne Island is to Grenada or Jamaica or Barbados. Characteristics identified with southern territory and attitudes have been inextricably wound into the story. Wright has constructed the story—written completely in dialogue—so that external knowledge of history and relationships between Blacks and whites in the South must be brought to bear upon it, to understand its multi-layers of personal interaction. An understanding of the role of the black maid in particular, both in stereotype and in reality, is essential.

"Man of All Work" is the story of Carl, a black man who, while his wife Lucy is recuperating from childbirth, dons her maid's uniform to go to work for a white family. A professional cook who has recently lost his job and is desperate, Carl pursues the disguise and the maid's job against his wife's wishes: the outrageous and hilarious circumstances in which he will find himself are in fact foreshadowed by her objections. And his story illustrates how quickly a role can re-define an individual. Carl, who the reader knows is male, puts on the uniform and immediately becomes hot momma maid, the sex object, to Dave Fairchild, the husband of his employer. Carl is just another body to fill the slot he has appointed for maids: he can see no individual black women, just bodies in the role of maid, bodies which certainly have no desire or power to resist his sexual advances.

Mr. Fairchild sees all black women who come to work in his house as objects for his personal use and abuse. Certainly they will drink with him, he believes, because all nigger bitches drink, and certainly they will respond to his pawing, because all of them want to be touched by white men. Besides, their black men are not doing them any good anyway. The irony of his beliefs becomes apparent as a white man tries to seduce a black man. Wright has eliminated the usual foci of competition between black men and white men—either black women or white women—and has made them confront each other directly. Instead of emasculating a black man by taking his woman, Mr. Fairchild is forced to try to seduce or conquer the black man directly. In his so doing, however, the white man's sexuality and power are minimized and ridiculed because he is seen as trying to commit a homosexual act. Mr. Fairchild's drinking intensifies his impotency and sets him up for yet further ridicule.

Unaware of Carl's masculinity, however, Mr. Fairchild has toward him all the attitudes he has toward black women generally. Because Bertha, the previous maid, has shared Mr. Fairchild's whiskey and "wrestled" with him, he expects Carl to do the same. (It should be pointed out that Mrs. Fairchild is aware of her husband's antics with the maids. They either quit or she fires them when she "discovers" what her husband does on his lunch hour.) When he comes home for lunch and tries to seduce Carl, the resistance he meets only inspires further assault. The more he suffers in defeat, the greater is his desire to conquer; Carl knocks him down more than once, but he keeps trying to get the upper hand, and when it looks as if he is conclusively losing the physical battle, he resorts to his whiteness for support, for what it represents in terms of power, control and superiority. When Carl urges Mr. Fairchild to leave him alone or he will twist his arm, the man responds with "Goddamn, this nigger woman says she'll lick me. We'll see!"[2] Mr. Fairchild cannot tolerate the possibility of physical defeat by a woman, or of racial defeat by a black person. He must "teach" the black woman a lesson, and the epithets he directs at "Lucy" show his increasing agitation. "She" is a "strong bitch" (p. 117), a "nigger woman" (p. 118) "a sassy nigger bitch" (p. 118), and finally a "black bitch" (p. 118) who will get her neck broken for hitting Mr. Fairchild.

Mr. Fairchild forgets that he is fighting a "woman" and, fighting for the essence of his identity, gives up fairness in favor of winning. When Carl has him pinned to the floor, he cries out: "Turn me loose or I'll kick you in the stomach!" (p. 118). Proverbially, Mr. Fairchild has bitten off more than he can chew, but his understanding of who and what he is will not allow him to quit even when Carl pins him again as his wife enters the house. He loses the fight, but he wins ultimately by keeping his good name and reputation; Carl wins the fight, but loses when he is shot and accused, ironically, of rape, then wins when he obtains two hundred dollars from the Fairchilds to pay off his mortgage (a Pyhrric victory at best).

Mr. Fairchild's response to Carl's resistance is deeply informed by his sense of place. The first to see Carl when he came for his job interview, he reported to his wife that the applicant "seems clean, strong. *Knows her place*" (p. 104, my emphasis). To resist his sexual advances is to step out of place, to be uppity. In her place, "Lucy" should be understanding and receptive, and Mr. Fairchild will do for "her" what "her" husband is unable to do. He tells Carl: "I just want to make you feel good" (p. 117). His assumption that he can make black women feel good and that the chosen woman will not have the

will or the audacity to resist presumably leaves only the option of
submission for "Lucy," unless "she" is ready simply to quit "her" job
and leave the house.

Carl's interaction with Mr. Fairchild provides the central satiric
hilarity of the tale, but his interaction with Anne Fairchild is equally
important. With her, Carl is in a real dilemma: what is expected of
him as a black "woman" and his pre-conditioned responses as a black
man in the presence of a white woman, one of Wright's recurring
themes, are in radical conflict. As maid, Carl is immediately assigned
cooking, cleaning, and child-care duties. These he takes in stride, but
when he is asked to scrub Mrs. Fairchild's back during her bath, he
almost collapses in panic. That scene will provide Mr. Fairchild with
his mad accusation of rape, and it deserves to be quoted extensively.

> —Lucy!
> —Yessum. I'm coming.
> —Come here, please!
> —Yessum. On the way, ma'am.
> —Lucy!
> —Yessum. Where are you, Mrs. Fairchild?
> —I'm here in the bathroom. Won't you come in?
> I want you to wash my back.
> —Hunh?
> —Come into the bathroom.
> —Ma'am?
> —Right here. I hear you. Open the door and come in. I want you
> to wash my back.
> —Yessum.
> —Lucy, can't you hear me?
> —Yessum.
> —Then open the door and come in.
> —Er . . . Er, yessum.
> —Well, what's the matter, Lucy? Why are you poking your head
> like that around the door? Come in. I want you to wash my back
> with this brush. Come on in. I haven't got all day, Lucy.
> —Yessum.
> —I don't want to be late for work. Well, come on. Why are you
> standing there and staring like that at me?
> —Er . . .

—Don't you feel well, Lucy?

—Yessum.

—Then come here and wash my back.

—Yessum.

—That's it. Scrub hard. I won't break. Do it hard. Oh, Lord, what's the matter with you? Your arm's shaking. Lucy?

—Ma'am.

—What's come over you? Are you timid or ashamed or something?

—No'm.

—Are you upset because I'm sitting here naked in the bathtub?

—Oh, no, ma'am.

—Then what's the matter? My God, your face is breaking out in sweat. You look terrible. Are you ill, Lucy?

—No, Ma'am. I'm all right.

—Then scrub my back. Hard. Why, your arms are like rubber. Well, I never. You're acting very strange. Do I offend you because I ask you to wash my back? Bertha always helped me with my bath . . .

—It's just the first t-t-time . . .

—Oh, I see. Well, I don't see why I should frighten you. I'm a woman like you are.

—Yessum.

—A bit harder, Lucy. Higher, up between my shoulder blades. That's it, that's it. Aw . . . Good. That's enough. Now, Lucy, hand me that towel over there. Where're you going? You're not leaving yet. I'm not through. Oh, I must be careful getting out of this tub. Tub's [sic] are dangerous things; you can have accidents by slipping in tubs . . . Lucy, give me the towel . . . WHAT IS HAPPENING TO YOU, LUCY? Why are you staring at me like that? Take a hand towel from that rack and wipe your face. Are you well? Maybe the doctor ought to take a good look at you. My brother-in-law, Burt Stallman, is a doctor. Do you want me to call him for you?

—It's just hot in here, ma'am.

—Hot? Why it's rather cold to me. I'm cold, you're hot. What's wrong with you? HAND ME THE TOWEL! Now, that box of talcum . . . Thanks (pp. 109–111).

The nearly speechless Carl, mechanically mumbling "Yessum" throughout the scene, shares the immobilization of Wright's other characters Bigger Thomas and Big Boy in their scenes in forbidden white territory. Bigger, who cannot overcome his fear at the thought of being caught in a white woman's bedroom, smothers Mary Dalton to death. Big Boy, less afraid but at first equally immobilized when he encounters a white woman near a forbidden swimming hole, springs into hysterical action and also kills. Carl, who is more in control of himself than either of the other two, manages, but not without difficulty, to survive the ordeal. He collapses on the back steps once he is allowed to leave the bathroom. Certainly "Man of All Work" has a lighter tone and a happier ending than *Native Son* or "Big Boy Leaves Home," but Carl can no more than Bigger or Big Boy escape his history as a black man in a white country. He knows as well as they that black men cannot possibly encounter nude white women or show their nakedness to them and claim innocent intentions.

Carl finds himself in double jeopardy, racially, in the bathroom scene. He suffers as a black man in the presence of a white woman, and, as a black female domestic, he is reduced to performing an act (scrubbing Mrs. Fairchild's back) which shows the low status he has in relation to the white woman. He has not been in the Fairchild household for more than two hours when the request for backscrubbing comes. Mrs. Fairchild does not stop to consider the maid's view of backscrubbing. Consider, further, the following part of the bathroom scene:

—Oh, Lucy, I've just got to watch my figure. Don't you think I'm too fat?
—Ma'am, some folks are just naturally a bit heavy, you know.
—But my breasts—aren't they much too large?
—Maybe . . . a little . . .
—And my thighs, aren't they much too large?
—Maybe . . . a little . . .
—Lucy, you are too polite to tell me what you really think. I wish I were as slender as you. How do you manage it?
—Just working hard, I guess, ma'am.
—Really, Lucy, I like you very much. Ha, ha! You're like a sixteen-year-old girl. I'm surprised that you've had two children (p. 112).

Carl does not need a Phi Beta Kappa key to know that he must respond diplomatically to Mrs. Fairchild's questions.

But that is not the only sort of tact required of him. In their initial interview, Mrs. Fairchild tells him that the previous maid, Bertha, "was a disappointment" to her. "She seemed so nice. But she drank. And when she did, her conduct was awful. Guess you know what I mean?" (p. 105) Of course the awful conduct involved Mr. Fairchild and of course Carl understands, but Mrs. Fairchild stops just short of being explicit about her guidelines for conduct between black women and white men. Later, after Mr. Fairchild has loudly enjoyed Carl's pancakes and gone off to work, Mrs. Fairchild decides she should pursue the matter of conduct a bit further. She starts the conversation:

— . . . There's something I must say to you and there's no better time than now, while I'm drying myself. I want to talk frankly to you, as one woman to another.
—Yessum.
—Now, I didn't tell you when you first came here why I had to get rid of my last maid. Now, look, my husband, Dave, likes to take a drink now and then—maybe a drop more than is good for him. Otherwise, he's perfectly sober, thoughtful, and easy to get along with. You know what I mean?
—Yessum. I think I know.
—Now, Bertha too did a little drinking now and then. And, when both of 'em started drinking—well, you can imagine what happened. Understand?
—Yessum.
—Now, Lucy, tell me: do you drink?
—No, ma'am. Not a drop.
—Good. As long as you don't drink, my husband won't bother you and you can very well defend yourself. Just push him away. Now, as one woman to another, do we understand each other?
—Mrs. Fairchild, your husband isn't going to touch me.
—Well, I'm glad to hear you say it like that. Dave's not so much a problem, Lucy. He gets the way men get sometimes. Afterwards he's ashamed enough to want to go out and drown himself or something. Understand? Any strong-minded person can handle Dave when he's like that. But if you're like Bertha, then trouble's bound to come.
—Yessum. You can depend on me, Mrs. Fairchild. . . .

—Listen, Lucy, what I've discussed with you about my husband is just between us, see?

—Yessum. I won't open my mouth to anybody, Ma'am.

—How do you and your husband get along?

—Oh, fine, ma'am (pp. 111–112).

Still without graphic details, the conversation nevertheless makes the problem of Mr. Fairchild's aggressive sexual promiscuity clear. Mrs. Fairchild demands her maid's denial that that aggressive promiscuity is any such thing. Mr. Fairchild is a devilish little innocent; his intended violations can be rebuffed easily. As Carl's fight with the man will indicate, neither of those things is true, but Mrs. Fairchild needs, as many of her antebellum sisters had needed, to cling to some fantasy of marital fidelity and family cohesiveness. She confides in "Lucy," exploiting their feminine ties, and assumes that the black woman will keep what is said to herself. After all, as Katzman suggests in his comment about invisibility, maids are looked upon as sponges; they soak up confidences but very seldom put them out again—at least not to the friends and neighbors whose good opinions matter to the Fairchilds. The pattern is an old one. Black women have not only had their labor exploited and their bodies abused: they have additionally had to soak up the intimate slime of their employers' personal lives. Grace Halsell, a white woman who dyed herself black and worked as a maid, recounts being *talked at* for hours when one of her employers needed to spill all the gossipy ugliness of her life.[3] Halsell was not expected to respond—that would have been presumption on the particle of humanity the white woman was confiding in—she was merely expected to listen. A "tactful" maid may thus be expected to deny both the truth and herself.

It is significant that Mrs. Fairchild asks "Lucy" about "her" relationship with "her" husband. If a black woman has a happy marriage and is indeed the hard, honest worker and good church-woman "Lucy" has presented herself to be, then perhaps she will be less inclined to engage in hanky-panky with Mr. Fairchild. But the fact that Mrs. Fairchild asks the question about the maid's personal life indicates that she has already admitted the possibility that "Lucy" might be tempted by Mr. Fairchild, a possibility which is irrelevant to "Lucy's" individual case. Rather, it is bound up in the stereotype of the hot momma black woman: a lascivious beast lurks just beneath the clean, presentable, respectable exterior of even the black woman much influenced by the social institutions of marriage and church.

This attitude of Mrs. Fairchild's combines with her need to keep up a facade of marital solidarity when she walks in on Mr. Fairchild "wrestling" with Carl. She initially admonishes her husband (DAVE, OH DAVE . . . YOU DRIVE ME CRAZY! EVERY TIME I TURN MY BACK THIS HAPPENS! AND YOU SWORE TO ME IT'D NEVER HAPPEN AGAIN!), then she turns her fury on the black woman (AND I THOUGHT I COULD TRUST YOU, LUCY! I'M SICK AND TIRED OF THIS! THIS IS THE END!). She grabs a gun which she furiously directs at "Lucy," who momentarily symbolizes Dave's promiscuity and Anne's acute sense of dissatisfaction with the deteriorating marriage her lying, cheating husband has created: "Get out of my way, Dave," she warns, "I'll be made a fool of no longer. For all I know, you might have sent this black bitch here to work . . . No wonder she came so early in the morning. Now, I'm going to kill her" (pp. 119–120). But she and her husband then join in a scapegoating ritual comparable to that in the battle royal scene of Ellison's *Invisible Man*. By attributing their basest sexual desires to the black boys they have forced to watch a nude white dancer, Ellison's respectable, upright white town leaders can cling to an untainted image of themselves. Similarly, in attributing sexual promiscuity and the disruption of their family to the black woman, the Fairchilds attempt to retain an image of themselves as morally pure and socially stable. When Anne Fairchild says "THIS IS THE END!" her husband responds:

—O.K., Anne. Send this bitch away, right now. Let's send her packing.
—No. Don't speak to me, Dave. I've got a better idea. Just wait.
—You see, Lucy. My wife saw what you were doing.
—You goddamn rotten white man.
—Lucy, get your damned things together and get the hell out of here. Be gone before my wife comes back in (p. 119).

Mr. Fairchild joins forces with his wife ("Let's") in establishing a union of power against which most black maids in similar situations would have been powerless.

When, instead of sending Carl away, Anne shoots him, Dave Fairchild resorts to every stereotype he can evoke about Blacks in order to worm his way out of responsibility for the situation. He calls Dr. Burt Stallman, his wife's brother-in-law, to come over and attend to the maid. He then advises Anne to "take it easy." "Look," he says, "I did the shooting. see? I'll take the blame." But he does not; he continues, "I found her stealing and I asked [sic] to halt. She ran. I shot her" (p. 122). Mr. Fairchild assumes it will be easy to make a case against a maid for stealing; "Lucy" will then be to blame for her wound, having "asked for it." Mr. Fairchild has an even better case at his disposal when he has discovered that the maid is a man:

> —Anne, Burt, listen . . . I've got it solved. It's simple. This nigger put on a dress to worm his way into my house to rape my wife! Ha! *See?* Then I detected 'im. I shot 'im in self-defense, shot 'im to protect my honor, my home. That's our answer! I was protecting white womanhood from a nigger rapist impersonating a woman! A rapist who wears a dress is the worst sort! Any jury'll free me on that. Anne, that's our case (p. 125).[4]

Mr. Fairchild knows that, from an historical point of view, he has Carl almost literally "by the balls." The one thing that can possibly save Wright's protagonist from lynching or imprisonment is Anne Fairchild's testimony, and she chooses not to lie. Significantly, she does not stop lying to herself about her husband's character; she simply says that in "this" case "I'll not lie. . . . You can't make me lie" (p. 125). Her refusal to do so offers Carl a shaky escape at best, for Mrs. Fairchild's motive is not to save him; she is merely thoroughly exasperated with her husband—for the moment. The fate of the black man who encounters a white woman is ever thus precarious.

Carl, of course, is aware from the beginning of the dangerous possibilities of the game he is playing. Interestingly, his identity is most consistently challenged by Lily, the Fairchilds' six-year-old daughter. Mr. Fairchild is preoccupied with an imagined "Lucy's" body, and Mrs. Fairchild is preoccupied with her own body; Lily, however, sees something strange in a maid who is as hairy and as muscular as "Lucy" is. She notices his arms as Carl is washing the breakfast dishes, and she takes him through an inquisition straight out of Little Red Riding Hood:

> —Lucy, your arms are so big.
> —Hunh?

—And there's so much hair on them.
—Oh, that's nothing.
—And you've got so many big muscles.
—Oh, that comes from washing and cleaning and cooking. Lifting heavy pots and pans.
—And your voice is not at all like Bertha's.
—What do you mean?
—Your voice is heavy, like a man's.
—Oh, that's from singing so much, child.
—And you hold your cigarette in your mouth like Papa holds his, with one end dropping down.
—Hunh? Oh, that's because my hands are busy, child.
—That's just what Papa said when I asked him about it.
—You notice everything, don't you, Lily?
—Sure. I like to look at people. Gee, Lucy, you move so quick and rough in the kitchen. You can lift that whole pile of dishes with one hand. Bertha couldn't do that.
—Just a lot of experience, Lily (p. 108).

The child is not aware of the implications of her observations, but she sees more than either of her parents does. Lily likes "to watch," and she sees much. She sees in Carl's collapse on the back steps that he is afraid (p. 113), but she does not understand the source of his fear. She has observed her father "wrestling" with Bertha, and she has seen Bertha giving drinks to the mailman, but again she does not have the context or the analytical skills for using the information she has. Yet, she can see through the illusions that have been created for her parents by both Bertha and Carl, and she can see through the facade her father has created for her mother. What Lily sees (as opposed to what others see and believe) underscores the extent of the discrepancy between illusion and reality.

What is as opposed to what appears to be gives substance to the story and becomes a major concern not only for Lily, but for her parents as well; clothing and language are central to this idea. As Mrs. Fairchild shows "Lucy" around the house, Lily asks: "Mama, does Lucy know about Little Red Riding Hood?" (p. 106). When Lily later questions Carl about the big muscles and the dangling cigarette, then, the Red Riding Hood idea of the wolf in sheep's clothing has already been introduced. In truth, although it is Carl who literally wears clothing other than his own, it is Mr. Fairchild who most clearly fits the role of the wolf. The "clothing" of his status at the bank and his general respectability disguise to the world an individual who is immoral and exploitative. Mrs. Fairchild's desire for respectability and a viable family unit blinds her to her husband's corruption. And the role to which both Fairchilds have relegated maids blinds them to Carl's disguise. Mr. Fairchild also tries to change reality for Lily by translating attempts at seduction into "wrestling," an innocent word which forgives his abuses.

Wright also shatters the illusion that the white middle-class father is invariably doting. For Mr. Fairchild, Lily is a pest, an object to be shunted off to bed at noon in order that he may proceed with his "wrestling." His angry impatience, when he comes home to find her still eating her lunch and delaying her nap, is clear:

> — . . . Finish your ice cream.
> —Ooowwa . . . Papa, don't be angry with me . . .
> —Aw, come on, Lily. It's bedtime, *now*. . . .
> —Will you shut your mouth and eat! . . .
> —Papa, did you bring me something?
> —Hunh? No, darling. I never bring you anything at noon. I'll bring you something tonight. Now, finish eating. . . .
> —Lucy, come and put Lily to bed . . . (pp. 115–116)

Meanwhile, Mr. Fairchild searches for his bottle and begins drinking. True, his wanting Lily out of the way might seem protective, but his harshness to her rather discredits the possibility.

By drawing Burt Stallman into complicity with him, Dave Fairchild ultimately seeks to make an illusion out of the series of incidents in his encounter with Carl. His urgent need to re-define reality and save his family from embarrassment appears in his plea to Stallman: "Burt, can we find a way of keeping this quiet? Anne won't help me to do this thing right [by lying]. Help us to get out of this. You're our friend. This scandal'll ruin me at the bank" (p. 125). While Burt does not lie, he does, by not reporting the shooting, refuse to tell the whole truth. He adopts the role of the heavy at the end of the story by emphasizing again and again that the "boy" Carl should appreciate getting off so lightly and should therefore keep his mouth shut about the Fairchilds. He, like Dave Fairchild, opts for white solidarity rather than true justice. He gets a signed statement from Carl that he will be satisfied to have his medical bills taken care of and to receive two hundred dollars in cash. Burt is concerned only with superficial solutions; neither he nor Anne nor Dave considers that Carl has a mind or emotions that may be affected longer than his body by the various sorts of violence they have done him.

And the Fairchilds go back to their illusion of happy home life. Although Anne Fairchild threatens to leave Dave, the threat very quickly dissolves:

> —I'm leaving, Dave.
> —No, Oh, God, no, Anne. Don't say that.
> —I can't help it, Dave.
> —If you leave me, I'll get plastered and stay plastered for a month.
> —Oh, Dave.
> —Say you'll stay, Anne.
> —Oh, God . . . I'll have to stay, I guess.
> —Good girl. I'll change. You'll see. Sh. Look, there's Burt leading that nigger to his car. He looks pretty weak to me. Hope he doesn't die. There. They're driving off. Thank God, it's over, Anne.
> —It's not over for me, Dave. Not as long as you drink, it'll never be over.
> —Baby, I swear I'm on the wagon from now on.
> —You always say that (p. 128).

Mr. Fairchild will go on with his drinking and chasing black women, and Anne will go on trying to believe in him.

The form of "Man of All Work" encourages mythmaking and the exploitation of stereotypes. The story is told completely in dialogue, without even the stage directions and notes for delivery of speeches of traditional drama. Characters call each others' names frequently as one way of providing stage directions, but the characters' voices are so clearly defined that we can distinguish one from another almost immediately. Still, the bareness of the form lends itself to imaginative filling in of details. We must infer tone and imagine happiness and tears. We must also attribute motives on the basis of what characters reveal about themselves and each other as well as on the basis of the historical background we bring to the story. Comparison to the proverbial tip of the iceberg is appropriate. We see surface action and dialogue, but that surface has a depth which assures that all the characters will play certain roles.

Against the backdrop of history, the role each character must live within or rebel against becomes clearer. Because we know how white women usually treat their black maids, the intimate conversation Mrs. Fairchild has with Carl is not surprising. Because we know that one of the stereotypes about black women is that they possess an olympian sexuality, we understand Mr. Fairchild's approach to "Lucy." Historically, many black women have found themselves in "Lucy's" sexually vulnerable position. As Baker and Cooke point out in their discussion of the Bronx slave market, white men often approached black women for purposes of prostitution as they waited on corners to be hired for day work.[5] Other women were hotly pursued in whites' homes. Halsell reported one incident in which, while she was working as a maid, the husband came home at midday and tried to force sexual favors from her. He got her into the bedroom under false pretenses and tried to wrestle her onto the bed and into submission. When she fought back, he replied: "Only take five minutes, only take *five minutes* . . . Now quieten down! Just gotta get me some black pussy!" (p. 196). Halsell left the house running, later to reflect on the many women who had not so escaped: "I have heard many Negro maids say that their greatest fear is being in the house alone when the white man comes in. As one bitterly commented, 'They pay you fifteen dollars a week, and then expect to get you too' " (p. 198). If the white men who seek sexual favors from their domestic help do not consider such services to be included in the pay, they are consistently, cynically convinced that the women are in such dire financial straits that they will jump at the chance to make extra money.[6] In fact, the very ad Carl answers, starting off Wright's wildly extravagant chain of events, prepares the alert, knowledgeable reader for what follows:

> Cook and housekeeper wanted. Take care of one child and small modern household. All late appliances. Colored cook preferred. Salary: fifty dollars a week. References required. 608 South Ridgway Boulevard. Mrs. David Fairchild (p. 99).

The preference for a "colored cook" is explicit and the extremely high salary, five or ten times the norm, will encourage so many black women to apply for the job that Mr. Fairchild can choose one precisely to his taste. It will further encourage the woman who takes the job to put up with hell to keep it.[7] Wright's story, then, depends upon readers' knowledge for its successful humor as well as for its pathos. Carl depends on the whites' stereotyping notions from the beginning. When he puts on Lucy's dress and tries to convince her that his scheme will work, he comments: "I've got on a dress and I look just like a million black women cooks. Who looks that close at us colored people anyhow? We all look alike to white people. Suppose you'd never seen me before? You'd take one look at me and take me for a woman because I'm wearing a dress. And the others'll do that too" (p. 100). In that comment, Carl stereotypes white stereotyping of Blacks. Thus they all exploit each other with types. Their financial and physical exploitation of each other, however, is not equal. Certainly the two hundred dollars Carl obtains from the Fairchilds is not nearly as destructive to them as is their overwork of him, the sexual harassment, and the gunshot wound. His financial exploitation of them, if it can accurately be called such, will not leave a dent in their purses; nor is it designed to reap the luxuriously tangible rewards that Ellie's and Vi's does in *Happy Ending*.

While "Man of All Work" might offer a superficially happy ending, it leaves things under the surface essentially as they were before the story began. Carl has gone into the white world and, considering his actions, should have disturbed it profoundly, but he has not done so. He returns home with his money and his thigh wound, and the Fairchilds go on amid their illusions. The portion of the submerged iceberg which might have been brought to the surface is, instead, submerged even deeper. Perhaps it is sufficient, however, for a story simply to expose issues, not resolve them.

One issue Wright plays with rather freely is that of black male sexuality, and it is here that the title of the work is important. Carl is called a man of all work, yet his original occupation—professional cook—is traditionally a female one. He puts on a dress and his wife goes into spasms: "Oh, God! I thought you were somebody else. Oh, Carl, what are you doing? Those are my clothes you got on. You almost scared me to death. . . . Carl, have you gone crazy? . . . Carl! Go 'way! TAKE OFF MY DRESS! No, no! . . . Carl, I don't want to talk to you. Leave me alone. AND GET OUT OF MY DRESS! *Now*! You hear!

Please . . . CARL, PULL OFF MY DRESS!" (pp. 99, 100, 101). Her very violent reaction draws attention to itself. She and Carl have discussed his desperate need to find work, but when he comes up with a scheme for doing so, she vehemently rejects it. Certainly Lucy's fear that Carl might be arrested for "impersonating a woman" is not unfounded, but can there also be something more in her reaction? Can she be thinking of the implications of emasculation that there are in a black man's doing a black "woman's work"? Is the emasculation involved in black women's being able to find jobs when their men cannot relevant to her overreaction here? Does Lucy also see a literalization in Carl's transvestitism of what John A. Williams's Sissie did to her husband? The theme of emasculation appears again when Carl, in Lucy's dress, is shot in the thigh by Anne Fairchild. Unintentionally, the white woman has joined her husband in symbolically stripping the black man of his sexuality. Paradoxically, black male sexuality can be reduced to insignificance when Fairchild wants to believe that he can satisfy "Lucy" better than "her" husband can, or it can be heightened to monstrous proportions when the pedestalized white female is its potential object. Even in its fearful, mythical proportions, though, it can also be destroyed, or at least stifled, as James Baldwin's "Going to Meet the Man" also clearly shows.

Although the protagonist of Wright's story is a man, it nevertheless presents those ideas that keep black women domestics confined to their positions as essentially powerless employees. History, attitude, stereotypes—work to a degree to Carl's disadvantage. He can win a small battle, but the war is still raging at the end of the story. Black women will still be considered promiscuous hussies, even as they are sought to care for white children, and white men will continue to pursue them and feel justified in that pursuit. Those black women who resisted merely spurred the white men on to intensify the efforts at conquest. For black women in the South, who were not as mobile or as independent as their northern sisters, such occupational hazards could be especially distressing. The percentage of light-skinned Blacks testifies to the fact that many women could not resist such pressures. It would take a different literary climate and a different time for writers to effect much-needed changes in the portrayal of maids.

CHAPTER FIVE

NORTHERN MAIDS:
Stepping toward Militancy

Mammy figures, Southern maids, are almost always presented as merely reacting, acquiescently and thoughtlessly, to the whites for whom they work. Transitional maids, the moderates, on the other hand, meditate on the inequality which separates them from the white women for whom they work, and they speculate about how things could be different; in other words, they have active imaginations and can conceive of states of existence beyond their present ones. Lutie Johnson, in Ann Petry's *The Street* (1946), imagines that it would be good just once for the white woman for whom she works to recognize her before other human beings as a human being. (Though the two women are about the same in age—they both are married and have small sons—the white woman pointedly relegates Lutie to the mere role of maid whenever they are in public.) Lutie will, ultimately, leave domestic work. Opal Simmons, in William Melvin Kelley's *dem* (1964), is audacious enough to order her white employer out of the kitchen and out of interference with her caring for his son. The transitional northern maids, then, may be just as hard working and apparently conformist as true southern maids, but they never fully accept the status that has been assigned to them. It does not stymie their operation in the world outside the white home as, though it may alter their relationships with their families, they have the ability to rise above it.

Lutie Johnson's story is that of a young woman who will still be paying in 1944 for decisions she had made under economic pressure during the Depression. Born and raised in New York, Lutie is at seventeen a beautiful girl whose grandmother believes that she should get married quickly so that her beauty will not be exploited by men. Lutie marries Jim at seventeen and shortly thereafter has a son. Glittering hopes for the marriage are dulled when Jim cannot find a job, when a scheme to take in welfare children backfires, and when Jim loses any desire to confront the powers that keep him unemployed. Lutie reflects on their plight at that time years after the break-up of the marriage:

> They were young enough and enough in love to have made a go of it. It always came back to the same thing. Jim couldn't find a job. So day by day, month by month, big broad-shouldered Jim Johnson went to pieces because there wasn't any work for him and he couldn't earn anything at all. He got used to facing the fact that he couldn't support his wife and child. It ate into him. Slowly, bit by bit, it undermined his belief in himself until he could no longer bear it. . . . Jim finally stopped looking for work entirely. Though to be fair about it he did help around the house—washing clothes, going to the market, cleaning. But when there wasn't anything for him to do, he would read day-old newspapers and play the radio or sit by the kitchen stove smoking his pipe until she felt, if she had to walk around his long legs just one more time, get just one more whiff of the rank, strong smell of his pipe, she would go mad.[1]

Jim and Lutie have what she describes as "a loud, bitter, common fight" (p. 116) on the evening the welfare children are taken away, and, in an effort to make mortgage payments on their house, Lutie accepts a live-in job as maid to a wealthy family in Connecticut, leaving her two-year-old son and Jim in New York. She has never had such a job before, but her experience with the welfare children had inspired her in the art of creative cooking, and she gets a white proprietor in her neighborhood, a Mrs. Pizzini, to write a recommendation letter for her. Like the title character in John A. Williams's *Sissie* (1963), also set in the Depression, she is forced to become the breadwinner in the family simply because her husband cannot find a job; all the same, the pride she feels as a result of finding a way to enable them to keep their house is not diminished when Jim asks how he, alone save on her four days off at the end of each month, will take care of Bub. Even his sullenness and silence in the days before she has to leave and his refusal to accompany her to the train station are not sufficient warning to her that their marriage is threatened; the fact that she will earn seventy dollars a month living-in in Connecticut is the only thing that seems important to her. The job will serve the immediate function of enabling them to make their mortgage payments, and all else, to Lutie, should be secondary. So off she goes to Connecticut.

Jim soon tires of her absence and takes another woman to cook for Bub and himself. Lutie leaves the Chandlers—after almost two years—but her marriage is dissolved and she and the eight-year-old Bub must make a new life for themselves. Bits and pieces of this story are revealed first as Lutie, now in her mid-twenties, searches for an apartment for herself and Bub, and then during the time they live together in a tiny fifth-floor walk-up.

Although Lutie's taking a job as a domestic has disastrous results, what happens to her should be distinguished from the dreadful things we have seen happen to other maids who have left their homes and families to go to work for whites. Lutie, unlike Mammy Jane, Granny, and Pauline, sees her job as a means to an end, not as an end in itself. She sees temporarily working for whites as a way of getting her family on solid financial ground. Therefore, she does not identify with whites as thoroughly or in the same way as the mammy figures. Lutie sees the black and white communities as distinct entities with all the economic advantages being on the side of the whites. She is acutely aware of discrimination and of the stress put on Blacks, particularly as a result of the Depression. Even before she goes to work for the Chandlers, she has to remind herself how self-destructive a thing it would be to allow herself to hate whites for her husband's and her father's inability to find jobs (Pop is evicted from his apartment when he is forced to shut down an illegal liquor operation and can't find a job to replace the lost income). Lutie has a political consciousness, a social awareness that the mammies have not. Seeing herself as connected to a black community which has been closed in and shut out by a white community, she is not an isolated individual responding to whites, as the earlier maids had been. Lutie knows how whites view her; she does not delude herself into thinking that she is to them an exception among Blacks, an ideal and indispensable Mammy Jane or Granny or Pauline. Her identity has been shaped by forces in the *black* community, especially by the grandmother who brought her up.

In her bid to break out of the pathology which often characterizes the urban black community, Lutie may resemble in a superficial way some of the maids who considered the best of everything to be in the white community. Unlike Granny in *God Bless the Child*, however, who sees the values and material goods of the white community as valuable in themselves, Lutie values them for their power to get her out of the ghetto, to restore integrity to black men she loves who have been beaten down by economic forces, and to ensure a better life for her child. What she sees and appreciates in the white world, then, is set against what she knows is true in the black world, and she would use the former to set the latter right. Yet, though she never becomes as fanatical as Granny in her appreciation of what the whites have, she does, during her two years with the Chandlers, sometimes come close to it. (In later years, after her separation from her husband, she is able to put things in clearer perspectives.) Her first glimpses of Mrs. Chandler and the Chandler house are a baptism into a new world:

> For Mrs. Chandler wore ribbed stockings made of very fine cotton and flat-heeled moccasins of a red-brown leather that caught the light. She had on a loose-fitting tweed coat and no hat. Lutie, looking at the earrings in her ears, decided that they were real pearls and thought, Everything she has on cost a lot of money, yet she isn't very much older than I am—not more than a year or so . . . . She never quite got over that first glimpse of the outside of the house—so gracious with such long low lines, its white paint almost sparkling in the sun and the river very blue behind the house (p. 28).

Nineteen and impressionable, she makes a resolution immediately. "Some part of her mind must have had it already, must have already mapped out the way she was to go about keeping this job for as long as was necessary by being the perfect maid. Patient and good-tempered and hard-working and more than usually bright" (p. 28). Seeing the interior of the house confirms her initial reactions:

. . . to Lutie the house was a miracle, what with the four big bedrooms, each one with its own bath; the nursery that was as big as the bedrooms, and under the nursery a room and bath that belonged to her. On top of that there was a living room, a dining room, a library, a laundry. Taken all together it was like something in the movies, what with the size of the rooms and the big windows that brought the river and the surrounding woods almost into the house. She had never seen anything like it before.

That first day when she walked into Mrs. Chandler's bedroom her breath had come out in an involuntary "Oh!" . . . The rest of the house was just as perfect as Mrs. Chandler's bedroom. Even her room—the maid's room with its maple furniture and vivid draperies—that, too, was perfect. Little Henry Chandler, who was two years older that Bub, was also perfect—that is, he wasn't spoiled or anything. . . . Yes. The whole thing was perfect (pp. 29, 30).

That perfection draws Lutie into the Chandler world in part because it is in such obvious contrast to her own life and experiences. Her response approaches Pauline Breedlove's; Lutie has been transported to the world of the movies Pauline so much admired. "As long as was necessary" will get longer and longer. She will faithfully send money to Jim, but there will be little indication that she misses her son or her husband; she will be bewitched by the glamour of the Chandler environment.

As an intimate in the Chandler house, Lutie is early exposed to what the Chandlers consider to be of value:

They didn't want their children to be president or diplomats or anything like that. What they wanted was to be rich—"filthy" rich, as Mr. Chandler called it.

When she brought the coffee into the living room after dinner, the conversation was always the same.

"Richest damn country in the world—"

"Always be new markets. If not here in South America, Africa, India—Everywhere and anywhere—"

"Hell! Make it while you're young. Anyone can do it—"

"Outsmart the next guy. Think up something before anyone else does. Retire at forty—"

It was a world of strange values where the price of something called Tell and Tell and American Nickel and United States Steel had a direct effect on emotions. When the price went up everybody's spirits soared; if it went down they were plunged in gloom.

After a year of listening to their talk, she absorbed some of the same spirit. The belief that anybody could be rich if he wanted to and worked hard enough and figures it out carefully enough. Apparently that's what the Pizzinis had done. She and Jim could do the same thing, and she thought she saw what had been wrong with them before—they hadn't tried hard enough, worked long enough, saved enough. There hadn't been any one thing they wanted above and beyond everything else. These people had wanted only one thing—more and more money—and so they got it. Some of this new philosophy crept into her letters to Jim (p. 32).

Lutie forgets momentarily what brought her into the Chandler home: she and Jim had tried all the other possibilities they had of making money and all had disappeared. She forgets how impossibly hard she had worked trying to feed five welfare children and her own family on thirty dollars a week, spending endless hours shopping, hunting for bargains, trying to make bland food interesting and nutritious. She forgets the diligence with which Jim had set out to search for jobs and Pop's determined efforts to find something to replace his liquor business. She never once stops to think that people like Jim and Pop have perhaps been victimized by the Chandlers of the world. She does not note that the countries her new mentors mention as exploitable are all of the third world, all countries of colored peoples, all countries easily exploited because they are powerless.

Her seduction by the American Dream, by the belief that dedication to getting money will solve all problems, leads Lutie to go home less and less, "pointing out to Jim how she could save the money she would have spent for train fare" (p. 32). She fails to realize until after her marriage is dissolved that seventy dollars a month will not pay for a house in the suburbs or put her on Wall Street. When a relative of her employer commits suicide on Christmas morning, Lutie is struck not so much by the insensitivity of the family in response to the death—"The nerve of him. The nerve of him. Deliberately embarrassing us. And on Christmas morning, too" (p. 35)—but by the power of the family's money.

She learned that when one had money there were certain unpleasant things one could avoid—even things like a suicide in the family.

She never found out what had prompted Jonathan Chandler to kill himself. She wasn't too interested. But she was interested in the way in which money transformed a suicide she had seen committed from start to finish in front of her very eyes into "an accident with a gun." It was done very neatly, too. Mrs. Chandler's mother simply called Mrs. Chandler's father in Washington. Lutie overheard the tail-end of the conversation, "Now you get it fixed up. Oh, yes, you can. He was cleaning a gun" (pp. 35–36).

As one of the powerless, the minimum-waged, Lutie sees the Chandlers as models of wealth, power, and prestige, and she holds their positions in awe.

Still, she does not completely dissolve into a Granny Huggs. She recognizes, partly through the suicide, that having money does not "necessarily guarantee happiness" (p. 35); and she has had experiences enough apart from the Chandlers to have a particle of pride in herself and what she is that contact with them does not diminish. When Mrs. Chandler joins Mr. Chandler in alcoholism, and goes on extravagant buying sprees, purchasing clothes she passes on to Lutie without wearing or after only a few wearings, Lutie accepts them "gravely, properly grateful":

> The clothes would have fitted her perfectly, but some obstinacy in her that she couldn't overcome prevented her from ever wearing them. She mailed them to Pop's current girlfriend, taking an ironic pleasure in the thought that Mrs. Chandler's beautiful clothes Designed For Country Living would be showing up nightly in the gin mill at the corner of Seventh Avenue and 110th Street (p. 36).

The hand-me-downs that Granny Huggs would have savored as the tangible confirmation of her unity with her employers and of her worth to them become symbols of her differentness and subservience to Lutie. She is aware of being more than the Chandlers are aware of her being, of being something other than what they think she is.

The same is true when she hears female visitors to the Chandler household expressing stereotyped notions about the virtue of black women—or their lack of it. "Whenever she entered a room where they were, they stared at her with a queer, speculative look. Sometimes she caught snatches of their conversation about her. 'Sure, she's a wonderful cook. But I wouldn't have any good-looking colored wench in my house. Not with John. You know they're always making passes at men. Especially white men.' And then, 'Now, I wonder—'" (p. 30). Lutie is initially angry, then "just contemptuous," because the white women are unaware that she has "a big handsome husband of her own; that she didn't want any of their thin unhappy husbands. But she wondered why they all had the idea that colored girls were whores" (p. 31). When Mrs. Chandler's mother arrives, she echoes the sentiments of the bridge club ladies. "She took one look at Lutie and hardly let her get out of the door before she was leaning across the dining-room table to say in a clipped voice that carried right out into the kitchen: 'Now I wonder if you're being wise, dear. That girl is unusually attractive and men are weak. Besides, she's colored and you know how they are—'" (p. 33). The women do not allow for the fact that Lutie is an individual black woman; she becomes representative of all black maids in all white homes, just as Carl does in the Fairchild home. But Lutie is proud of the way in which Granny has raised her, and thinks especially of her grandmother's admonitions not to let any white man touch her:

> Something that was said so often and with such gravity it had become part of you, just like breathing, and you would have preferred crawling in bed with a rattlesnake to getting in bed with a white man. Mrs. Chandler's friends and her mother couldn't possibly know that, couldn't possibly imagine that you might have a distrust and a dislike of white men far deeper than the distrust these white women had of you. Or know that, after hearing their estimation of you, nothing in the world could ever force you to be even friendly with a white man (pp. 33–34).

Lutie denies that the stereotype of the hot momma, sexually loose black woman is a part of her upbringing and thereby denies the women any power to define her; and she turns out to be far more broadminded in her evaluation of them than they are in their evaluation of her. The white women's preoccupation with the sexual habits of black women is a course in the brick wall Lutie had noted earlier as standing between Blacks and whites. The wall might break down a bit in moments of tragedy, but it is soon rebuilt.

And Mrs. Chandler adds bricks to the wall even at those moments when Lutie has begun to think that they two can meet as human equals, not as mistress and maid. On their rides into New York together, they talk about newspapers or clothes or movies. Once they arrive at the station, however, Mrs. Chandler says loudly, "I'll see you on Monday, Lutie" (p. 37):

> There was a firm note of dismissal in her voice so that the other passengers pouring off the train turned to watch the rich young woman and her colored maid; a tone of voice that made people stop to hear just when it was the maid was to report back for work. Because the voice unmistakably established the relation between the blond young woman and the brown young woman.
>
> And it never failed to stir resentment in Lutie. She argued with herself about it. Of course, she was a maid. She had no illusions about that. But would it hurt Mrs. Chandler just once to talk at the moment of parting as though, however incredible it might seem to anyone who was listening, they were friends? Just two people who knew each other and to whom it was only incidental that one of them was white and the other black? (p. 37).

Pauline Breedlove and Granny Huggs would perhaps have had their pride titillated just to be out in the presence of their rich white mistresses; if passers-by had noticed, the pleasure would have been intensified. The quality in Lutie which places her a step beyond the mammies is her instinctively putting her humanity first and the job second: even when she must play the role of the maid, her evaluation of herself goes beyond that role. Even as she revels in the riches of the Chandler household, she still can judge it, visualizing herself as apart from it.

She leaves the Chandlers when Pop writes to tell her that Jim has taken up with another woman. It is too late for her to save the marriage; and perhaps the same pride that has helped her to keep at least a part of herself inviolate to the Chandler influence also interferes with the possibility of a reconciliation. But four years after the Chandler experience has ended, Lutie concludes that "that kitchen in Connecticut had changed her whole life" (p. 39) and indeed it had:

it had solidified her determination to achieve upward mobility. Even if she does not make it to Wall Street, she will not be satisfied to have her son grow up on 116th Street, *the* street of the title, with winos, prostitutes, pimps, and litter, in a stale and unsafe walk-up apartment building with a demented superintendent. She spends a year and a half mastering typing, a year taking civil service examinations, and a year waiting for an appointment before she finally gets one as a file clerk. During those four years, she has worked at a steam laundry: none of the mammies would have had such gumption. None would have seen herself as building an identity apart from the white domestic world. And none would have severed connections with a rich white family, either to take care of her own children or to attempt even minimally to salvage a marriage.

Alone on 116th Street in 1944, Lutie keeps before her the image of possibility that the Chandlers represent. When she is acutely conscious of her poverty or when adversity strikes, she thinks of them again and again. She thinks of their large house and wide yard when Bub must make his sport of counting dogs from the tiny window of their fifth-floor apartment. What the Chandlers represent becomes ever more important to Lutie than any consideration of them as people, which is perhaps not a reaction many other maids would have—though, as we have seen, it is a reaction many people have to maids. She thinks of what money can accomplish, for example, when she learns that a man she knows has bought his way out of the army just as the Chandlers had bought an "accident with a gun" in the newspapers. She tries desperately to push the low ceiling of possibility Baldwin refers to in "Sonny's Blues" to greater heights in an effort to ensure that she and her son will escape the crushed hopes that have awaited so many young Blacks in urban areas. Her image of the Chandlers is the light which always beckons her to that higher ceiling.

Lutie's struggle is constant, for the men who control money offer it to her only at the price of her body. When Boots Smith, a piano player who has obvious connections, the man who had bought his way out of the army, offers her a job as a singer in a casino, she sees it as a long awaited opportunity to escape the ravages of the street. Her hopes are short-lived, however, for the white man who owns the casino, Junto, wants her; and he directs Boots to give her presents instead of the money she so desperately needs, believing that this will wear her down until she accepts financial favors from him in return for sexual ones. While she is still heroically rejecting his proposals, Bub is caught taking letters out of mailboxes on the street, having been led to do so by Jones, the super of Lutie's apartment building, who had informed him that he would be helping the police capture a thief by taking the letters and bringing them to him. When an attempt of his to rape her was foiled, and when he then learned that Junto was interested in her, Jones had concluded that Lutie liked white men—and would get back at her for that unforgivable sin by devising a scheme to cause her son to be taken away from her. When Bub does end up in Children's Shelter, Lutie ends up at Boots Smith's apartment asking for two hundred dollars for a lawyer. Then, when Boots takes advantage of Lutie's situation by bringing Junto to his apartment and telling Lutie to "be nice to him" in return for the money, the rage which has been building in her explodes. Shouting, she forces Junto from the apartment; she kills Boots when he decides that he will rape her and then pass her along to Junto. She discovers that Boots has a wallet full of money, two hundred dollars of which he could have easily given her. She takes a portion; she decides to leave Harlem, leaving Bub in the care of the Children's Shelter, and to go to Chicago. She believes she is an utter failure, that the street has indeed broken her. Petry's point about determinism is made.

After all her efforts have backfired, after all her hopes have come to naught, after Bub has been taken to Children's Shelter, Lutie reflects on the circumstances which have made black lives what they are:

> Her thoughts were like a chorus chanting inside her head. The men stood around and the women worked. The men left the women and the women went on working and the kids were left alone. The kids burned lights all night because they were alone in small, dark rooms and they were afraid. Alone. Always alone. They wouldn't stay in the house after school because they were afraid in the empty, silent, dark rooms. And they should have been playing in wide stretches of green park and instead they were in the street. And the street reached out and sucked them up.
>
> Yes. The women work and the kids go to reform school. Why do the women work? It's such a simple, reasonable reason . . . .

The women work because the white folks give them jobs—
washing dishes and clothes and floors and windows. The women
work because for years now the white folks haven't liked to give
black men jobs that paid enough for them to support their families.
And finally it gets to be too late for some of them. Even wars don't
change it. The men get out of the habit of working and the houses
are old and gloomy and the walls press in. And the men go off,
move on, slip away, find new women. Find younger women.

And what did it add up to? . . . Add it up. Bub, your kid—
flashing smile, strong, straight back, sturdy legs, even white
teeth, young, round face, smooth skin—he ends up in reform
school because the women work.

Go on, she urged. Go all the way. Finish it. And the little
Henry Chandlers go to YalePrincetonHarvard and the Bub Johnsons graduate from reform school into DannemoraSingSing.

And you helped push him because you talked to him about
money. All the time money. And you wanted it because you
wanted to move from this street, but in the beginning it was
because you heard the rich white Chandlers talk about it. "Filthy
rich." "Richest country in the world." "Make it while you're
young."

Only you forgot. You forgot you were black and you underesti-
mated the street outside here (pp. 240–241).

No one, Lutie maintains, can stay on 116th Street and stay decent,
"for it sucked the humanity out of people—slowly, surely, inevitably" (p. 144). She has witnessed a scene in which a woman's cry that
her purse was snatched was met with "Aw, shut up! Folks got to
sleep," "What the hell'd you have in it, your rent money?" and "Go
on home, old woman, 'fore I throw somp'n special down on your rusty
head" (p. 143). She has seen a woman resignedly refuse to cry at the
knifing death of her brother (p. 125); the woman simply had accepted
that as the fate of those like herself. She has seen the same resignation
in the face of an old black man in a hospital emergency room (p. 127)
and in the face of a young girl who had been "cut to ribbons"
(pp. 128–129). They had all accepted the fact, Lutie observes, that
there was nothing better for them in this life; they refused to protest
against the conditions of their lives and they could not even envision
any ways to make things better.

And Lutie becomes increasingly angry, feeling her space compressed by those who have money, feeling herself trapped like the animals she and Bub had seen in the zoo (p. 201). She begins to see her neighborhood as being directly linked, negatively, to the powerful and the wealthy:

> Streets like the one she lived on were no accident. They were the North's lynch mobs, she thought bitterly; the method the big cities used to keep Negroes in their place. And she [thought] of Pop unable to get a job; of Jim slowly disintegrating because he, too, couldn't get a job, and of the subsequent wreck of their marriage; of Bub left to his own devices after school. From the time she was born, she had been hemmed into an ever-narrowing space, until now she was very nearly walled in and the wall had been built up brick by brick by eager white hands (pp. 200–201).

When, a few weeks after the Casino fiasco, Lutie discovers that to get other singing jobs she needs one hundred twenty-five dollars' worth of lessons, and that the white teacher to whom she has gone will gladly forget about the fee if she allows him to do as he wishes with her body, the man's whiteness sticks out in her mind as the source of all her problems. The white Junto had tried to control her. The white Chandlers and their friends control so many other people. They who created the street will make sure that an attractive black woman, in spite of her moral vision of the world, cannot change her circumstances without compromising her virtue. Their money equals power, and power is not beneficent in the Harlem/Connecticut world. Their street will offer her no salvation.

In essence, Lutie is crying out against the status quo, against those forces which have assigned an inferior place to Blacks; her reflectiveness, her imagination, her understanding, and her awareness of the black social condition distinguish her from the mammies, the southern maids. She has a sense of the community that she perhaps feels more than she is able to articulate. She certainly wants to improve things specifically for Bub and for herself, but in her awareness of what the street does to all Blacks there is no view of herself as the "exceptional nigger," a perfect maid to be splendidly appreciated in token fashion by whites and set apart from other Blacks. Lutie's ultimately realistic vision is in distinct contrast to the outlooks of

Mammy Jane, Granny Huggs, and Pauline Breedlove—she having, unlike them, ultimately recognized the corruption inherent in the glamour of rich white families. And emphasizing as it does the power of the white world, *The Street* provides a natural transition to the satirization of whites which is the focus of *dem.*

A great part of the satire in William Melvin Kelley's *dem* (1964) is centered upon its white family's interaction with their black maid, Opal Simmons. The Pierces, Mitchell and Tam, representative of middle-class whites in urban areas, have a decent apartment, a small son, friends in the suburbs, and that amenity which will cause them the most problems: Opal. Mitchell is in advertising and Tam spends her days visiting art galleries and pursuing the leisurely life. They have all that which would seem to separate them from the majority of Blacks in America. The neatness of their little world is shattered, however, when Tam gives birth to twins, one black and one white. In the rarest of fabulously rare occurrences, Tam is impregnated by both Mitchell and Cooley Johnson, a black man whom she has met through Opal and whom she has been dating. The shock of the births sends Mitchell through a series of hilarious scenes in which he tries to find the black man responsible for the black baby, which he wants to turn over to him, thinking perhaps that the removal of the tangible evidence of his wife's violation, and his home's, will restore his peace of mind. Mitchell finds himself attending black parties and passing as a Black, and he finds himself being pursued by black women. By the time the "problem" is finally resolved, it is clear that Mitchell's life will never be the same.

The focus of the novel is on Mitchell's odyssey. The maid, however, is important: first of all, because she is key to Cooley's getting together with Mrs. Pierce. If anyone should be curious as to why a black man is entering the Pierce apartment, Opal can simply say, as she says to Mitchell, that Cooley is her friend. And how Mitchell views Opal foreshadows how he will conduct his investigations later. Mitchell's image of himself is of someone in control. He is successful in his advertising job and likes the status and material comforts he and his family have; Opal is an expected accompaniment of success and the birth of children. As the person in power, he expects her to be submissive and recognize his power; as the person who pays her salary, he expects a nearly slavish amount of deference from her. But though he tries to turn her into a southern maid, she refuses to be consistently submissive, in fact almost insulting him and often laughing at him. And it suggests the hopelessness of his bid for superiority that while he suspects the un-mammyish Opal's under-cutting of his power and attitudes and her behind-the-mask laughter, he can focus on no precise evidence of them and is unable quite to articulate what he finds disrespectful in her.

He comments to Tam: "We've got what everybody wants. . . . A nice place to live. A good maid. What do your buddies call her—a treasure? She does all the boring stuff and you have time to do the things you want to do, like go to the art gallery tomorrow."[2] (The irony is that Tam is going to the art gallery—if indeed that is the place she is going—to meet Cooley.) Here Mitchell has Opal's role clearly defined as that of THE MAID whose primary function in life is to make things easy for her mistress. Many points of his own relationship with her can be seen in the scene wherein he comes home from work to find her feeding carrots to his son, Jake. He interferes, insisting that Jake must hate the strained vegetables instead of liking them as Opal suggests, as she tries to coax him into eating them; but she contradicts him:

"I said he loves it. Don't you, Jakie? Love those carrots, don't you?"

Jake clamped his teeth, refused to open his mouth.

"Look at him, for Christ's sake. He hates the stuff. Don't you, Jake-boy?"

"I can't have you breaking down all the discipline I build up during the day." She smiled up at him. There was a black space between her two white middle top teeth.

Mitchell put his hat on a stool and began to rummage in the cabinets for a towel to dry the papers.

"What're you looking for?" She turned from Jake, a spoonful poised halfway to his open, waiting mouth. "Don't mess around in there."

"I'm looking for a dishtowel. I dropped these God-damn papers in the street. I want—"

"Give them here." She put down Jake's spoon, got up, and

extended her hand to him. "Men don't know anything. Never try to wipe anything when it's wet. Wait until it's dry. Then you'll be able to shake off the mud. A little wrinkled, but you'll be able to read them."

"Where the hell do you pick up knowledge like that?"

"My job." She smiled. "I get hired to take care of you" (p. 34).

Opal makes it clear to Mitchell that she has been hired to take care of the baby and that he should not interfere with what she does; she essentially tells him to mind his business and not to bother things in the kitchen. Mammy Jane would never have given her two commands to Mitchell—"Don't mess around in there" and "Give them here"—to Major Carteret. Nor would Pauline have spoken so to the Fishers. Opal obviously doesn't see her existence in the Pierce home as the be-all and end-all of her life. But with her smiles she maneuvers back into the maid's role out of which she has stepped. She refuses at bottom to accept Mitchell's sense of her place; but, like Childress's Mildred, she is able to avoid jeopardizing her job. Her comment on men suggests again that she does not respect walls Mitchell has tried to erect between them; conversely, his question about her knowledge is another indication of that wall he wants to maintain in certain instances. And her comment that she was hired to take care of Mitchell has buried in it the implication that he cannot take care of himself. "You" may also refer not just to Mitchell in particular but to whites in general. In spite of their efforts to separate themselves from Blacks, whites still need Blacks, especially maids—if only to do the "boring stuff."

Opal is playing with Mitchell, making fun of the situation they are both in. It is Mitchell's life; for Opal, it's a job. She knows that she is in control, knows that Mitchell is on territory unfamiliar to him—the kitchen, "her" kitchen—and she knows, most importantly of all, that he does not have the courage to reclaim the kitchen, or the baby, or even what is in the kitchen drawers. She takes advantage of his weakness of character to assert her own, but to assert it in a teasingly playful way that Mitchell cannot clearly identify as out of bounds. After all, she has been hired to care for the baby, and to oversee the kitchen.

Opal's duties connect her to her southern sisters, as her name connects her to generations of southern Sapphires and Beulahs; but Mitchell wishes to resemble his southern counterparts in a more fundamental way—counterparts like Bob Stone in Jean Toomer's "Blood-Burning Moon." We have seen him observe the gap between Opal's teeth almost subconsciously, and we may recall that a popular stereotype holds gap-toothed people to be morally loose, inclined to few restraints in their sexual activities.[3] As Opal feeds Jake thereafter, Mitchell's awareness of her body increases. "Under the white nylon dress [the traditional uniform] Opal wore to work, her white bra cut into dark brown skin. He wished sometimes she would wear a cotton dress or at least a full slip" (p. 34). Mitchell goes out of the kitchen and into his wife's bedroom still thinking about Opal's body and presuming on a second generalizing stereotype. "It was a shame to see her getting fat. Colored people ate too much rice" (p. 35). And when he returns to the kitchen for his dinner he notes that "she was wearing a pink half-slip under her nylon dress. A brown strip of stomach separated her white bra and the pink half-slip. . . . She bent down and the dress stretched over her buttocks and thighs" (p. 37). In these comments, Mitchell seems to be concerned simply with the proprieties of dress, but it is obvious that he has at least a latent sexual interest in Opal. The thought of her getting fat—i.e., losing her sex appeal—depresses him. But although he sees breasts, buttocks, and thighs, Mitchell still tries to remain detached from what he sees, as evidenced by the declarative sentences used to provide the information. He may wish to be Toomer's Bob Stone, but in the matter of sex as in kitchen matters he lacks the courage to assert himself with Opal. Indeed, he is embarrassed even when his wife catches him watching her breasts. Powerful white men who desire to exploit maids may delight in sexual conquest, but Mitchell Pierce has not the will or the ability to conquer.

It is precisely because he wants Opal and cannot dare allow that thought to surface in his conscious mind that he responds irrationally when Cooley comes to take her home. Cooley comes to the kitchen entrance and rings the bell; Mitchell opens the door, is slightly puzzled to see a black man, hears Opal's explanation and her hasty good-bye, and immediately becomes angry. "Mitchell found himself tasting vinegar; his eyes began to water. He paid her enough to expect better service than this, a decent report on how she had left the house, a respectful good-bye. And how dare she have such a person as this Cooley, in his outlandish bowling jacket, call for her at his house? Mitchell could not let her go without expressing his disapproval" (p. 38). Mitchell tells Opal to ask Cooley to wait outside. Then he confronts her:

> "Yes, sir?" She buttoned her coat, starting at the collar. Her brown hands moved down the row of black, shiny buttons.
>
> He could not speak until her hands stopped. "Look, Opal, I don't want to hurt your feelings, but I'd be grateful if you didn't have your boy friends coming to the door."
>
> "I'm sorry, Mr. Pierce. This is the first time and—"
>
> "Well, make sure it's the last, God damn it! Don't run your social life out of my house. You can meet your *men* on the corner. I don't want them hanging around."
>
> "He just came. He wasn't hanging around, Mr. Pierce." She was being too submissive, almost as if she were willing to accept his insults to keep him from discovering a more serious crime.
>
> "Listen! I don't want any God-damn excuses from you! Just don't have a whole lot of guys coming to my door!"
>
> She lowered her head. "Yes, sir" (pp. 38–39).

One encounter and *one* man are projected into *men* and *a whole lot of guys*. In her role as all black women, Opal, from Mitchell's point of view, is clearly a promiscuous and lewd woman, and he is jealous of Cooley—just as his wife was jealous of Opal earlier (p. 36). Cooley, in his unapologetic blackness, is able, he concludes, to do with Opal what he himself would like to do. Mitchell believes what James Baldwin has argued in several of his works, that sexual prowess is a source of racial control.[4] If you can make those who would oppose you submissive and helpless as individuals can often be in the sexual act, you confirm your image as a conqueror in other areas. Mitchell, too weak to exert such control, is understandably jealous of the Cooley who has, he suspects, the sexual power that he himself lacks. With classic irony, however, his jealousy is misdirected; he should be jealous of Cooley over Tam, not over Opal. Indeed, it is hinted that the submissiveness Mitchell notices in Opal's demeanor in the doorstep scene is perhaps an attempt to smooth over the situation before Mitchell gets too curious about Cooley—and perhaps connects him to Tam.

Mitchell regularly uses stereotyped attitudes to reassert his own superiority comfortingly in his own mind, and he does it again after Opal's last "yes, sir." Convinced that her submissiveness does cover some more "serious crime" and eager to assuage his own helplessness in the situation, he falls back on a stereotype that he and his wife had shown their belief in earlier: black domestics will steal. He grabs Opal's purse to prove it to himself:

> Now, very subtly, she was insulting him. She was very good at it; they all were—so good that he was not even sure what about her was insulting. That made him even more angry and before he was fully aware of what he was doing, he had pushed her to the floor, wrestled the brown handbag from her, dumped its contents on the kitchen table and was searching amid hairpins, coins, lipsticks, and scraps of paper for the things he was certain now she had stolen from him (p. 39).

The maid who will steal is projected from Mitchell's own mind. Clinging to the idea of her, he gets back what Cooley has taken away as well as what he had lost earlier when Opal ordered him around in the carrot scene. "If you can't help in here . . . Don't you think it's time you said hello to Mrs. Pierce?" (p. 34) He had been able to tolerate the way she talked to him as long as he thought he and his wife and son were the sole beneficiaries of her talents—talents for cleaning, ironing, cooking, and child-care; but the moment he sees that she might have and exercise other talents—that she has a life, a romantic life, beyond his apartment—his tolerance dissolves like snowflakes in warm water.

Mitchell fires Opal for stealing although he has not a shred of evidence that she has done so: "And she must have sold everything quickly, for cash; he had never found any of it in her possession, had never even been certain what she had taken" (p. 99). He and Tam go on about their lives. But he must encounter Opal again when Tam's twins are born and he learns that the black father is Cooley, a friend of Opal's nephew Carlyle. He goes to Opal's apartment seeking information; they have the following conversation:

> He took a deep breath. "I'd like to find your friend Cooley." He watched closely for her reaction, saw a tear pop into her eye. "Opal?"

"He cause you more trouble, Mr. Pierce? I'm sorry I ever brought him to your house. Of all the men I ever met, he was the most trouble-causing . . . " She shook her head.

"Wait a minute, Opal."

"That man was a jinx." She looked at him, a tear stalled on her cheek, like brown wax. "Why'd you fire me, Mr. Pierce? It was for going around with men like Cooley, wasn't it."

"Now Opal . . . "

"The best job I ever had and I lost it because of a common, ordinary nigger. Excuse me, Mr. Pierce, but we both know what he was." She wiped her tears with a chubby hand. "A nigger."

"No, Opal," Mitchell shook his head. "We fired you because you were stealing. That's why I went through your purse. Don't you remember?"

"Me?" She sat up, snorted. "I never stole from you, Mr. Pierce. Not even leftover food. My pay check was always enough."

Mitchell suddenly realized that at very least she believed what she was telling him. Either she had forgotten or had gone insane. He was certain he would know if she was lying. "No, Opal, you were stealing from us."

"What kind of person would I be to steal from you, as good as you was to me?"

He had often wondered that himself. "But, Opal . . . " He stopped because he knew now why the livingroom seemed so familiar; it was a poor copy of his own—designed by Tam—even to the reproduction.

"What did I steal, Mr. Pierce?"

He hesitated. "Well, Opal, I don't really know." That too seemed strange; they had never really missed anything. He tried to remember why he had even believed Opal to be a thief.

"You see?" She was triumphant, but not angry. "It was because of that Cooley. You were right to fire me, Mr. Pierce. I never should've had that nigger come to your house. I didn't even like him. I only went out with him three times." She stopped "What you want him for, Mr. Pierce?" (p. 104)

The first question that comes to mind here is whether Opal has actually undergone a change of character or whether she is putting on an act for Mitchell. If she has changed, was it the accusation of theft that broke her spirit? If she is putting on an act, how does the act relate to her earlier one? If on the other hand her true character is here being expressed, whence came her seeming defiance and confidence earlier? Had that defiance with which she ordered Mitchell around been simply a function of kitchen freedom?—a question which immediately raises another. Why should Opal be less free in her own living room? And is that living room really a copy of the Pierces', or would Mitchell with his glazed eyes just see it as such when Opal is apparently identifying with him again? Even if it were a copy, would it suggest the kind and degree of identification that Mitchell would like? Most importantly, how much of the joke that had been played on Mitchell by Cooley and Tam is Opal aware of? Was she merely the medium through whom Tam first met Cooley, or has she consented to or at least been aware of Cooley's and Carlyle's bid to hit whitey where it obviously hurts most?

Further questions follow. Opal uses almost the same hard language Carlyle will use later to describe Cooley's character. Yet Cooley and Carlyle, at least, are apparently friends; later, at a party Mitchell attends with Carlyle, Carlyle and Cooley (the latter unrecognized by Mitchell) put their heads together in an intimate conversation. Would Carlyle do that with a reprehensible criminal? Opal tells Mitchell she has met Cooley through Carlyle, her nephew, yet she maintains that she does not know Cooley's last name. Would a woman go out on repeated social occasions with a man whose last name she does not know? Would a nephew who seems to be as concerned as Carlyle is about his aunt's welfare introduce her to a villain whose last name cannot be revealed?[5] In fact, once Mitchell arrives at Carlyle's apartment, Carlyle questions him about the firing of Opal, his questions indicating both concern about his aunt and a very subtly concealed animosity toward the man who has caused her pain. (Cooley, remember, was just outside the door when Mitchell knocked Opal down to search her purse; certainly he has passed on information about that incident to his friend Carlyle.) Is Opal, then, being truthful when she says "that man was a jinx" (p. 104) and "the best job I ever had and I lost it because of a common, ordinary nigger" (p. 104), or has she, forewarned that Mitchell will perhaps look her up, decided to use deception to steer him to Cooley and Carlyle so they can abuse him further? Is she wearing a mask of submissiveness to gain Mitchell's trust and to hasten him to a losing encounter with his partner in conception?

Opal's last few comments in the conversation should be further considered. Mitchell, who wants almost desperately to believe that she is on his side, offers her her old job back with a twenty dollar raise. She is to come to work in two days, after he has had the opportunity to fire the German maid he had hired to replace her. "Me? Work for you again? Even after what I done? . . . I'd love to work for you. And I promise never to go out with any nigger like Cooley again" (p. 105). But *has* Opal done anything? The exaggerated gratefulness of her words makes their import questionable. Is she gleeful because she knows Carlyle and Cooley will repay Mitchell for what he has done to her? Or is she genuinely happy about the job prospect? Is she, perhaps, realizing that if she were to return to work for the Pierces, her knowledge about them would enable her to indulge in blackmail if she so desired? We are never sure because the novel ends before the two days are up, with Mitchell still fantasizing that Opal will show up to pretend that the black baby, which Cooley has refused to take, is really her own child. (The white twin has died). Though Mitchell is almost certainly deluded about that, Kelley leaves the facts ambiguous.

Though Opal has been out of the book since the pocketbook-searching incident, and though she does not appear again after this conversation about the whereabouts of Cooley, she serves to send Mitchell on his labyrinthine journey through black nightlife, and she serves as part of the inspiration for the fantastic sexual dream he has later in the novel (pp. 125–130). And Opal is not painted as being a stupid woman; therefore, her insistence that she was fired because of Cooley is presumably a way of keeping him before Mitchell's eyes, thereby spurring him on to pursuit of the man—and further humiliation. (Given Cooley's determination to exact money from Mitchell and still not take the black baby, and given Carlyle's desire to see Mitchell suffer for having fired Opal, the white man's downfall is assured.) Opal's reference to Cooley as a "common, ordinary nigger" may flatter Mitchell in addition to separating her from his enemy; if she emphasizes that she is unlike Cooley and emotionally more tied to Mitchell, he will perhaps trust her word more quickly and be more quickly punished. He is soothed in this conversation into believing that Opal is a good maid—to the point that he cannot "remember why he had eve[r] believed [her] to be a thief." Opal's submissive crying act thus puts her in control of the gullible Mitchell. His ineffectiveness, his inability to see when he is being fooled, his acceptance of orders from his lecherous mother-in-law—all of which cause him to accomplish less and less as the novel progresses—all increase the probability that Opal is really in control in her last scene. The evaluation of Mitchell as a failure, in his attempts to imitate a southern planter, still stands, and the evaluation that Opal is a transitional northern maid is substantially supported.

CHAPTER SIX

BEYOND THE UNIFORM

In 1956, Alice Childress published *Like One of the Family . . . conversations from a domestic's life*—sixty-two "conversations" which had all been previously published in either *Freedom* or *The Baltimore Afro-American*.[1] The publication of the conversations marked the beginning of a sassiness in black literary maids which would lead to the confrontation dramas of the 1960's. Childress has commented on the creation of Mildred, the major character in the volume, as well as on the response to her conversations' publication:

Mildred is based upon my aunt Lorraine who was a domestic worker all of her life, a wonderful woman who refused to exchange dignity for pay. I wrote the pieces originally for Paul Robeson's newspaper *Freedom* for no compensation at all, then for five dollars per column. *The Baltimore Afro-American* ran them all (one per week) for twenty-five dollars each and then I wrote new ones for them (unpublished) for the next year or two. Floods of beautiful mail came in from domestics (male and female) telling me of their own experiences. I had done domestic work myself for about three or four months and not because I was studying the people . . . but because it was the only work I could get at the moment.[2]

The structure of the conversations shows they were written with an audience in mind. They are Mildred's accounts of what has happened to her in a white woman's house a couple of days or a week or more ago; she is always speaking in dramatic monologue to Marge, a fellow domestic and neighbor. Marge never speaks, and her presence is indicated only in Mildred's observations on or responses to her unseen and unheard reactions. Marge identifies with and wonders at Mildred's exploits, and is astounded when Mildred seems to stretch the truth, just like the domestics who were reading *Freedom* or *The Baltimore Afro-American*. Thus Childress enables her audience to interact with Mildred in more personally satisfying ways than if they were mere readers; through Marge, they are allowed instead to be participants on the page. This is as true of any audience reading *Like One of the Family* today as it was of Mildred's audiences in 1956—and especially so if that audience has any knowledge of the black domestic's life.

Mildred is substantially unlike any of the maids covered so far in this discussion. First of all, she is single; she therefore has no dependents whose needs could complicate the relationships she defines with the white women for whom she works. Second, although Mildred is thirty-two, a little older than Lutie Johnson and about the same age as Pauline Breedlove, she has not allowed herself to become so settled in her work that she silently acquiesces in whatever her mistresses say and do. If she had been Lutie, at the train station, she would have told Mrs. Chandler what she thought. If she had been Pauline Breedlove, she would not have been content to let the matter go if a white woman had held back her pay. Third, Mildred is thoroughly independent. She never tells of accepting cast-aways or service pans; she is proud of her health and gumption and of the fact that she makes enough money to buy things she wants (and indeed to buy many things for other people). Fourth, Mildred is a day worker, a fact which contributes greatly to her iconoclastic attitude. If polite conversations with the mistress cannot straighten out problems on a job, she always has the option of quitting and trying for another one, the more conveniently because of her New York location and her singleness. As a day worker, she probably has several employers within a short period of time instead of having her entire income derive from a single source. She therefore does not have the kind of dependency that many of the maids had who worked for a single family for years. She can therefore take off work for a few days or even a week (though she never speaks of doing so) if things do not go well. But even on the jobs she holds for months, Mildred is unwilling to let others define her, unwilling to accept the definition of her place accepted by so many of the earlier maids.

Whereas Pauline Breedlove looks upon her job as an art to be selfishly practiced, Granny Huggs sees hers as a lifestyle, and Lutie Johnson hers as a means of achieving the American Dream, Mildred views hers as a profession. She goes to her jobs not with the attitude that her employers are doing her favors by allowing her to work, but with the attitude that she has something of value to offer, something the white women can benefit from and something which in turn can serve her in good stead. Her career is not, in her eyes, just something she has been forced into because she is black, or single, or living in New York; although she never mentions the possibility of getting another sort of job, what we learn of her would indicate that she knows she would do very well in any job situation.[3] Forever strong and confident about her work and about her ability to do good work, she has a positive sense of self—of an identity which cannot be reshaped and/or damaged by contact with whites—that ultimately differentiates her from the literary maids previously discussed. The compliments she receives, and the other rewards of her domestic work, therefore do not negate her worth as a human being—and they certainly do not come about as a result of her effacing herself. She could never be mistaken for the stereotypical maid who accepts insults or nasty insinuations from whites and wavers about her own identity in their presence. She is generous and loving toward other Blacks, especially the children who live in her apartment building. Her creativity in work and in capturing her experience borders on the artistic, in the very best sense of that word.

From the beginning, Mildred sees her job as an arena for asserting herself, and at times she turns it into a forum for discussing black causes and attitudes toward Blacks. She rejects right away the notion that she is "like one of the family." That rejection enables her to keep her cultural identity intact and to make it clear to her white employer that she is still a part of a group which is distinctly separate from the white world. To be one of the family would be to become a possession, as Pauline Breedlove does, or to adopt completely the values of the whites, as Granny Huggs does. But Mildred's perspective is uniquely realistic and uniquely non-white. In the title conversation, she recounts to Marge how Mrs. C[4] drools over her to a friend: "I could hear her talkin' just as loud . . . and she says to her friend, 'We *just* love her! She's *like* one of the family and she *just adores* our little Carol! We don't know *what* we'd do without her! We don't think of her as a servant!'"[5] Mildred decides it is time to talk with Mrs. C, and the conversation reveals her confidence in herself and her refusal to be intimidated:

When the guest leaves, I go in the living room and says, "Mrs. C . . . , I want to have a talk with you."

"By all means," she says.

I drew up a chair and read her thusly: "Mrs. C . . . , you are a pretty nice person to work for, but I wish you would please stop talkin' about me like I was a *cocker spaniel* or a *poll parrot* or a *kitten*. . . . Now you just sit there and hear me out.

"In the first place, you do not *love* me; you may be fond of me, but that is all. . . . In the second place, I am *not* just like one of the family at all! The family eats in the dining room and I eat in the kitchen. Your mama borrows your lace tablecloth for her company and your son entertains his friends in your parlor, your daughter takes her afternoon nap on the living room couch and the puppy sleeps on your satin spread . . . and whenever your husband gets tired of something you are talkin' about he says, 'Oh, for Pete's sake, forget it. . . . ' So you can see I am not *just* like one of the family.

"Now for another thing, I do not *just* adore your little Carol. I think she is a likable child, but she is also fresh and sassy. I know you call it 'uninhibited' and that is the way you want your child to be, but *luckily* my mother taught me some inhibitions or else I would smack little Carol once in a while when she's talkin' to you like you're a dog, but as it is I just laugh it off the way you do because she is *your* child and I am *not* like one of the family.

"Now when you say, 'We don't know *what* we'd do without her' this is a polite lie . . . because I know that if I dropped dead or had a stroke, you would get somebody to replace me.

"You think it is a compliment when you say, 'We don't think of her as a servant. . . . ' but after I have worked myself into a sweat cleaning the bathroom and the kitchen . . . making the beds . . . cooking the lunch . . . washing the dishes and ironing Carol's pinafores . . . I do not feel like no weekend house guest. I feel like a servant, and in the face of that I have been meaning to ask you for a slight raise which will make me feel much better toward everyone here and make me know my work is appreciated.

"Now I hope you will stop talkin' about me in my presence and that we will get along like a good employer and employee should" (pp. 2–3).

Direct confrontation is the essence of Mildred's deviation from the stereotype of the domestic, and since this particular confrontation occurs at the beginning of the book, it sets the tone for her self-assertion and sassiness throughout the volume. And Mildred is almost unrealistically accepted by her employers—accepted in the sense of not being fired or beaten or treated even more violently in retaliation for her verbal blasts.

Mildred begins the conversation discussed above by challenging the limits of the psychological and physical space usually allowed domestics. Before the opening of my quotation, Mildred, having gone into the living room to remove a platter, has indicated her disapproval to Mrs. C and her guest by giving them both "a look that would have frizzled a egg"—a look which changes the conversation immediately. The bold weaponry of the eye achieves its desired purpose. And the conversation will also accomplish its purpose of enlightenment. Mrs. C, Mildred says, "was almost speechless but she *apologized* and said she'd talk to her husband about the raise. . . . I knew things were progressing because this evening Carol came in the kitchen and she did not say, 'I want some bread and jam!' but she did say, '*Please*, Mildred, will you fix me a slice of bread and jam'" (p. 3). Mildred has won recognition that she is a human being instead of the family mascot her mistress has believed her to be: in Mildred's world, a word to the wise is sufficient. That would have given hope to those newspaper readers who had undoubtedly encountered Mrs. Cs in their jobs as domestics. While their reactions may have been as nervous as Marge's—"I'm going upstairs, Marge. Just look . . . you done messed up that buttonhole!" (p. 3)—they would ultimately feel a sense of pride, vicariously identifying with Mildred. If they themselves did not have the aggressiveness to complain about their jobs and assert their own humanity, they could live out their wishful thoughts through Mildred. So had generations of Blacks appreciated Brer Rabbit and John Henry and Staggolee. For those in confined positions who must confront those in powerful positions, a story of a confined someone who does so and who succeeds in doing so must carry its own reward.

Added to the thrill of what Mildred says in "Like One of the Family" would have been the pleasure in how and where she says it. She does not wait for Mrs. C to come into the kitchen, the territory usually associated with black domestics; she goes into the living room in a deliberate violation of the space taboo. And not only does she go into the living room, she draws up a chair without being asked to be seated, and without any consideration of how her employer might respond to that symbolic equalization of their human conditions. Mildred's body language clearly indicates that she is not a toy, an oversized plaything for the amusement of the white woman and her guest. By assuming that she *can* confront the white mistress, and by doing so, Mildred broadcasts loudly that she is a proud woman and a professional, not a poor soul comfortable in a cubbyhole.

By confronting the white woman, Mildred gives the lie to the myth that most black maids love and accept being adopted by their white families. She denies what Pauline Breedlove sees as the reality of her existence, a reality which, as we have seen, is a mirage. In assaulting those feelings of generosity the white woman maintains are hers, and in not being met with a rebuttal, Mildred establishes that white mistresses and black maids are distinct entities, just as the black community is distinct from the white. To assert anything else is to foster illusion. No matter how much Mrs. C may "love" Mildred, she has yelled out to her in the presence of a guest that Mildred should "eat *both* of those lamb chops for your lunch!" (p. 1), a comment by which she is simultaneously showing off the quality of her servant's food (she has already told Mildred to eat the chops) and the fact that Mildred is having lunch somewhere other than in the living room with herself and her guest (probably the kitchen). If things were so loving and non-discriminatory, that certainly would not be the case. Observing that Mrs. C's theories about their relationship have no counterpart in her practice, Mildred forces her to realize that she is not as liberal-minded as she believes herself to be.

Mildred gets at the truth, and she gets at it with humor and good will. The woman, who in a different setting might have been angry with Mildred, recognizes instead the truth as it is presented and acts upon that truth. We see the result in the change in her daughter's behavior and conclude that if she has been interested enough to follow through in that instance, she will probably also follow through on Mildred's raise and the general changes she suggests in their working relationship. Mildred's mention of the raise, of course, would also encourage her audience to identify with her. The mistresses' attitudes made money a problem in the usually non-unionized maid situation, and fair wages were often not forthcoming. Requests for additional wages could cost a maid her job, and the accusation of being ungrateful was added to the charge that she was uppity if the majority of her pay had come from service pans and cast-aways. Mildred's straightforward request for money and her comments on the positive effects a raise would have in themselves made her heroic to Childress's newspaper readers—who would look forward to the next installment to see what other come-uppances she had planned for the whites.

The wait would not have been long. In "Let's Face It," Mildred further rejects the concept of physical spatial limitations; she deliberately sits down in the presence of a visiting white southerner who is lecturing her on the proper place for "Nigras." He has waited restlessly for the opportunity to talk with Mildred because he has stereotyped her as the "right" sort of "Nigra." He has called her "sister" (tantamount to Auntie) and has complimented her on the good, stable sort she seems to be in these changing times; because of examples like her, he is not losing his faith in "Nigras." In an effort to rebuke his southern references to her as "sister" and "girl," northern Mildred politely tells the man he can call her "Mildred." That only stops his assault for a moment, and his deliberate pursuit of the subject of race enables Mildred to violate the space assigned to her:

Billy Alabama looks a little shook up for a minute and then he says, "All right, *Millie*, now, as I was sayin', I am not goin' to lose *my* faith in the Nigras no matter what *anybody* says. I have known some really *fine* Nigras over the years and I say that they were some of the *greatest* people I ever met."

By this time, Marge, he decided to settle down to business and really chat a while so he takes a seat in Mrs. M . . . 's leather chair. Well, you know there's two of those armchairs that sits facin' each other right in front of the fireplace. So I sat down in the other one. Girl, he got a look on his face like somebody had just slammed a automobile door on his finger.

Sure, he had to go on or else get *ungenteel!* Well, I could see him strugglin' for strength. He swallowed hard and started in again . . . (pp. 185–186).

Billy Alabama tries to remain calm in the face of the presumed insult, but Mildred does not allow him to keep his composure. When he relates the tale of one of his coloured friends, a black minister, the epitome of an Uncle Tom, she upsets him further by threatening to go to Alabama and whip his model "Nigra." By settling herself in the living room of the white family for whom she works, at the same eye level with Billy and in a chair similar to his, Mildred eradicates the physical symbols of inequality. In being sassy, she refuses to recognize psychological inequality. Once again her body language initially affirms her humanity, and in her retorts to Billy's prejudices she extends the realm of her freedom. Here is a "crazy nigger" who gets away with overstepping her bounds because Billy is too amazed at her unusualness to respond immediately.

Mildred also redefines physical and psychological boundaries in "Interestin' and Amusin'." Given a small amount of time to do some yea-saying, she uses it to make a nay-saying speech on World War II. Serving at a buffet cocktail party for Mrs. H., Mildred is struck by the company's overuse of the words "wonderful" and "amusing"; it represents to her their thoughtlessness and shallowness. When they stop ringing their changes on the words of the evening long enough to ask her opinion of the war, Mildred mentions that she has work to do. Why try to explain anything to such people?

"Oh, Mildred," Mrs. H. squeals, "don't be stuffy. I've told everyone how *wonderful* you are."

So I put down the silent butler and says short and quick, "I'm against war and if most of the people feel like that there'll be peace."

Well, honey, I could tell by the laughter in their eyes that they thought me "amusin'." Anyway, one arrogant young man speaks up. "Why are you for peace . . . do you have a son?"

"No," I says, "I do not have a son, but I got *me* and I have hope for better days and I'd like to be here to see 'em and I'm lookin' forward to someday bein' as much of a woman as I can be. . . . I also consider that all children belong to us whether we birthed them or not, be they girls or boys."

At this point, Marge, Mrs. H. starts wavin' her hands and smilin' as if to say that was enough, but I wasn't payin' her no mind whatsoever. . . . "Furthermore," I said, "I do not want to see people's blood and bones spattered about the streets and I do not want to see your eyes runnin' outta your head like water. . . . When there is true peace we'll have different notions about what is *amusin'* because *mankind* will be *wonderful*" (pp. 160, 161).

Having been given an inch, Mildred takes ten miles. She has been given permission to speak and she thoroughly exploits the opportunity. Technically, she has not violated "place," but she has certainly violated the substance of the concept. Mrs. H., who is presumably in control, is not; Mildred becomes the manipulator, "doing her own thing." Mildred has deftly taken the subject her listeners and employer have given her, expounded upon it graphically, and handed it back to them. She succeeds not only in refuting by the simple sanity of her arguments their low opinion of her intelligence (" . . . one of 'em got the bright idea of tryin' to make a fool out of me by callin' me in and askin' my opinion . . . "), but she uses forcefully and meaningfully the very language that in their mouths has been hollow and meaningless, when they very likely had expected her to speak the comically childish and inaccurate English of a minstrel-show sideman.

By putting Mildred on the side of life, meaning, and substance, and by placing her in the living room, Childress succeeds in passing judgment on the people at the cocktail party who really engage with none of those things. Mildred, the assumed bottom rail culturally and intellectually, becomes the top rail morally and racially, for as a black maid Mildred represents Blacks whether she wants to or not. But thus representative as she is, she is also decidedly individual. She has her individual triumph as the audience recognizes the truth and seriousness of what she says in contrast to the falsity and triviality of what the whites have said. One *Mildred*, a black maid whom they have considered inconsequential and utterly lacking in gray matter, turns the intellectual tables on them all.

The broad vision and sound reason Mildred exhibits in both "Let's Face It" and "Interestin' and Amusin'" is also apparent in her attitude toward the organization of domestic labor in "We Need A Union Too." Because she recognizes that women will hire maids as soon as their income allows that luxury, that those employed will probably be overworked and underpaid, and that domestics have jobs that "almost nobody wants," she figures they need protection.

> That is why we need a union! Why shouldn't we have set hours and set pay just like busdrivers and other folks, why shouldn't we have vacation pay and things like that? . . . Well, I guess it would be awful hard to get houseworkers together on account of them all workin' off separate-like in different homes, but it would sure be a big help and also keep you out of a lot of nasty arguments!
>
> For example, I'd walk in to work and the woman would say to me, "Mildred, you will wax the floors with paste wax, please." Then I say, "No, that is very heavy work and is against the union regulations." She will say, "If you don't do it, I will have to get somebody else!" Then I say, "The somebody else will be union, too, so they will not be able to do it, either." "Oh," she will say, "if it's too heavy for you and too heavy for the somebody else then it must be also too heavy for me! How will I get my floors done?" "Easy," I say, "the union will send a *man* over to do things like paste wax, window washin', scrubbin' walls, takin' down venetian blinds and all such" (pp. 140–141).

Mildred suggests that if the woman should complain that that would be too costly, and decide instead to hire non-union labor, her apartment would be picketed—the nonconformist being identified as such publicly.

Mildred sees the same obstacles to organizing domestics that Gerda Lerner pointed out: she is not too blunted by her work to see problems and envision solutions. Her awareness that the mistress/maid relationship is exploitative and her belief that something can be done about that both set her apart from the likes of Mammy Jane and Pauline Breedlove. Her accumulated experiences have inspired her support of unionization, and one of those experiences is of particular interest. The one time she had applied for a permanent job, her prospective employer had spoken at first in terms of working out arrangements satisfactory to both of them—but something else happened.

Marge, before I can get in a word about what'll make me happy she takes a sheet of paper out of her desk and starts readin' off how things will go. "Mildred," she says, "on Monday you will report at eight o'clock in the mornin' and after the breakfast dishes you will do the washin'. Of course we have a machine." "Naturally," I says, then she starts runnin' her finger down this devilish list: "After the washin' you will take care of the children's lunch, prepare dinner, clean the baby's room *thoroughly* and leave after the supper dishes, that's Monday." "So much for Monday," I says, "and how about Tuesday?" "Well," she says, "you don't come in until noon on Tuesday, then you fix the children's lunch, iron, give the kitchen a thorough cleaning, prepare dinner and leave after the supper dishes." "Well," I says, "here we are at Wednesday already." "Yes," she says, "on Wednesday you come in at eight in the mornin' and do all the floors, fix the children's lunch, do the mendin', give the foyer and the baths a thorough cleanin', prepare the dinner . . . " ". . . and leave after the supper dishes," I says. "That's right," she says, "and the schedule remains pretty much the same for the rest of the week; on Thursday you thoroughly clean the bedrooms, on Friday the livin' room, on Saturday the pantry shelves, silver, and clothes closets and on Sunday you fix early dinner and leave after one-thirty."

Marge, I must have looked pure bewildered because she adds, "Do you have any comment?" "A little," I says, "When is my off-time?" "Oh that," she says. "Yes mam," I says, and then she begins to run her finger down the list again. "Well, you have one half-day off every Tuesday and one half-day off every Sunday and every other Thursday you get a full day off, which makes it a five and a half day week."

How 'bout that Marge! I was never too good at arithmetic, but I really had to tip my hat to her. Even somebody as smart as Einstein couldn't have figured nothin' as neat as that. Before I could get a word in on what I considered the deal of the year, she played her trump card, "I will pay you two weeks pay on the first and fifteenth of each month." "But that way," I says, "I lose a week's pay every time the month has five weeks." Well, she repeats herself, "I pay on the first and fifteenth" (pp. 97–98).

As outrageous as those demands may seem (and part of the outrageousness is due to the way Mildred tells the story), they are not far different from the demands put on many black women who had no choice but to do the work assigned to them if they wanted to keep their jobs.[6] Mildred's independent circumstances give her the leeway to respond rather flippantly to them. But unlike Mildred, many other women had no choice about submitting to a mistress's exorbitant demands; it was either submit and pay the bills and feed the family or refuse to submit and let the bill collectors come and the family go hungry. Such women simply girded themselves up and did the work.

Mildred leaves. As she explains: "I could see me workin' myself into such a lather that there wouldn't be nothin' to do but crawl into the doctor's office on the first and fifteenth and give every blessed nickel I had in order that he could try and straighten me out in time to meet the second and the sixteenth" (p. 98). Still, she sees additional humor in the situation: "How come all of them big-shots in Washington that can't balance the budget or make the taxes cover all our expenses, how *come* they don't send for that woman to help straighten them out? Why, in two or three weeks she'd not only get everything on a payin' basis, but she'd have enough money left over to buy every citizen a free ice cream cone for the fourth of July, not countin' all the loot we'd have left over to bury at Fort Knox! Genius like that just pure takes your breath away. It's almost beautiful in a disgustin' sort of way, ain't it?" (p. 98).

The conversation is appropriately entitled "I Hate Half Days Off,"[7] a title which reflects Mildred's attitude toward what the woman tries to force upon her. How the title unfolds in the conversation reflects the woman's sense of power, her belief that she can and will force that amount of work upon some black woman. Mildred's refusal to compromise makes this northern white woman like many of her southern sisters who viewed the black worker primarily as a beast of burden—as Zora Neale Hurston has it, as the mule of the world. For all of them black women existed primarily to liberate white women from the unpleasantries associated with housework, and never mind if they ended up with bad feet and bad backs, under doctors' care. Mildred's interviewer has organized the schedule of work to make it an enemy which exacts the sacrifices of a brute of a stone god. It demands complete submission of body and mind and promises the survival of neither. It relishes self-degradation, self-denial, and de-humanization. It delights in those varicose veins, lower back pains, and raw hands. It wants, most importantly of all, to destroy the human spirit of any black woman who would submit to such disci-pline. Mildred will *not* worship it.

In another sketch, one in which she is left a note describing what she should do and appropriately titled "On Leavin' Notes!", Mildred is equally emphatic in setting limits on the work expected of her. Here the problem is not so much the difficulty of the work as the fact that it is slyly imposed:

> Well girl, I done come up with my New Year's resolution. . . . That's right, I made just one, and that is this: NOBODY THAT I DO DAYSWORK FOR SHALL LEAVE ME ANY NOTES . . . You know what I mean. Whenever these women are going to be out when you come to work, they will leave you a note tellin' you about a few extra things to do. They ask you things in them notes that they wouldn't dast ask you to your face.
>
> When I opened the door this morning I found a note from Mrs. R . . . It was neatly pinned to three cotton housecoats. "Dear Mildred," it read, "please take these home, wash and iron them, and bring them in tomorrow. Here is an extra dollar for you. . . ." And at the bottom of the note a dollar was pinned.
>
> Now Marge, there is a laundry right up on her corner and they charges seventy-five cents for housecoats. . . . Wait a minute, honey, just let me tell it now. . . . I hung around until she got home . . . Oh, but I did! And she was most surprised to see the housecoats and me still there. "Mildred," says she, "did you see my note?"

"Yes," I replied, "and I cannot do those housecoats for no dollar."

"Why," she says, "how much do you want?"

I give her a sparing smile and says, "Seventy-five cents apiece, the same as the laundry."

"Oh," she says, "well it looks as though I can't use you. . . . "

"Indeed you can't," I say, " 'cause furthermore I am not going to let you."

"Let's not get upset," she adds. "I only meant I won't need you for the laundry."

"I am not upset, Mrs. R . . . ," I says, "but in the future, please don't leave me any notes making requests outside of our agreement. . . ." And you know, THAT WAS THAT. . . . No, Marge . . . I did not pop my fingers at her when I said it. There's no need to overdo the thing! (pp. 154–155).

In the sort of confrontation that characterizes *Like One of the Family*, Mildred makes it clear to her employer that she expects to be treated as a human being who has the right to say no, even to that employer. The fact that Mildred and Mrs. R have an agreement of sorts that Mildred expects the woman to honor must have in itself made Childress's readers blink; as Mrs. Burton and other women pointed out in my interviews with them, in reality there were no such understandings. If a maid had a moment of spare time, the mistress thought she was not getting her money's worth and gave her additional duties as a matter of course. Yet the fictional deviation from the norm gave hope and vicarious satisfaction to Marge and the newspaper audience as Mildred once again triumphed over the conditions that weighed so many of her sisters down.

Mildred does not always speak with blunt, unindulgent briskness. In "Listen for the Music," she insists on the necessity of explaining things to children with both patience and imagination (pp. 4–8). In her effort to show a little boy where music comes from, she becomes a model of wise motherhood, a sharp contrast to the child's real mother, who is exasperated by his questions. But she is no ever-doting mammy, as she shows in "Inhibitions." In that conversation (pp. 132–136), instead of telling a trying child that she loves him and politely explaining at length why he cannot play in the hamburger she is trying to prepare, Mildred simply says "Because I *said* not, that's why!" (p. 133). His mother is shocked and spends some time soothing the shocked child. Once he has quieted down, she returns to Mildred with a lecture on the necessity of dealing with children in unabrupt ways. Mildred counters by identifying the true problem before them:

> You have spoiled that boy so rotten 'til you've made it impossible for anybody to have any dealin's with him at all. If I was to tell him why he couldn't play in the dinner, I would *have* to talk about you some. If I did that, it would put you and me in a awful strain, so I just go along and tell him don't do it 'cause I *said* so (p. 133).

When the woman asks for clarification, Mildred continues:

> here it is: the reason he can't do any and everything that strikes him is 'cause somebody has given him some wrong ideas about his *rights*! In spite of what you tell him, it is not his *right* to walk over everybody, to be rude and sassy, to hold me up from doin' my work, to make everybody sick 'cause he feels like playin' in their food. No, it is not his right to do these things or to get rewarded for *not* ruinin' the supper. He needs to be told that there are things that everybody ought to do whether they feel like it or not, and the sooner they get used to the idea, the better they will get along in the world (pp. 133–134).

What a great psychological distance between Mildred and Mammy Jane! There is no worshipful acquiescence here, or even polite tolerance. Mildred calls a brat a brat, and she does not feel compelled to suffer the brat's tantrums. She is iconoclastic toward traditional ideas of the proper relationship between black maid and white child, between white mother and black child-tender, striking down one more stereotype with which the majority of her audience must often have been confronted.

More often than not, Mildred is able to make her points in relatively polite and certainly witty ways. Not in "Ain't You Mad?" The racial anger underlying many of the conversations surfaces blatantly in this one, and it is here that Childress comes closest to being a propagandist, introducing themes which will be seen in the work of John A. Williams, Douglas Turner Ward, Ted Shine, and Ed Bullins.

Message is consciously allowed to become more important than art and direct lecturing takes the place of witty manipulation. Mildred turns the domestic territory into a battleground:

Marge, I am sick to my soul and stomach. . . . Well, this morning I report on the job, and Mr. and Mrs. B. are finishing their breakfast. Mr. B. is finishing on the last piece of buttered, jellied toast when he looks up from his paper and says to me, "Isn't it too bad about this girl tryin' to get into Alabama University?" And then Mrs. B. swashes down her bacon with a gulp of coffee and says, "Tch, tch, tch, I know *you people* are angry about this. What is going to be done?"

My hand started jumpin' and I was twitchin' my pocketbook, tryin' my best not to pop her in the mouth with that heavy plastic bag. All of a sudden, Marge, something hit me! I could feel a hotness creepin' over me from my feet on up and when it hit my head, bells started ringin'[8] and I hollered at her, "What the hamfat is the matter with you? *Ain't you mad*? Now you either be *mad* or *shame*, but don't you sit there with your mouth full 'tut-tuttin' at me! Now if you mad, you'd of told me what *you done* and if you shame, you oughta be hangin' your head instead of smackin' your lips over them goodies!"

. . . Now wait a minute, Marge. Please let me finish. Mr. B. stops chewin' with the jam fairly skeetin' out of his mouth and says, "Don't upset Mrs. B. We were only tryin' to be sympathetic." Marge! I whammed my pocketbook down on the table, put my hands on my side and started pattin' my foot, and I yelled at him: "Don't you worry about Mrs. B. bein' upset 'cause if she gets too wrought up she can *scream* and the law, the klan and them men that ganged up on that young lady to keep her out of school, that's right, every one of 'em will come runnin' in here and move me off the premises piece by piece!"

At this point, Marge, he was gaspin' and sputterin' while she was puffin' and blowin' and I wheeled on him and said, "You tryin' to tell me about you bein' sympathetic . . . how do I know you wasn't in sympathy with them grown-up men that was throwin' eggs and stones at a defenseless colored woman? In the first place, you are white and you haven't opened your mouth to do a thing but

put toast in it, and first thing I walk in you come askin' me what am
I gonna do."

Then guess what, Marge! Mrs. B. jumps up wavin' her newspaper at me, talkin' about "Go home, go home *immediately*, you're
in no condition to work here today!" Honey, never fear! I reached
over and snatched that paper out of her hand and says, "Don't you
be wavin' and fannin' nothin' in my face! My mama don't do that!"
Then Mr. B. jumps up and hollers "Are you out of your mind,
snatching things like that!" . . . . "Well," I told him, "you can thank
your lucky stars that paper is the only thing I'm snatchin' this
morning!" He tried to cut me off, but I wouldn't let him, "If you
ain't got the grace to stand up and fight for your own decency and
good name, don't you dare ask me what *I'm* gonna do, because as
long as *you* ain't *doin'* I ain't gonna tell you, 'cause then you'd know
as much as I do, and that might be too much!"

Marge, I didn't want to cry because it do look so weak, but the
tears were streamin' down and it seemed like their faces were
floatin' in a sea of water. I could hear their voices but no words,
just a rush of murmurin' in my ears. "Yes," I went on, "black folks
want decent educations and the right to work at decent jobs and
also every kind of right there is! And we bein' mobbed and killed
and shot at. . . . That's right, they're shootin' at little children ridin'
school buses! They're shootin' down their fathers for tryin' to get
'em into the schools, they won't sell us no food because we want
our children educated, they turnin' us off of jobs and tryin' to drive
us out of our homes, they draggin' people out of their beds in the
middle of the night and burnin' them with oil and fire. And you ask
me what *I'm* gonna do!"

Marge, the next thing you know he says real nasty-like, "When
there's a Negro crime wave, I don't throw it in your face." . . . Sit
down, Marge, keep still. Girl, I opened up on him and said, "You
better not! 'Cause whenever a Negro does somethin' it's a *wave*,
but your doggone newspapers is full of nothin' but white folks
murderin' and robbin' *every day* that the Lord sends ever since
there's been a newspaper and you folks done got so numb inside
'til you think that's how it *should be!*" Then I says, "Why, I can't
turn on the television without seeing you all killin' each other up
just for the sake of *entertainment*. So you just keep on eatin' your

breakfast same as ever, you just keep 'tut-tuttin'. The world's just goin' to pass you by." He jumps up again and says, "Go home!" . . . "I'm goin'," I says, "but remember this: everybody that don't like the idea of white folks warrin' on my people, everybody that feels they don't want to be included in the mob crowd, all those kind of folks speak up and let the world know!" Yes indeed, I told him, "All those that keep quiet are with the mob whether they agree with 'em or not!"

And with that, Marge, I walked out and left them sittin' there big-eyed. . . . Yes, dear, I'll take a cup of coffee—strong. Yes, your friend Mildred is *upset*! (pp. 171–173)

Mildred is conscience and concern; her employers are insensitivity and condescension. By noting the casual way Mr. B. finishes the "last piece of buttered, jellied toast" and the offhand way Mrs. B. swashes down her bacon "with a gulp of coffee" as they consider the wretchedness in Alabama, Mildred emphasizes the distance between black and white: between the security, stability, and complacency of the B.s' life on the one hand and the insecurity and disruption that Autherine Lucy must have been experiencing—insecurity and disruption that Mildred herself shakes at the thought of—on the other. Mildred selects detail here to make the B.s seem like villains whose places in society prevent them from ever sympathizing with or even understanding what vitally concerns the black community.

Everything which might have been expected of Mildred THE MAID has been pushed into the background in this conversation. Perhaps attention should be called to her employers' insensitivity and short-sightedness; but Mildred's forceful, successful breaking down of all barriers between mistress/master and maid is—to put it bluntly—quite incredible. Childress has a statement to make about the historic attempt of Autherine Lucy to enter the University of Alabama; and in the intensity of her anger, she forces upon her angry Mildred a much more propagandistic stance than usual. Dictates of character are forgotten as Mildred's tale becomes a polemical essay.

Marge, of course, and doubtless Childress's newspaper audience with her, have on many occasions responded to Mildred's tales with a wonder that was tinged with real skepticism; but she and they have also probably seen some slight possibility that the incidents Mildred relates did indeed occur just as she says they did. Thus when Mildred relates to Marge that she has set straight the woman who considered her as one of the family, the audience may, with Marge, find themselves uneasily messing up their buttonholes, as it were; but they can hope, and in their wishful thinking believe, that Mildred might have indeed thus confronted the woman. Again, when Mildred has stretched credibility so far as to make Marge drop a pan of beans (p. 27), there is still, at least, the delightful possibility that she has indeed confronted the woman who had implied that she would steal. But in none of those other conversations had Mildred actually shouted at her white employers or physically assaulted them, as she does when she snatches the newspaper out of Mrs. B.'s hand. In other words, elsewhere even the never-never land Childress creates to promote wholesome fantasy has its boundaries in terms of what it expects its audience to accept as truth or probability.

"Ain't You Mad?" is the only conversation in which Mildred is sent home. Significantly, she is not fired though she radically violates every sort of spatial bountary set for the domestic; but also significantly, only in "Ain't You Mad?" do she and her employers fail to reach a new level of understanding. Usually, the people she enlightens as to their ignorance accept their enlightenment. They are shocked that they have been so narrowminded concerning racial issues; they evince an eagerness to change. They and Mildred recognize their mutual humanity and Mildred works harmoniously with them for at least a few more days or weeks—a pattern which might occur once or twice in real life, especially in Mildred's New York and in the life of a maid with so vivacious a personality as Mildred's, but which surely could not be the norm. "Ain't You Mad?" is striking, therefore, in that it is the least realistic confrontation in the conversations, yet it has the most realistic, least optimistic ending.

Even as late as 1956, real life was still not quite ready for a Mildred. Dragon-slayer in a segregated, pre-Stokeley Carmichael world, dominant figure in the traditionally submissive role of domestic, Mildred, real as she herself is, does not represent herself in the conversations as living in what Marge and Childress's readers knew was the real world. Instead, she shapes and orders her experiences to give them entertainment value, to point up their ironies, and with the wisdom of hindsight and poetic license, to bring out the psychological and symbolic truths that had been in them. There is also the possibility that she is exploiting her experiences not only to encourage catharsis in Marge but to feel it herself: *that* Mildred confronted Mrs. C might be one truth; *how* she confronted her might have been another; and anything she might have lost at the moment of the real encounter might be being regained in her telling about it. What happens to truth in this process?

Certainly there is no suggestion that Mildred is dishonest. Marge is an attentive audience, and she and Mildred are spiritual compadres. Both women work for gushing white females, both experience stupidity and insensitivity, and both are black. The truth of those circumstances is ultimately more significant than any other. And Childress is more concerned with Marge's response—with her newspaper audience's response—than with anything else. Her purpose is to give back to those domestics who have "refused to exchange dignity for pay" a self-affirming identification with a woman facing the circumstances they must face daily. When maids read about Mildred, they must have felt something similar to what steel-driving men must have felt upon hearing stories of John Henry, or what slaves who worked from four in the morning until nine at night must have felt in response to tales about John or Brer Rabbit getting out of work that the master or other animals required of them. Mildred's very real moral strength, independence, assertiveness, and positive conception of herself must have served to inspire many domestics to dare to recognize such things in themselves, even if they knew they could never use them as Mildred unrealistically does. And to see the possibility of breaking out of the maid's confining space, even as an abstract possibility, was liberating: all was not hopelessness. By giving Mildred the opportunity to create a legend of herself through the process of her story-telling, Childress offered spiritual flight to thousands of black women—and men—confined in the cage of domestic drudgery. Perhaps Mildred is representative of those instances, heightened because of the compactness and intensity of her experiences, in which black women historically "refused to exchange dignity for pay." My interviews revealed a few of these women—though they were not the norm—who gave up their jobs when required to do too much, who struck out at their mistresses when intimidated, and who grabbed weapons to defend themselves when necessary. One of these women, almost legendary in what she relates, had the following story to tell—very dramatically and passionately, as if her feelings in 1980 were as strong as they had been four decades before—about a job she quit in Greene County, Alabama, in the late 1930's or early 1940's. She had requested a day off from work to help her sister and her brother-in-law (Bro' John) finish chopping cotton. She was given an ultimatum: either come to work that day or not come again.

[Miss Lucille] told me, "If you can't come here, you can't work here no mo'," and I told her it didn't make me no difference if I didn't work anymore. So I come on that morning. She met me, she come out and met me when I was crossing the road going on up [to get to the sister's house]. She say, "Is you gon come here today?" And I say, "I'm not going there today. I'm going to help my sister git thoo [through] chopping cotton." I started off; she come out again and when I found myself I was up on the porch cause she came out wiping the butcher knife, but she wasn't coming at me, but I reckon she just hated for me to overdo her. She come out wiping, but I thought she was at me. I jumped up on the top step and grabbed one little stick of wood and I caught myself. Bro John was coming telling me to come down and I caught myself and walked on back down and went on and she called me 'til I got to the road: "I wanna know is you gon work?" I told her, "No-o-o." "If you ain't gon work for me, you don come, don't git on my place no more." I say, "You can't keep me from coming up the highway." I say cause the highway made for the come. I say I'm coming up the highway and I'm going out here to he'p her chop. I went on out there and hope her chop and went on down the highway home. And when I got home—we stayed over there in a little small house—when I got home, some of them tole me, say, "She'll be there in the morning." I say, "I'm gon be ready for her." So that morning when she knocked on the do' I come to the do' putting one arm in my dress . . . She said, "I wanna know is you coming back to work," and I said, "No, Miss Lucille." I say you stay over there in yo' fine house and let me stay in this hut. Cause, I say, "if I git in the house working for you and you do something to me, it's gon be too wet to plow . . ." I told her she didn't raise nary a daughter named Charlie Mae. She didn't raise me. My momma raised me. I say you can't change me. . . . I say I done told you you ain't raised nary daughter named Charlie Mae. . . . So that ended me and her. I didn't go back there no mo'.[9]

At that time, Mrs. Burton was alone with two small children and a sick father; she had to have a job. Yet, like Mildred, she refused to allow the white woman to dictate to her, or to bow and scrape as she was expected to. She managed to survive by asserting herself and continued to work in domestic positions for years after that incident. Other women I interviewed likewise quit their jobs after they had been cursed at or otherwise victimized by the whimsical and moody women for whom they worked.[10]

Mildred's backtalk has, therefore, at least some historical precedent. Mildred's many accounts of understandings reached with white women also have a measure of historical validation. My interviews show that some women were able to get apologies from the women who had abused them, or, if not from the women themselves, from other family members.[11] In order to accomplish her purpose of spiritual flight, Childress gave a new sort of black domestic to literature. Her Mildred is and remains intellectually vibrant, going to lectures during Negro History Week and challenging the lecturers on the substance of the material they present; calling her minister to account for the sermons he preaches; questioning Jim Crow everywhere it applies—in busses, in schools. She takes time to have a party for neighborhood children and to tell them some of the black history that is not written in books. She has not, then, been mentally dulled by the work she does, or sacrificed her humanity and her own sense of history just because she does what the world classifies as menial work. Significantly, too, Mildred is proud of that work. Nor is her pride dependent upon white approval of what she does: her pride is that of a worker who has a skill and who executes her work with an artful attention to detail. When she cooks a meal or makes a bed to her own satisfaction, that the white mistress may approve is merely coincidental. In pleasing herself, and in having a strong sense of racial and cultural identity, Mildred is noticeably a more complex character in her relationships to whites than either Pauline Breedlove or Granny Huggs, and more forceful in her assertion of herself than

Lutie Johnson. In giving Mildred such complexity, Childress was not attempting to elevate the status of scrubbing floors. Her attempt was to help black domestics expand their conception of themselves. In doing so, she restored individuality and life to a worn-out literary pattern. In the particular way her Mildred defies the pattern— *acting*, at least in her mind, in ways not to be expected of a maid—she is a bridge between the transitional northern maids who espouse freedom of mind and the revolutionary maids who exhibit freedom of action.

CHAPTER SEVEN

THE ICONOCLASTS

"Son in the Afternoon" (1962) is the first of a series of works in which a black maid or her family (either her immediate family or the community of black people) deliberately and openly violates the sanctity of the white home into which she has gone to work. In it, John A. Williams focuses on the son of a maid and the aggressive expression of his long-simmering hatred for the whites who had had more of her attention over many years than he had.[1] In Douglas Turner Ward's *Happy Ending* (1964), two black maids unscrupulously exploit their white employers to assist an extended family in Harlem and in the South. In Barbara Woods's "The Final Supper" (1970), Ed Bullins' *The Gentleman Caller* (1969), and Ted Shine's *Contribution* (1968), the last three works in the series, maids commit serious acts of physical violence against their white employers. All of the works show the influence of the Black Arts Movement upon them as is apparent in their outspokenness and violence. Confrontation that had affected Blacks in other walks of life touched domestic servants as well, and these women on the bottommost of the bottom rail joined their brothers and sisters across the country in expressing their displeasure with their conditions and in aggressively asserting themselves.

"Son in the Afternoon" ties in with the three plays which follow it and the works which preceded it because it relies upon its audience ultimately to judge the actions committed. Wendell, the narrator and main character in the short short story, is as concerned about his audience's reaction and as anxious for their approval as Mildred is. He opens his narrative by recounting an incident in which he, as a writer, had tried to get a word in a script changed; the incident had occurred just before he was scheduled to pick up his mother, Nora, from her job as a maid. Someone he refers to as a "Hollywood hippie" had insisted that a black character "slink" when Wendell thought he should "walk"; the black actor playing the part had simply been quiet, "had played Uncle Tom roles so long that he had become Uncle Tom" (p. 288). Realizing that he is passing judgment, he asks the reader to "hear me out," because his mind has turned to Nora, who may be considered an Aunt Thomasina by some. Wendell's awareness of an audience, of the fact that he is consciously telling a story, creates a set of circumstances more representative than the isolated incident with Kay Couchman, the white woman for whom Nora works.

The story's climactic incident is rather simple and rather quickly over. Wendell arrives at the Couchman house to discover that Nora cannot leave because Kay Couchman has not returned home and Ronald, her nine-year-old son, is slightly ill. Nora suspects that Kay is "out gettin' drunk again," and Wendell is resentful both that he is being delayed and that Ronnie is getting more attention from Nora than he or his siblings ever had. Nora goes off to put Ronnie to bed; Kay arrives "high" and invites Wendell—how the times have changed—to have a drink. He then goes into his "sexy bastard routine," embraces and kisses Kay, and refuses to let her go when Ronnie, realizing his mother is home, rushes into the room. His actions are quite deliberate, the last one being designed to give Ronnie an image and a sense of loss to haunt him throughout his life. Wendell succeeds in taking Ronnie's mother away from him to repay the many Ronnies who have taken Nora away from her children. As Nora and Wendell leave, Ronnie is still slapping Kay's consoling hand away. The "contest" has been decidedly unfair, between a grown man and a nine-year-old boy, but Wendell feels little remorse; and, significantly, he does not expect his audience to judge him harshly.

For that audience not to judge harshly, they must have a knowledge of maid/mistress/white child relationships as well as of what happens to little black children when their mothers must go off to work as maids. Nora has been working as a maid all her adult life, from the time when her husband could not get work in their poverty-stricken early years on. It is the only work she knows and, although she now has children upon whom she could depend for support, she refuses to give up working. Maybe it is her way of keeping busy since her husband's death and of fulfilling the urge to motherhood now that all of her own children are grown and gone. In any case, the job with the Couchmans is one in a long line of domestic jobs she has had.

And Nora, like many domestics we have seen prior to this point, has very clear ideas about what mothers should and should not do. Kay, Wendell notes, is "a playgirl," a fact which causes Nora not to think well of her: "My mother didn't like her too much; she didn't seem to care much for her son, Ronald, junior. There's something wrong with a parent who can't really love her own child, Nora thought" (p. 289). Nora, consequently, fills the gap Ronnie's often-absent mother leaves. "Nora loved him," Wendell concludes, as other domestics we have seen loved "their" white children:

> Couchman was gone ten, twelve hours a day. Kay didn't stay around the house any longer than she had to. So Ronnie had only my mother. I think kids should have someone to love, and Nora wasn't a bad sort. But somehow when the six of us, her own children, were growing up we never had her. She was gone, out scuffling to get those crumbs to put into our mouths and shoes for our feet and praying for something to happen so that all the space in between would be taken care of. Nora's affection for us took the form of rushing out into the morning's five o'clock blackness to wake some silly bitch and get her coffee; took form in her trudging five miles home every night instead of taking the streetcar to save money to buy tablets for us, to use at school, we said. But the truth was that all of us liked to draw and we went through a writing tablet in a couple of hours every day. Can you imagine? There's not a goddam artist among us. We never had the physical affection, the pat on the head, the quick, smiling kiss, the "gimmee a hug" routine. All of this Ronnie was getting (p. 291).

If *The Bluest Eye* had been told from Pecola's point of view, if she had been articulate, perhaps she would also have expressed the feeling of

deprivation that Wendell does. Wendell's reflection is a response to
Ronnie's running to Nora after Wendell has yelled at him. Because
Nora was not ready when he arrived, Wendell had walked into the
living room to wait for her; little Ronnie had come through and
thrown a scene reminding him of the power that all little white
children have over black maids:

> "Nora!" he tried to roar, perhaps the way he'd seen the parents of
> some of his friends roar at their maids. I'm quite sure Kay didn't
> shout at Nora, and I don't think Couchman would. But then no one
> shouts at Nora. "Nora, you come right back here this minute!" the
> little bastard shouted and stamped and pointed to a spot on the
> floor where Nora was supposed to come to roost. I have a nasty
> temper. Sometimes it lies dormant for ages and at other times, like
> when the weather is hot and nothing seems to be going right, it's
> bubbling and ready to explode. "Don't talk to *my* mother like that,
> you little—!" I said sharply, breaking off just before I cursed. I
> wanted him to be large enough for me to strike. "How'd you like
> for me to talk to *your* mother like that?" (pp. 290–291)

Little Ronnie is appropriately shocked and dashes to Nora, who
comfortingly gathers him into her arms. Ironically, Nora thus protects "her" white child from the black child she had actually borne.
Wendell is left to stand alone with his anger and his reflections. Nora
comforts Ronnie by telling him Wendell is jealous, a fact Wendell
himself recognizes but cannot overcome. His efforts to blame his loss
of temper on the weather and on things going badly in his job mask, in
a degree even from himself, his resentfulness about what his mother
is doing and has done and toward those who have reaped the benefits
of her actions. The intensity of his anger comes from many years of
knowing that his mother did not wholly belong to him, and years,
perhaps, of envisioning her in tender scenes with those to whom she
did belong.

The sacrifice to others' children of the black maid's motherly
affection has been an accompaniment of the job, intentionally or
unintentionally, since the first black mother went to work for a white
family. The deprived children, however, have seldom if ever had an
outlet, as Wendell did, for venting their anger at the loss of their

mother. And, many of them have been too timid or frustrated even to think of doing so. Consider Pecola Breedlove again; she simply becomes a shrinking violet when her mother rejects her in favor of a white child. Or consider Rosie Fleming, who creates a fantasy world revolving around the Liveseys for whom her unaffectionate grandmother works. Pecola may enter the kitchen where her mother works, at least once, but neither she nor Rosie goes into a white home there to revenge herself for what she feels she has lost. Wendell does: he is not afraid to do so and only slightly ashamed to have done so.

But even Wendell has learned, as the son of a maid, to make certain gestures of humility automatically. When he arrives at the Couchman household, for instance, he goes around the house to the kitchen door, even though it may be as late as 1962.[2] He explains why:

> I don't like kitchen doors. Entering people's houses by them, I mean. I'd done this thing most of my life when I called at places where Nora worked to pick up the patched or worn sheets or the half-eaten roasts, the battered, tarnished silver—the fringe benefits of a housemaid. As a teen-ager I'd told Nora I was through with that crap; I was not going through anyone's kitchen door. She only laughed and said I'd learn. One day soon after, I called for her and without knocking walked right through the front door of this house and right on through the living room. I was almost out of the room when I saw feet behind the couch. I leaned over and there was Mr. Jorgensen and his wife making out like crazy. I guess they thought Nora had gone and it must have hit them sort of suddenly and they went at it like the hell-bomb was due to drop any minute. I've been that way too, mostly in the spring. Of course, when Mr. Jorgensen looked over his shoulder and saw me, you know what happened. I was thrown out and Nora right behind me. It was the middle of winter, the old man was sick and the coal bill three months overdue. Nora was right about those kitchen doors; I learned (pp. 289–290).

The young Wendell had focused on the back-door custom as a personal affront, while Nora had concentrated on what was necessary to keep a job and keep one's family in coal. Wendell knows as an adult that "no one shouts at Nora," which says something about her strength and self-identity; he recognizes that going through kitchen doors has not destroyed Nora and that it will not destroy him.

Wendell's understanding of the forms of subservience and of the class distinctions inherent in them is reflected not only in his going in the back door to the Couchman home, but also in his encounter with Kay. He must brave a growling Great Dane tied to a backyard tree to get to the back door. The dog, put there to attack burglars, growls appropriately, for Wendell in effect "steals" little Ronnie's mother away from him—mercilessly pulling her down from her pedestal, roughly touching the untouchable white woman who represents everything forbidden to black men and everything black children must give up their maid mothers to. The scene in which he thus embraces and kisses Kay and violates Ronnie's image of her is filled with racial and class tensions, as well as sexual ones. When Kay arrives and aims her car at him playfully, she refers to him as "Nora's boy," her comment bringing to mind the historical status of all black men, no matter their ages. Wendell's correction that he is "Nora's son" and his observation that he is "as old" (p. 292) as she is both go unnoticed by Kay. Invited to drink with her, he mixes their drinks—feeling how many different impulses to do so?—with hers stronger. When she makes small talk about Nora's having such a talented son, Wendell translates it: "What she was really saying was that it was amazing for a servant to have a son who was not also a servant. 'Anything can happen in a democracy,' I said, 'Servants' sons drink with madames and so on.' 'Oh, Nora isn't a servant,' Kay said. 'She's part of the family.' Yeah, I thought. Where and how many times had I heard *that* before?'" (p. 293). And when he kisses her, Kay responds "completely." Knowing that he has conquered her, that she has responded to him as a man, not as the servant's son, Wendell decides that Ronnie should see her flesh and blood reaction: he has not planned his "robbery," but he readily seizes the opportunity when it presents itself. By the end of the scene, Ronnie too will know tension.

Wendell's profession as a writer and his awareness of his audience are both clear as he describes his assertion of power:

We could hear Ronnie running over the rug in the outer room. Kay tried to get away from me, push me to one side, because we could tell that Ronnie knew where to look for his Mom: he was running right for the bar, where we were. "Oh, please," she said, "don't let him see us." I wouldn't let her push me away. "Stop!" she hissed. "He'll *see* us." We stopped struggling just for an instant, and we listened to the echoes of the word *see*. She gritted her teeth and renewed her efforts to get away.

Me? I had the scene laid right out. The kid breaks into the room, see, and sees his mother in this real wriggly clinch with this colored guy who's just shouted at him, see, and no matter how his mother explains it away, the kid has the image—the colored guy and his mother—for the rest of his life, see?

That's the way it happened. The kid's mother hissed under her breath, "*You're crazy!*" and she looked at me as though she were seeing me or something about me for the very first time. I'd released her as soon as Ronnie, romping into the bar, saw us and came to a full, open-mouthed halt. Kay went to him. He looked first at me, then at his mother. Kay turned to me, but she couldn't speak (p. 294).

And Wendell and Nora depart, leaving Kay trying to repair the damage that has been done. Wendell's "Me?" is a response to an assumed question from his audience: "And what are *you* doing, Wendell?" He has his "scene laid right out," as a playwright would lay out a scene, so that it has the maximum dramatic effect on all its audiences: on us, on Ronnie, and on Kay. He repeats the word *see* seven times in the short passage to drum into our minds the vivid image of sullied motherhood he creates for Ronnie in the final tableau of his little drama. Wendell is plotting in several senses, and he is deliberately and vindictively aware of what he does. He had talked earlier of the habits behind the scenes of these rich folks for whom his mother works; now he uses his skills as a writer to bring some of that immorality to the light, even if he has to taint his own image in the process. Besides, he does not care about Ronnie's opinion of him, and Nora does not witness the scene.

But it is not just as a craftsman that Wendell cares about his audience's response. From the point at which he asks us to hear him out, it is clear that he is aware of an audience watching, listening, and judging. When he tells of Nora's buying the tablets for him and his siblings, and their using them up so thoughtlessly, his "Can you imagine?" is a request for understanding. He pleads his childish ignorance of the parental sacrifice. When he stops to explain that he had "been that way too," in speaking of the Jorgensens' amorous fit, he at once bespeaks sympathy for himself and shows a sympathetic understanding of the Jorgensens. He seems to be asking for understanding, too, when he explains about his nasty temper—rather apologetically—just before shouting at little Ronnie.

The reiterational *see* (as in "for the rest of his life, see?") becomes an insistent plea for the audience to understand Wendell's point of view and to be lenient in judging him. When he victimizes, he wants us to see him as also a victim, as someone who is only doing unto another what was done unto him. Ronnie happens to be the representative white child whom Wendell repays for the "psychic injuries sustained . . . during his childhood and youth."[3] Kay, too, represents a chance to make a point, and he uses her perhaps in the same unfeeling way that many black women have been used by white masters and mistresses. Thus using Kay and Ronnie, Wendell runs the risk of becoming—and of appearing in his audience's eyes to be—Baraka's slave, the black person who wields power after the revolution just as unscrupulously as the whites had before it. But if we respond sympathetically to all of what he tells us, perhaps we may understand and forgive him for what he does to Kay and Ronnie. We may conclude that just a little turnabout is fair play. The taboos that Wendell violates—going into the Couchman library and living room, shouting at Ronnie, having a drink with Kay and embracing and kissing her—may all be looked upon as cases in which the bottom rail again pushes itself to the top, a blow being struck for the black community against the forces which work to stifle it. And the fact that Wendell is not a thoroughly heartless, thoughtless villain does much to save him from potential rejection by the audience. He has his moment of glee when he thinks, "*There you little bastard, there*"; but he also has an active conscience. He feels "many things," he says, in the wake of his vengeance, and he hates the long drive back to Watts. Reflection may bring pangs of guilt, but not, necessarily, bitter regret.

Wendell's action takes on revolutionary overtones in spite of his pangs of conscience over it and its rather childish nature. Wendell, in acting, joins characters in other works from the 1960's who not only refuse to adhere to the status quo but take active steps to alter it; and though he acts for himself as an individual, his action has meaning for nearly all black people.

Tricksters in Afro-American folklore are almost always male. In the worlds of Brer Rabbit, John the slave, black folk preachers, and the Signifying Monkey, roles are divided along traditional lines. Males, if not breadwinners, at least live much of their lives outside the home. Males venture out into a world of violence, greed, and cruelty; they trick other people or other animals in order to take the gains back to their own families—or merely for self-gratification. Females stay home and take care of children or little rabbits; they are otherwise absent from the tales and toasts unless they serve as tricksters' rewards. Brer Rabbit steals butter from other males, using the birth of his offspring as an excuse to slip away from the other animals and eat the butter himself. John tricks Old Massa and other men with his lucky guess about the coon under the box; if he is married, his wife is not important to the tale. When she does appear, as when Massa plays God and calls for John, it is to be offered up as a sacrificial substitute for her husband or to cover up his whereabouts. Females seldom appear in Signifying Monkey toasts. The elephant and the lion rip and tear each other considerably, and the Monkey swears and cheers at the lion's downfall. The traditional male world of the trickster is one of lying, cussing, antagonism, brutality, and bloodshed; one of violence, power, and the violation of all positive relationships.

In Douglas Turner Ward's *Happy Ending* (1964), two women who would put Brer Rabbit to shame invade the male sanctum of the trickster. Ellie and Vi, the two domestics who provide the central action for the play, are tricksters in the classic Brer Rabbit tradition. Like Brer Rabbit is on occasion, they are motivated by concern for family members. Like John the slave, they serve whites and manipulate them to their advantage by successfully wearing masks. Like Brer Rabbit and the Signifying Monkey, they evince no respect for conventional morality. Indeed, it is the extent to which they set aside morality that clearly indicates their kinship to the tricksters of tradition.

The action of the play takes place in Ellie's kitchen. She and her sister Vi are passing a handkerchief and crying when the curtain rises. Their nephew Junie comes in and, after much bopping and bantering about his intended conquests of the evening, notices that his aunts are crying. Through cajoling, he discovers that the source of their grief is the intended divorce of the Harrisons, the white couple for whom they work. Junie's scorn is bottomless and he prances around orating about his aunts as the shame of Africa. But when they reveal to him the reason for their crying, he asks them to pass him the handkerchief. Ellie and Vi are crying because they are about to lose the "pigeons" (p. 24) from whom, over a nine-year period, they have taken everything from furniture to nightgowns. Ellie, indeed, has been promised a lifetime pension if she works for the Harrisons for one more year—until their oldest child is ten—a pension which will be lost if the Harrisons are divorced. Thus the grief.

These women have gone out into the world and manipulated it, setting aside morality to appropriate thousands of dollars worth of food and merchandise for their families. Brer Rabbit might have done so as a twentieth-century maid. Yet an important distinction must be made between the presentation of their activities and those of Brer Rabbit. We always see Brer Rabbit in the process of his cheating or stealing or robbing. Ellie and Vi, on the other hand, sit onstage and tell us what they have done offstage. Like Mildred, they are not shown with their white employers. There is no reason for us to doubt what they say, especially as we get testimony of their successes from Junie and from Ellie's husband Arthur, and obviously their grief at the possibility of having to go straight is genuine, but we do not see them being tricksters: we hear of it. The credibility of their actions offstage depends on the audience's coming to grasp how drastically they deviate from the stereotype of the black maid. They are in their "late thirties or early forties," have gone through two husbands each and are working on thirds, and have *chosen* their profession; they, like Nora and to a lesser extent Mildred, do not do domestic work either because of financial or educational necessity. Members of the audience may wonder about the importance of these facts and perhaps store them for further reflection; but they very likely respond to Ellie's and Vi's crying in the same initial way Junie does.

They respond, that is, with outrage and censure:

> Acting like imbeciles! Crying your heart out 'cause Massa and
> Mistress are go'n' break up housekeeping!!! . . . Here we are—
> Africa rising to its place in the sun wit' prime ministers and other
> dignitaries taking seats around the international conference
> table—us here fighting for our rights like never before, changing
> the whole image, dumping stereotypes behind us and replacing
> 'em wit' new images of dignity and dimension—and I come home
> and find my own aunts, sisters of my mother, daughters of my
> grandpa who never took crap off no cracker even though he did
> live on a plantation—DROWNING themselves in tears jist 'cause
> boss man is gonna kick bosslady out on her nose . . . !!! Maybe
> *Gone With the Wind* was accurate! Maybe we jist can't help "Miss
> Scarrrrrrrleting" and "On Lawdying" every time mistress white
> gets a splinter in her pinky. . . . So you work every day in their
> kitchen, Ellie, and every Thursday you wash their stinky clothes,
> Vi. But that don't mean they're paying you to bleed from their
> scratches! . . . Look—don't get me wrong—I'm not blaming you
> for being domestics. It's an honorable job. It's the only kind
> available sometimes, and it carries no stigma in itself—but that's
> all it is, A JOB! An exchange of work for pay! BAD PAY AT THAT!
> Which is all the more reason why you shouldn't give a damn
> whether the Harrisons kick, kill or mangle each other![4]

Members of the audience watch in further bemused contempt as
Ellie recreates the scene in which she tried to get Mr. Harrison to
reconsider his decision to divorce his wife:

Ellie. (As if to Harrisons) "Y'all please think twice befo' you do
  anything you'll be sorry for. You love each other—and who's in
  better position than Vi and me to know how much you love each
  other—" (Junie ceases dressing to listen closely.)
Vi. 'Course she love him, just can't help herself.
Ellie. "—When two hearts love each other as much as we know y'all
  do, they better take whole lots of time befo' doing something so
  awful as breaking up a marriage—even if it ain't hunert-percent
  perfect. Think about your reputation and the scandal this will

cause Mr. Harrison. Jist 'bout kill your po' mother—her wit' her blood pressure, artritis, gout, heart tickle 'n' everything. But most of all, don't orphan the kids! Kids come first. Dear li'l angels! Just innocents looking on gitting hurt in ways they can't understand" (pp. 11–12).

The idea of two full grown, healthy, middle-aged black women crying dolorously over the intended divorce of their white employers, begging the two to reconcile, is uniquely preposterous. They would even have plopped down on their knees to beg Mr. Harrison to give Mrs. Harrison another chance, they tell Junie, if they had thought of it at the time. The audience undoubtedly seconds Junie's response to his aunts' question as to what they will do if the Harrisons follow through on the break up: "Git another job! You not dependent on them. You young, healthy, in the prime of life. . . . In fact—I've always wondered why you stagnate as domestics when you're trained and qualified to do something better and more dignified" (p. 19). But Junie and the audience have a lot to learn, for Ellie and Vi are not at all the trite, stupid, servile creatures that they think.

For Ward's characters have chosen their jobs as maid and laundress to the Harrisons for their "fringe benefits." And what they have managed to appropriate for themselves and their families, mainly the latter, is astounding. Ellie and Vi do not have dependent children; nevertheless, they are virtually the sole supports of an entire extended family, ranging from Junie, their handsome but parasitical live-in nephew, to their husbands and cousins and Junie's mother and all the folks "down home." They manage such support by their trickery. As the person who orders the food, pays the bills, and balances the budget for the Harrisons, Ellie takes care of her own family's needs as well. This, she explains to the obviously naive and critical Junie, "means that each steak I order for them, befo' butcher carves cow, I done reserved TWO for myself. Miss Harrison wouldn't know how much steak cost and Mr. Harrison so loaded, he writes me a check wit'out even looking. . . . Every once in a full moon they git so good-hearted and tell me take some left-overs home, but by that time my freezer and pantry is already fuller than theirs . . . " (p. 22). She goes on to tell Junie that all the strikingly fancy suits he wears to impress women have come from Mr. Harrison and that other male relatives have benefited similarly:

Jim, Roy, Arthur and Ben can't even fit into the man's clothes, but that still don't stop 'em from cutting, shortening, altering and stretching 'em to fit. Roy almost ruined his feet trying to wear the man's shoes. . . . Now, I've had a perfect record keeping y'all elegantly dressed and stylishly—fashion-plated—'cept that time Mr. Harrison caught me off-guard asking: 'Ellie, where's my brown suit?' 'In the cleaners,' I told him and had to snatch it off your hanger and smuggle it back—temporarily (p. 22).

Aunt Doris has been put to rest in one of Mrs. Harrison's nightgowns, "the costliest, ritziest, most expensest nightgown the good Lord ever waited to feast his eyes on" (p. 22), and Ellie and Vi have both appropriated furniture when the Harrisons moved. And to make things even clearer to the bopping but unenlightened Junie, Ellie and Vi continue:

Ellie. Add all *our* bills I add on to *their* bills—Jim even tried to git me to sneak in his car note, but that was going too far—all the deluxe plane tickets your ma jets up here on every year, weekly prescriptions filled on their tab, tons of laundry cleaned along wit' theirs and a thousand other services and I'm earning me quite a bonus along with my bad pay. It's the BONUS that counts, Junie. Total it up for nine years and I'd be losing money on any other job. Now Vi and I, after cutting cane, picking rice and shucking corn befo' we could braid our hair in pigtails, figure we just gitting back what's owed us. . . . But, if Mr. Harrison boots Mrs. Harrison out on her tocus, the party's over. He's not go'n' need us. Miss Harrison ain't got a copper cent of her own. Anyway, the set-up won't be as ripe for picking. My bonus is suddenly cut off and out the window go my pension.
Vi. Suppose we did git us another job wit' one-'r them penny-pinching old misers hiding behind cupboards watching whether you stealing sugar cubes? Wit' our fringe benefits choked off, we'd fall down so quick to a style of living we ain't been used to for a long time, it would make your head swim. I don't think we could stand it. . . . Could you?
Ellie. So when me and Vi saw our pigeons scampering out the window for good today, tears started flowing like rain. The first tear trickle out my eyes had a roast in it.

Vi. Mine was a chicken.

Ellie. Second had a crate of eggs.

Vi. Mine a whole pig.

Ellie. Third an oriental rug.

Vi. A continental couch.

Ellie. An overcoat for Arthur.

Vi. A bathrobe for Ben.

Ellie. My gas, electric and telephone bills in it.

Vi. Three months' rent, Lord!

Ellie. The faster the stream started gushing, the faster them nightmares crowded my eyes until I coulda flooded 'em 'nuff water to swim in. Every time I pleaded "Think of your love!—"

Vi. She meant think 'bout our bills.

Ellie. Every time I begged "Don't crack up the home!—"

Vi. It meant please keep *ours* cemented together!

Ellie. "Don't victim the chillun!—"

Vi. By all means insure the happiness of *our* li'l darlings! (pp. 23–24)

Finally Junie understands that Africa has not been embarrassed, and he joins in the crying. Members of the audience join in appreciation of the joke that's been played on the Harrisons, on Junie and on themselves. They can now sit back, released from their emotional agitation, and wait to see what the rest of the play will reveal. Or they can remain strongly partisan, emotionally, but change sides, hoping things will work out to Ellie's and Vi's satisfaction and advantage.

Ellie and Vi, who would perhaps be staunch church-women in another situation, have set aside morality when it comes to the Harrisons. They have met exploitation with exploitation. Ellie and Vi understand, as their slave ancestors did, that morality can be forgotten when avenging cruelties or injustices suffered at the hands of whites. If whites stole millions of Blacks from Africa, exploited black women sexually, and brutalized Blacks generally, why, the slaves reasoned, should Blacks adhere to the golden rule which their masters clearly did not? Therefore, they and the tricksters about whom they created tales saw themselves as existing in a world which recognized only the necessity of survival; Ellie and Vi do the same. The Harrisons get an excess of work—washing, cooking, cleaning, ironing, child-rearing, budgeting, marriage counseling, and more—in exchange for the small pay they offer.[5] "Money I git in my envelope,"

Ellie says, "ain't worth the time 'n' the headache. . . . *But—God Helps Those Who Help Themselves*" (p. 21). For Ellie and Vi, the adage has exploitation—not Christianity or any other ethical source—as its basis, for the emphasis is upon helping one's self, which is precisely what they do. They help themselves to everything they can and to everything they want. In the amoral world of the Harrison household, Ellie and Vi, like Brer Rabbit in his amoral world, have no consciences.

What they appropriate from the Harrisons is traditional trickster plunder. They take food, first of all—steaks of all kinds, chicken, roast beef, lobster, squab, and duck. As these are luxuries, far more substantive and valuable than the little lemon dessert pies Granny brought home in *God Bless the Child*, the pleasure of the trickery is increased. Ellie and Vi, like Brer Rabbit and other tricksters, are not content with basic survival; they want wealth, prestige, success, and power, which all can be had by the weak who can outwit the strong. By historical analogy, Ellie and Vi are clever slaves and the Harrisons are masters who deserve to be duped. By analogy to folklore, they are rabbits pitted against wolves and elephants. No matter how hard they work, they will never be as well off as the Harrisons; their thefts are their protest against that imbalance and injustice in the distribution of the world's goods.

We do get one glimpse of the manipulative control Ellie wields over her employers. After an entire act of excessive grief, the somber mood onstage is interrupted by a telephone call from Mr. Harrison; he has decided to give his wife another chance, and he wants Ellie to babysit that evening while the reunited couple go out to celebrate. Ellie is initially jubilant when she hears to what Mr. Harrison wants her consent: "If it's all right?!!! . . . Tell him I'm climbing on a broomstick, then shuttling to a jet!" (pp. 28–29). As her husband Arthur starts back to the phone to relay the message, however, Ellie comes to her senses.

> "Wait a minute! . . . Waaaait a minute! Hold on!—I must be crazy! Don't tell him that. . . . Tell him he knows very well it's after my working hours and I'm not paid to baby-sit and since I've already made plans for the evening, I'll be glad to do it for double-overtime, two extra days' pay and triple-time off to recuperate from the imposition. . . . And, Arthur! . . . Kinda suggest that *you*

is a little peeved 'cause he's interrupting me from taking care of
something important for you. He might toss in a day for your
suffering" (p. 29).

The Harrisons never suspect the upper hand they have had, and Ellie
wants to make sure that the power quickly reverts to her. She will go
to them, but on her own terms. This glimpse of Ellie manipulating
the Harrisons is the key validation of what has occurred offstage: the
story told within the story, the offstage action, clicks into its frame,
the action onstage.

Ellie and Vi are themselves a tale even as they present a tale, a tale
which functions to educate, as much folklore does. Junie and the
audience learn from them a tactic for survival, a mechanism for
dealing with sometimes overwhelming, nearly impossible circumstances. They teach the advantages of mother wit over schooling.
Apparently Ellie and Vi had never bothered to explain their clandes-
tine activities to Junie, but how he could still be so naive at the time
the play opens is a mystery to Ellie. He has continued to believe,
apparently, that **Santa Claus** delivers all of his fancy suits and that **the
tooth fairy** is responsible for the fine furnishings he uses to impress
his dates. Ellie tells him: "I know you went to college for a coupler
years, boy, but I thought you still had some sense, or I woulda told
you . . . " (p. 20). The notion that college breeds common sense out of
people is a recurring strain in Afro-American folklore. As the farmer
tells his college-bred son who insists upon the validity of the formula
πr^2: pie are round, cornbread are square.[6] Junie believes in square
pies, and his lack of savvy constrasts strongly with the understanding
his aunts have of historical and cultural techniques of survival.

Ellie and Vi further reveal to Junie and to the audience that
appearances are indeed deceiving. They encourage Junie to move
from revulsion at to acceptance of their actions, and perhaps Ward
wants the audience to do the same. The toast at the end of the play is
to Ellie's and Vi's continuing in their roles as strong, enduring,
matriarchal pillars of support for their families. But questions remain. Is the audience merely to appreciate the women's slick actions
as slick, or is it ultimately to approve their way of life? Instead of
feminizing male trickster values, Ellie and Vi have fully taken on the
traditional roles of men; it is as if they were Brer Rabbit and John

masquerading as women. They are prominent breadwinners. They give sharp orders to their nephew and husbands. Junie suggests that they are unemotional and only slightly tolerant of human frailty. He responds to their initial show of concern about the Harrisons with: "Why, I've seen both of you ditch two husbands apiece and itching to send third ones packing if they don't toe the line. You don't even cry over that!" (pp. 14–15) Does Ward approve?

Again: Junie's aunts know how superficial he is, know that his primary goal in life is studding. Ellie and Vi take him through a kind of catechism to illustrate the extent of his dependency:

Vi. (Standing at Junie's right as Ellie sits to his left.) Every time you bite into one of them big tender juicy steaks and chaw it down into your belly, ever think where it's coming from?

Ellie. The Harrisons.

Vi. Every time you lay one of them young gals down in that plush soft bed of yours and hear her sigh in luxury, ever think 'bout who you owe it to?

Ellie. The Harrisons.

Vi. When you swoop down home to that rundown house your ma and pa rent, latch eyes on all that fine furniture there, you ever think who's responsible?

Ellie. The Harrisons.

Vi. You ain't bought a suit or piece of clothes in five years and none of the other four men in this family have. . . . Why not?

Ellie. Mr. Harrison.

Vi. Junie, you is a fine, choice hunk of chocolate pigmeat, pretty as a new-minted penny and slick 'nuff to suck sugar outta gingerbread wit'out it losing its flavor—but the Harrisons ain't hardly elected you no favorite pin-up boy to introduce to Santa Claus. Took a heap of pow'ful coaxing to win you such splendid sponsorship and wealthy commissions, 'cause waiting for the Harrisons to voluntarily *donate* their Christian charity is one sure way of landing head-first in the poor-house dungeon (pp. 20–21).

Junie's dependency has lasted five years. He comes onstage referring to his visit to the employment office; viewers will later realize that that is one of his ritual locations for showing off his fancy suits. He scorns the positions he is offered. Among his first lines in the play are these: "Sure got them petty tyrants straight at the unemployment office today. (Dripping contempt.) Wanted me to snatchup one of them jive jobs they try to palm off on ya. I told 'em no, thanks!— SHOVE IT! . . . If they can't find me something in my field, up to my standards, forgit it!" (p. 7) His standards, like Mr. Parker's in Lonne Elder's *Ceremonies in Dark Old Men* (1969), were formed out of Starlight long ago, in a galaxy far away. When the amount of time Junie has spent waiting for something to measure up to his standards is revealed, the ways in which he is using Ellie and Vi are underscored. He is a moocher of the worse sort: like a pig feeding on acorns, he never looks up to see the source of his bounty. Nor does he care what it is, simply assuming that it will continue to exist. The irony of the gap between the shamelessness of his own mooching and the shame he feels for his aunts' behavior is blatant.

Thus, when Junie says he is ashamed of them, and they ask when he has bought food for the house, he responds: "I know I'm indebted to ya. You don't have to rub it in. I'll make it up to you when I git on my feet and *fulfill* my potential. . . . But that's not the point!" (p. 18) But it is precisely the point. Junie's idleness and parasitism have been motivations for Ellie's and Vi's trickster activities. Theirs is almost a pimping/whoring relationship, the women supporting a fancy man—Junie is a very fancy man—by means which are generally seen as not only illegal but degrading. He is a parody of militancy; he spouts fashionable words without ever looking beneath their superficial meanings. The incongruity between what he says and what he is undercuts his manhood as well as the militancy he espouses. Does Ward want us to accept that negative evaluation of his characters? Of all his characters, for, more or less consciously and in their different degrees, Arthur, Bob, Jim, and Aunt Doris exploit their exploiting relatives even as Junie does. Arthur and other male relatives may appreciate what Ellie and Vi take from Mr. Harrison, but they, too, lose a portion of dignity and self-worth in accepting it. At the end of the play, when Ellie consents to feed Mr. Harrison into gaining ten pounds more so that his clothes will still fit the expanding Junie, are we to conclude that these patterns of exploitation will continue indefinitely? When, finally, Junie suggests that Ellie encourage Mr. Harrison to change clothing styles, and Vi comments that Junie will "make it," what does that mean? That he is henceforth to copy his aunts' style of exploitation with our approval?

A comment from Clinton F. Oliver and Stephanie Sills seems relevant here:

> The ironies evidenced in this play are manifold and the admixture of laughter and venom should not go unnoticed. Junie, unquestionably is a clod and a parasite. Ward is wielding a double-edged sword in this play which is considerably more than an extended vaudeville sketch as some critics regarded it. The whites are vicious and parasitically dependent upon the blacks for their existence. The blacks must counter parasitism with parasitism in order to survive. The matriarchal nature of black society is also, in this play, demonstrably underscored and demonstrably, although subtly, deplored.[7]

The irony and our sense that what is shown is deplored emerge from our recognition of Ward's exaggerations. Ellie's and Vi's manipulation of the Harrisons is too perfect, and it goes on too long without consequences—even Brer Rabbit is brought low, sometimes, and John can get a whipping from Old Massa as quickly as he can win his freedom. The Harrisons are too naive and even Junie is perhaps a bit too unsuspecting. Like that of Swift's *Modest Proposal*, the logic of Ward's play is just too superficially flawless for it to be anything but ironic. A world view that would force an Ellie and a Vi to go to the extremes they do must be fantastic in itself. Imagine the logistical difficulties in removing suits and ducks from under the noses of two adults and two children—the latter of whom are perhaps underfoot constantly. Imagine a world that would allow Mr. Harrison to order his best friend out of Mrs. Harrison's bedroom in so civilized and polite a manner as he does. Imagine a world in which black men encourage their aunts and wives to be amoral and then celebrate that amorality. Surely that was not the world of the 1960's and positive images of blackness and black consciousness.

Set against its historical backdrop, then, the play becomes an elaborate statement on the inappropriateness of indirection in black/white relationships and on the ambiguous status of trickster psychology—on the need to adapt cultural forms to new situations. What was effective in one historical period may not be appropriate, even if effective, in another; the underhandedness that is an essential component of trickery lessens its appeal and acceptability in a world where directness and confrontation are, ideally, the norm. Although a new strategy for survival is not formulated explicitly in *Happy Ending*, the need for it is implicit in Ward's ironic treatment of all of his characters. In contemporary urban folktales, Brer Rabbit is not subtle; he takes a shotgun and gets what he wants.[8] Ellie's and Vi's tricks might be successful, but the women are always potentially at the mercy of forces over which they have no control—"forces" as trivial, at bottom, as one white couple's divorce. And if their actions are to form the stable base for black life, why are they working on their third husbands? It would seem, therefore, that when Brer Rabbit visits the ghetto, his actions must be focused in a new political direction; he must be direct in asserting black rights and in assisting black people.

But these are reactions of a reflective critic. By the majority of the audience watching the play, Ellie and Vi would, on the simplest level, be appreciated as tricksters who have pulled the wool over the Harrisons' eyes for years. They would be viewed as black women who are thoroughly aware of how to manipulate their masks successfully. Unlike the invisible man, who, even when he tries to play the role of the trickster, cannot distinguish illusion from reality, Ellie and Vi understand perfectly the invisible man's grandfather's advice. They know who they are and do not distort their own reality when they play handkerchief-headed servants for the Harrisons. Their method of surviving, and their determination to do so luxuriously, makes their actions more revolutionary than those of those black maids historically who stole food from white mistresses merely to keep their families alive. Ellie and Vi have consciously chosen to be manipulative, to collect for what they have been denied. Their actions, then, are in the realm of the political, and they have philosophical justification for what they do. They have become subtly defiant and consciously revolutionary. With these dimensions added to their characters, they find their invisibility as black maids an asset. They are certainly not as actively violent or as destructive as Ted Shine's maid in *Contribution* or Ed Bullins's in *The Gentleman Caller*, but they nevertheless redefine the dimensions of that mindless role others consider them to occupy.

CHAPTER EIGHT

THE MILITANTS

Douglas Turner Ward's Ellie and Vi work indirectly to achieve ends for others than themselves, indeed for a family community, but because they do not commit violent acts or change in any dramatic way the world they encounter, they do more to point out the faults in both the black and white worlds than to undermine either. Barbara Woods, Ted Shine, and Ed Bullins move beyond stirring the water to draining the lake. They create characters who, directly and indirectly, work to overthrow the society which has fostered oppression of Blacks and particularly of black domestics. It is significant that Woods's and Shine's works are set in the South. If revolution can be effected in this land of the most ingrained image of the stereotyped domestic, then perhaps there is hope for all Blacks. If the lowest of the low, in terms of earning ability and status, can be awakened enough to fight back, then those who are already inspired to fight can garner further inspiration. If, as Frederick Douglass pointed out, human beings who have been made into beasts can reverse the process and become men and women, then there is hope for us all. Shine and Bullins are conscious of their domestics as representative of those Blacks least suspected of objecting to the status quo. By using them as the perpetrators of revolutionary activity, they suggest that the movement of the 1960's could have been an all-embracing phenomenon within the black community; even those who had been traditionally associated with whites could be made to reject them. Such a victory at the level of the powerless and the victimized could only forecast major victories at other levels of black society.

To Woods, Shine, and Bullins, the rejection by maids has to be total. Not one of their domestics forgives the white world for what it has done to Blacks. They choose weapons, fight, and kill. They are soldiers in an army of revenge and rebuilding, and none allows sentiment to interfere with her battle. The Christianity that Ellie and Vi merely ignore is rejected or reoriented in "The Final Supper," *Contribution*, and *The Gentleman Caller*. In them, nothing stands in the way of the assertion of the humanity of Blacks and in slashing through territory to give that humanity room to blossom.

Slashing imagery is especially appropriate when speaking of Barbara Woods's Rosa Lee in "The Final Supper" (1970); when her white master invades the privacy of her bed once too often, she cuts his throat with a butcher knife. Set in Virginia in 1822, near Richmond and the site of Gabriel Prosser's intended rebellion, the story is an account of Gabriel's wife Nanny, who is a cook in the Van Evrie big house, and her fellow domestic Rosa. The two women are barometers of the increasing dissatisfaction among the slaves that leads to the preparation for Gabriel's rebellion; they reflect, too, the peculiar situation of dark-skinned house servants who, in their refusal to be properly appreciative of their privileged position, are disliked by their fellow house servants—though they manage, for the most part, to lead rather inconspicuous lives. Though Nanny and Rosa have been, flatteringly, put in charge of all cooking (they live in a room off the kitchen in the big house), and though they have daily close contact with the Van Evrie family, their sympathies are with the slaves in the quarters. Nanny, indeed, has enough of Gabriel's spirit to risk her house slave status by carrying as much food as she can to them. Nanny suggests that, just as Toussaint led his people to freedom and as God had led the Israelites out of the land of Egypt, surely too the slaves will be delivered.

Rosa, who had endured "two cruel masters in South Carolina," is at first pleased with the more relaxed environment near Richmond; but she is soon distressed by the sexual attentions that are thrust upon her by Van Evrie. He is only the last in a long line of such unwanted admirers, and Rosa, who still remembers vividily the love she had shared with Joe Henry, her deceased husband, reflects upon her situation as not so much that of an isolated individual but as the common plight of all black women in slavery. This sense of community makes her later action a blow struck for black womanhood, not simply for Rosa Lee.

> *Lord, will we Black women ever have the right to decide who's gonna be in our bed with us and who ain't, whose chillun we want to have? It just got to be a curse! A sinful curse on the daughters of Africa. But we done suffered enough for it! Ma, Nanny and me, countless others befo' and with us, and probably now my daughters, forced to be whores for these ol' White devils! Lord, I wish I could help my daughters. I got to do something, somehow! If that no-good Van Evrie ever try to put me to bed again, I'm gonna bust the hell out of him!*[1]

Rosa's internal monologue suggests that she would overthrow the present society if it were in her power to do so, and that she would do it in the interest of all black women.

Rosa has these thoughts while she is recuperating from a beating Van Evrie has given her for resisting his advances. He had waited until his wife and daughter had gone to visit the wife's sister in Richmond, and he had confronted Rosa when she came to bring clothes into the bedroom. He was drunk and wanted to force her to bed. Instead of submitting, she had smashed a liquor jug against his head, an act which momentarily made him forget that she was a woman he desired; he literally beat her unconscious. As further punishment for her resistance to him, Van Evrie has sold Rosa's son Tommy, who is also his son—and the third of their children he has sold. Rosa is nursed back to health by Nanny, but she promises on her sickbed that she will repay Van Evrie for what he has done to her and for what he has now come to represent: the exploitation of all black women. *"God, just give me strength, if Gabe's attack don't work, I'm gonna do something I shoulda done a long time ago. I know I is going to hell for it, Lord, if you don't forgive me!"* (p. 105)

In order to plan for her vengeance, Rosa wears the mask of the ideal servant to lull Van Evrie into a false sense of her defeat: "She moved about her work mechanically and she could tell by the satisfied look on Van Evrie's face that he thought that at last he had broken his nigger wench" (p. 108). She submits to his renewed sexual advances and bides her time, waiting to see if Gabriel's rebellion will succeed.

When it fails, a few weeks of despair only renew Rosa's role playing: "Rosa smiled, hesitantly at first, and then she began to laugh again. Lately, Rosa had been very attentive to Van Evrie and of course, he had not rejected her advances. She was polite, obedient and industrious, a real 'good nigga.' Van Evrie had remarked to a visitor that Rosa was the best negress he had ever owned" (pp. 109–110). Rosa's "good nigga" facade, however, hides an unforgiving heart. She gets her opportunity for vengeance at a Thanksgiving dinner which signals the return of normalcy after Gabriel's rebellion. Rosa makes "meats and cakes and pies" for the Van Evries and their numerous guests, all delicious and well deserving of the compliments she receives. But the "fine dinner" turns out to bring down upon each diner a fine death, for Rosa has laced the food with a poison that will do its fatal work just after the guests have returned to their own homes and beds.[2]

After enjoying his meal with the others and after his guests have departed, Van Evrie finds his way to Rosa's room. Not only is Rosa "not surprised" at Van Evrie's entrance—for he "always came to her at night when he felt secure and at peace with the world" (p. 110)—she is well prepared for it.[3] She invites him to rest beside her, and his confidence that he has conquered her, that he has restored proper race relations, soothes him into complacency, a complacency from which he will never rise.

He lay breathing heavily beside her on the old bed. When she was certain that he was sound asleep, she slowly pushed herself up. She was feeling weaker each minute. She gasped for a moment as she held her upraised hand over his head. Sweat poured down from her forehead. Her throat was hot and dry. But she could no more control the movement of her hand than she could stop the rapid pounding of her heart. Swiftly, she jerked the sharpened butcher knife across his throat. His eyes bulged as he tried to make a sound. In a wild frenzy, she stabbed him again and again in the chest. She saw the flesh separate. She felt the hot blood on her hands, felt it soaking through the mattress (pp. 110–111).

Van Evrie would have died of the poison as surely as his family and friends, but Rosa is not content to grant such a refined death to this personification of villainy. The stabs with the butcher knife are the most brutal form of repayment she can think of for what Van Evrie has brutally done in forcing himself upon her and in selling the children that they, together, had conceived. Nor is Rosa content with striking the blows; her fury must be given verbal vent. Whether Van Evrie hears or not, the reasons for his death and the others' must be articulated:

> Nothing matter no mo', boss! By now, yo' family, and yo' friends all dead. Dead! And you, always so holy, is baptized. I had to baptize you in yo' blood to get you right! And now you dead, and me . . . I ain't long for this world . . . but boss, the knife in yo' throat is for all the nigga men you done killed and castrated, the bastards you don birthed and sold, and all the nigga women you fucked over! This is the fruit of our love, boss (p. 111).

Rosa's references to Van Evrie's baptism refer to his delusion that in spite of his moral degeneracies he was a Christian soul. He and his family attended church and "on Sundays the house slaves had a chance to rest because the master reminded the household 'to remember the Sabbath and keep it holy'" (p. 103).[4] The moral disjunction between his pious carefulness on that point and his selling little children and freely indulging in adultery is gaping. So Rosa mocks Van Evrie's mockery of Christian ideals and rituals in proclaiming his death; and her action becomes itself ritualistic. It at once destroys Van Evrie and purges Rosa of the intense hatred to which she has clung. She symbolically frees herself at the same time that she is aware that her action will bring about her own death: she is satisfied to have done what she could, at whatever cost, to help Blacks by eliminating one species of vermin from the earth.

Woods ends the story with this sentence: "Rosa closed her eyes and rested in peace, fulfilled at last" (p. 111). She will wait for the mob to come and get her (there has been no indication that she has eaten of the poisoned food). When the guests are discovered dead, it will be easy to trace their steps during the holiday; when Van Evrie's family is discovered, and especially when his own sliced body is discoverd in her bed, Rosa will go quietly to her own death. Acting directly, Rosa has abandoned the mask, an abandonment which brings her revolutionary potential to fulfillment—and to an end. She has conclusively negated the subservience which her master had associated with the position of the domestic, and certainly Van Evrie will not perform any more violent acts; but, significantly, neither will she. Her death, which will bring her revolutionary activity to an end, is what distinguishes her from the maids in *Contribution* and *The Gentleman Caller*, each one of whom sees her activity as the beginning of a community-wide revolution.

Ted Shine's *Contribution* is a work set in the South, about a maid who understands perfectly the limitations of place and uses trickery to maneuver around those limitations. The maid operates within the paternalistic system, is aware of the definitions whites would impose upon her, and uses both to her advantage in making her "contribution" to the revolution of the 1960's. Copyrighted in 1968, performed in 1969, and set in "A Southern Town," the play has ties in its political stance to Ward's *Happy Ending* (1964) and to Bullins's *The Gentleman Caller* (1969). It shows clearly that black pride and revolutionary activity were not limited to the urban North or to the younger Blacks in SNCC and SCLC. The central character in the play, Mrs. Grace Love, is a beer-drinking "Grandmother in her seventies." Although the sixties provide the moment for her to reveal her revolutionary activity, she has been devoting herself to it for several decades.

The play depicts an encounter between Mrs. Love, her grandson Eugene, and Katy Jones, a neighbor. The action occurs on the morning that Eugene, freshly arrived from the North, is planning to sit in at a local lunch-counter with a few other Blacks. His near-sanctimonious attitude about his activism as compared with the passivity of his handkerchief-headed grandmother, a woman of "the grin and shuffle school," he believes, is the central irony in the play. Eugene and the others have their blackness fresh upon them; Mrs. Love has been aware of the implications of her blackness for quite some time. Although she is contemporary in age with Mammy Jane and Granny Huggs, she has a much more heightened sense of who she is and what is necessary to hold on to an essence of self in a world which would negate any effort at dignity. The world she confronts is like that of Mammy Jane in its determination to keep Blacks in their place and like that of Pauline Breedlove in its exploitation of the labor of the maid.

Sheriff Morrison, the white sheriff for whom she works, expects Mrs. Love to get up early in the morning, cook the cornbread he loves so much, and bring it or have it delivered to his office. On this morning, Katy will deliver the bread as she has apparently done on other mornings. But it is not a chore she relishes for the sheriff, she says, is always "patting me on the behind like I'm a dog. He's got that habit bad."[5] If the sheriff has made other sexual advance, it is not mentioned. His assumption that Katy is property of sorts, that she can freely be patted on the behind, indicates the place to which the sheriff has assigned black women, and his vision of them as cornbread-cooks does the same. That place for black women and for Blacks generally is more graphically illustrated when it becomes clear that the sheriff is planning to direct an attack on the demonstrators Eugene is preparing to join, an effort in which the citizens of the community and surrounding area are only too prepared to assist him. Katy reports early in the play that "white folks have been coming into town since sun up by the truck loads. Mean white folks who're out for blood!" (p. 372). The crowd of whites prepared to punish the demonstrators' violation of the place taboo and restore the status quo is the crowd which has rushed to every lynching and burning in history where the good white citizens came into town for the picnic/roast of the black offender. Eugene asserts after the sit-in that "every white person in the county was on that street! They had clubs and iron pipes, dogs and fire trucks with hoses" (p. 385).

All power—political, economic, legal, social, and physical—seems to be on the side against the demonstrators. The mayor has maintained on television that whites and Blacks get along well in his town, and Eugene has recognized the implication: "So long as 'we' stayed in our respective places" (p. 373). The owner of the targeted lunch-counter is threatening to "sic the dogs" on Eugene and his companions; and the sheriff, "the law," maintains that "he'd die before a nigger sat where a white woman's ass had been" (p. 385). But before the sheriff can voluntarily make his threat real, he falls to the street and dies—cussing, moaning, thrashing around, and foaming at the mouth. His assertions that place will be maintained come to naught, as the horrible nature of his death causes the momentary quiet in which Eugene and others are enabled to integrate the lunch-counter. The girl working there thinks the Blacks have put a curse on the sheriff and begs them not to put one on her. The curse, however, had been one the sheriff had brought on himself and it had been fulfilled through Mrs. Love's revolutionary activity: the cornbread she had sent him had been laden with poison.

We discover, later, that the seventy-six-year-old grandmother has managed to poison a number of the town's prominent citizens over a period of years. The sheriff, an authority figure responsible for keeping Blacks in their place, has been just another carefully selected victim. Mrs. Love knows that if she kills him, her grandson and his companions will be safe, for the spectacle of his ghastly death will make the holders of the iron pipes and clubs think again about what they are planning to do to the demonstrators. Eugene begins to understand that the grandmother he has called "ludicrous" for her attempts at hip language and her efforts at cursing is not at all the acquiescing, stereotypical domestic he had assumed her to be.

Had Eugene been more sensitive to things she said, sometimes quite in passing, he might have suspected that his grandmother had quite a different kind of personality. Mrs. Love's action is foreshadowed early in the play and hinted at throughout. She sings, as she prepares the sheriff's cornbread, "I SING BECAUSE I'M HAPPY—I SING BECAUSE I'M FREE—" (p. 372); and her songs continually affirm her sense of divine sanction for what she is doing ("HIS EYE IS ON THE SPARROW AND I KNOW HE WATCHES ME!" p. 372). Many comments she makes to Katy and Eugene have just a hint of something beneath the surface about them, some encouragement to evaluate them carefully. When Katy says Mrs. Love's heart could never take the stress of demonstrating, Mrs. Love responds: "You'd be amazed at what my heart's done took all these years, baby" (p. 372). When Eugene sarcastically asks if the sheriff had let her have the day off to nurse his, Eugene's, wounds, she replies: "You ain't gonna get no wounds, son, and you ain't gonna get this nice white shirt ruined either" (p. 373). She suggests that the cornbread is suspect when she repeatedly warns Katy not "to pinch off it" (p. 375). She consistently tells Eugene to stop worrying and relax, using words which in a different context might have been taken at their surface value but which become suspect here because of the setting. Mrs. Love tries several times before the climax of the play to get Eugene to see things in a different perspective, one which would admit the possibility that she is not the old Thomasina he assumes her to be.

Mrs. Love. You young folks ain't the only militant ones, you know!

Eugene. You work for the meanest paddy in town—and to hear you tell it, he adores the ground you walk on! Now you're a big militant!

Mrs. Love. I try to get along with folks, son.

Eugene. You don't have to work for trash like Sheriff Morrison! You don't have to work at all! You own this house. Daddy sends you checks which you tear up. You could get a pension if you weren't so stubborn—you don't have to work at your age! And you surely don't have to embarrass the family by working for trash!

Mrs. Love. What am I supposed to do? Sit here and rot like an old apple? The minute a woman's hair turns gray folks want her to take to a rockin' chair and sit it out. Not this chick, baby. I'm keepin' active. I've got a long way to go and much more to do before I meet my maker (pp. 377–378).

She fights against the idea that old people have no place in the revolution, and she fights against age prejudice generally. But Eugene is intent: he insists that things won't get any worse "Thanks to *us*" (p. 379), the "us" referring only to young, demonstrating Blacks like himself.

He takes more credit than he deserves, for it is he who is nervous and timid about the sit-in; his grandmother is insistent on courage and confrontation, ironing his clothes, cooking his breakfast, and forcing him to get to the demonstration on time. Her courage comes from having witnessed Ku Klux Klan raids and lynchings and burnings, among other things. When Eugene sarcastically suggests that the mere seeing of those things was his grandmother's contribution to bettering conditions, she says: "You'd be surprised at *my* contribution!" (p. 380)

She is disgusted that he honestly thinks Blacks from the North had to come down and rescue the darkies in the South. Instead of being satisfied in the North, she tells Eugene, "you had to come down here and 'free' us soul brothers from bondage as if we can't do for ourselves! Now don't try to tell me that your world was perfect up there—I've been there and I've seen! Sick to your stomach! I get sick to my stomach everytime I see how disrespectful the world's gotten! I get sick to my stomach, baby, because the world is more ruined now than it ever was! You lookin' at me like that 'cause I shock you? *You* shock me! You know why? Your little secure behind is down here to make history in your own way—and you are scared 'shitless'" (pp. 378–379). As she reveals to him her activities over the years, Eugene goes further and further into shock. Even after the sit-in, he has not yet been baptized by fire, and he still has the innocence to be shocked at his grandmother's attitude toward whites and finally to sit in speechless silence before her.

Before he quite loses his voice, however, he blurts out that she can be sent to the electric chair for what she has done. "Who?" she responds, "Aunt Grace Love? Good old black auntie? Shoot! I know white folks, son, and I've been at this business for a long time now, and they know I know my place" (p. 387). She has used that place, that image of the good old black servant, to win the trust of those for whom she worked, and has then destroyed them. Like John the Slave and Brer Rabbit, she has understood the nature of her opponents, and she has kept the mask of the trickster intact enough to accomplish her goals. When she steps out of her place, there are no witnesses; her response to Katy's description of the sheriff's death illustrates this point:

Mrs. Love. Oh, I've seen it before, child! I've seen it! First Dr. Crawford—After his whole family had died out one by one—Called me to his own death bed and asked me to hold his hand. "I ain't got nobody else to turn to now, Auntie." "You related to me in some way?" I asked him. He laughed and the pain hit him like an axe. "Sing me a spiritual," he said. I told him I didn't know no spiritual. "Sing something Holy for me, I'm dyin'!" he says. (She sings.) "I'LL BE GLAD WHEN YOU'RE DEAD, YOU RASCAL, YOU! I'LL BE GLAD WHEN YOU'RE DEAD, YOU RASCAL, YOU!" Then I told him how come he was dyin'.

Katy. He was a doctor, didn't he know?

Mrs. Love. Shoot!" Dr. Crawford, didn't know his liver from his kidney. "Dr. Crawford," I said, "how come you didn't treat my husband? How come you let him die out there in the alley like an

animal?" I gave him an earful and when I got through openin' his
nose to what was happenin', he raised up—red just like the sheriff,
his hands outstretched toward me and he fell right square off that
bed onto the floor—dead. I spit on his body! Went down stairs,
cooked me a steak, got my belongings and left.

Katy. You didn't call the undertaker?

Mrs. Love. I left that bastard for the maggots. I wasn't his "auntie"!! A
week later the neighbors found him stinking to hell. They came by
to question me, but I was grieved, chile, so they left me alone.
"You know how nigras is scared of death," they said. And now the
sheriff. Oh, I have a great peace of mind, chile, cause I'm like my
grandson in my own fashion. I'm too old to be hit and wet up, they
say, but I votes and does my bit (pp. 383–384).

Mrs. Love has instituted a tradition of death using the little bag of
poison she keeps in her bosom. She has set herself up as a vigilante,
an avenger who corrects wrongs she believes have been committed.
Her little bag of poison becomes more potent than a charm. She
almost acts as a conjure doctor and, in her combination of Christian
song-singing and folk medicine, she shows kinship to Tante Rosee in
Alice Walker's "The Revenge of Hannah Kemhuff" (1973).[6]

Mrs. Love comments on the Crawfords' deaths to Katy, but she
talks of what she has done to the sheriff to Eugene. "I gave him peace!
Sent him to meet his maker! Sent him in grand style too. Tore his
very guts out with my special seasoning! Degrading me! Callin' me
'nigger'! Beating my men folks!" (p. 387) Eugene is still innocent
enough to ask "Why?"

Mrs. Love. Because I'm a tired old black woman who's been tired,
and who ain't got no place and never had no place in this country.
You talk about a "new Negro"—Hell, I was a new Negro seventy-
six years ago. Don't you think I wanted to sip me a coke-cola in a
store when I went out shoppin'? Don't you think I wanted to try on
a dress or a hat when I bought it? Don't you think I wanted to have
a decent job that would have given me some respect and enough
money to feed my family and clothe them decently? I resented
being called "girl" and "auntie" by folks who weren't even as good
as me. I worked for nigger haters—made 'em love me, and I put
my boy through school—and then I sent *them* to eternity with

flying colors. I got no regrets, boy, just peace of mind and satisfaction. And I don't need no psychiatrist—I done vented my pent-up emotions! Ain't that what you always saying? (p. 387)

Eugene gets a glimpse at the reality of an existence he has not considered.

Mrs. Love has been consistent in her political stance. She has known what she wanted to accomplish. She thus joins other maids in literature who act with a purpose in mind and who understand the reasons for their actions. And she cannot lose her sense of identity when she goes into the homes of whites because she always knows why she is there:

Mrs. Love. I worked to feed and clothe [my son] like Katy's doin' for her children, but I had a goal in mind. Katy's just doin' it to eat. I wanted something better for my son. They used to call me "nigger" one minute and swear that they loved me the next. I grinned and bore it like you said. Sometimes I even had to scratch my head and bow, but I got your daddy through college.
Eugene. I know and I'm grateful—he's grateful. Why don't you go and live with him like he wants you to?
Mrs. Love. 'Cause I'm stubborn and independent! And I want to see me some more colored mens around here with pride and dignity!
Eugene. So that Sheriff Morrison can pound the hell out of it every Saturday night? (p. 380).

And if he is too flabbergasted to appreciate her killing the sheriff, Mrs. Love says, perhaps "some of the colored boys who ain't been to college, who's felt Ol' Man Morrison's stick against their heads" (p. 388) might appreciate what she has done. She tells Eugene she is planning to go shed a tear over the sheriff, then take off for Mississippi where college students are sitting in but not making much headway because of the governor. She asks if Eugene knows the governor's name, because "I have a feeling he just might be needing a good cook" (p. 388). She has extended her goals from her family to cover all those involved in the Civil Rights movement. She will continue poisoning and doing her "bit" to make things better for Blacks. By so doing, she joins the many maids historically and in literature who actually did poison or were accused of poisoning their masters.[7]

Shine, like many of the black writers of the 1960's, has expanded the implications of territory for the southern maid; he has turned her into a militant. For women like Mammy Jane, even stealing from whites was out of the question. Although Granny Huggs might have taken things, she could never have envisioned hurting Miss Helen or Miss Emilie or Miss Iris. Mrs. Love goes beyond either of these and commits the murder that many maids may have desired to commit but for which they lacked the courage, opportunity, and the necessary tendency to violence. In dealing with an unfair and degrading set of circumstances, she sets aside morality to gain personal dignity. She sings her religious songs even as she plots murder, and she kills for her children instead of negating their familial relationship. She is a complex bundle of grace, love, and hatred. As her name implies, she loves black people; she has grace that comes from religious contentment, and she has grace (peace of mind) that comes from killing whites in positions of authority.[8] Her hatreds are obvious. In her, the powerless have become powerful. Her power is secure and content to be secret unto itself; it does not need publicity, only the trickster's pride in successful completion of a trick. Mrs. Love's motivations to violence need only her own sanction; as a trickster, she sees a problem which needs taking care of, and she takes care of it.

Rosa's revolutionary activity ends the moment it is born. Mrs. Love's, however, has not only a past but a future. Hearing of it could possibly influence Eugene or Katy to engage in similar sorts of guerilla warfare. And after Mrs. Love tells Eugene to get out of his good clothes and hints that she is off to have an ice cream soda at the fountain which has been recently integrated, she warns the whites in Shine's audience that they could become victims of her poisoning scheme: "(She wanders to the apron of the stage.' . . . I wonder who will be next? I'll put me an ad in the paper. Who knows, it may be you or you, or you . . . " (p. 388), and she disappears from the stage singing "WHERE HE LEADS ME I SHALL FOLLOW." Her brand of revolutionary activity, then, is set forth as having its future not just onstage, in fiction, but offstage: it is made explicit that what has happened on the stage could also happen in the world beyond the stage, in real life. The short distance between life and art represented by this domestic could make other domestics see that revolution was not so out of their reach. If these women could find the force of will to advance to political activity, then certainly the gap between white

opportunity and black denial could be bridged, and the forces of
oppression could be rendered ineffective.

The revolutionary activity of the domestic is extended directly to
include all members of the black community in Ed Bullins's *The
Gentleman Caller* (1969), a drama from the Revolutionary Black
Theatre of the 1960's which, through symbols and direct statement,
worked to contribute its share to the black revolution. Bullins focuses
on representative characters who, through their stylized actions or
comments on stage, reflect a history of interacting with each other in
predetermined ways. The gentleman in the play represents all Blacks
who, like Lutie Johnson in her Chandler period, have ever dreamt
the decadent illusory American dream—with, as his own particular
Dream involves possessing a representative white woman, an ele-
ment of sexuality complicating his case. The play's maid, Mamie,
appears to be the representative stereotyped, acquiescing, and self-
effacing domestic—in fact, THE MAID. The unseen Mr. Mann represents the controlling power in white society which keeps Blacks
confined even as it encourages them to believe that there is liberation
for them in the American Dream. Madame is all white mistresses to
all black maids; she is also all white women who ever felt an attraction
to black men and encouraged the men's attraction to themselves. The
play opens with the gentleman's entrance, his search for what Mr.
Mann's beard represents, which may be middle-class status or economic advantage, among other things. What he wants must be
inferred from what Madame says, since the gentleman has no actual
lines; at intervals, the phone rings and a conversation occurs in which
the maid, who had at first been upset at the gentleman's appearance,
tells an insistent caller that no calls are being taken. The maid is
constantly at Madame's beck and call: she is fired and rehired,
caressed and corrected. Then she quits: she exits, apparently kills
Mr. Mann, drags his body onstage, kills Madame, and finally kills the
gentleman caller when he persists in pursuing that illusory beard.
The play ends with the maid transformed into a Queen Mother,
calling forth to all Blacks to join the revolution.

The major theme of the play is change, and the primary change in
the play is that of the maid from a true, southern, stereotypical
mammy to Queen Mother. Her first words in the play are "Hello . . .

Nawh . . . Madame's not takin' no calls. Sho I'm sho. Nawh . . . nawh . . . can't do that."[9] As long as she remains a southern, stereotypical maid, Mamie will thus make a mockery of the English language. She initially prides herself on having a privileged position in the white household. When the gentleman arrives, she vehemently reminds him that he has violated a taboo, stepped out of his place, by knocking at the front door: "Deliveries in the rear, boy!" (p. 371) She is just as put off by his uppity assumptions as Mammy Jane had been by those of the new nurse in *The Marrow of Tradition*. She refers to Madame as "Missy" in that politely deferential, protective way that might have been second nature to Mammy Jane, and the word she utters more than any other in the opening scenes of the play is "Yas'sum." Her dialect, her condescension toward other Blacks, and her bowing and scraping before the Madame are as stereotypical as her large, heavy stature and bandanna-covered head.

Madame is helplessly dependent upon Mamie even as she ruthlessly exercises her power over her. When she is first left alone with the gentleman, she calls out for Mamie and "whines" when the call is not immediately answered. She maintains to the gentleman that Mamie is a "blessing," but one which is slowly outliving its practicality.

Madame. . . . I don't know what I'd do without her. (Warming up.) She's been with the family for years. One of the truly worthwhile possessions my father left us with. . . . She's getting old now and times are changing. . . . Yes, changing, quite a bit. . . . And Mamie's getting to be something of an inconvenience . . . but tradition, family sentiments and loyalty are so much better than what the times would declare . . . (p. 372).

Madame gets lost in her own sense of what the past represents. Embedded in her comments are notions that slavery was the best state for Blacks and that it was well when there were real mammies. But Madame can change moods, and her sentimental feelings evaporate when Mamie starts to question the direction given to her to serve tea to the gentleman first. She admonishes the maid, "(Warning.) Don't question me, Mamie"—a warning which culminates in a furiously neurotic outburst to the gentleman once Mamie has made her exit. "This is the trouble with keeping people with you too long.

They feel that they can question your authority as if they had some priority. Now I knew how I wanted it all done. (Becomes more angry.) How dare she question me! Me! How dare she?" (pp. 373–374) What the maid has missed she more than receives upon her return to the room:

Maid: (Worried and sullen.) Is there anything else, ma'am?
Madame: Is there anything else? You meant to say is there anything wrong, didn't you? . . . Of course there's not! What would make you think that there was anything wrong?
Maid: Why I jest thought there might . . .
Madame: (Rises.) How dare you to think! (Points to exit.) Excuse yourself and leave us, Mamie Lee King. . . . At once! Do you hear?
Maid: (More sullen, avoids visitor's eyes.) 'Scuse me . . . yawhl. (She exits.)
Madame: (Sits.) How dare she take it upon herself to return? . . . And to ask questions? . . . And to think? Ohhhh . . . what are the times coming to? What are they coming to? There's only one solution. I have failed to face up to it before now. She must go (p. 374).

The concept of place informing the relationships between maid and mistress in the earlier southern portraits is relevant here. The maid must be able to recognize that there are times when she cannot overstep her bounds even to show concern for her mistress. And at no point is she to think; the mistress emphasizes labor over gray matter. The white woman's power can remain dormant, but it is there to be exercised at her discretion.

The precarious status of the mistress/maid relationship is emphasized in Mamie's and Madame's case when the conversation continues:

Madame. . . . Mamie! Mamie, come here at once! (The Maid enters.)
Maid. Yas'sum.
Madame. You are fired.
Maid. Yas'sum.
Madame. Get your things and be off at once.
Maid. Yas'sum. (Maid turns to go.)
Madame. Is that all you have to say?
Maid. Yas'sum.

Madame. Why?

Maid. 'Cause I didn't want to upset lil Missy anymo'.

Madame. Ohhh . . . how sweet. You're such a living doll, Mamie. (To visitor.) Isn't that simply divine. . . . So innocent . . . so childlike and naive.

Maid. Yas'sum. (Phone rings; Maid answers.) Wha? . . . Ya don' say? Nawh, I ain't gonna call her . . . wouldn't if I could. Thank ya, sah. (Hangs up.)

Madame. (Inspired.) You know . . . you know, Mamie, dear . . . I don't think you'd better go after all.

Maid. Nawh, Ma'am.

Madame. In fact, I'm thinking of giving you a two dollar a month raise . . . and . . . and . . . now listen to this, Mamie, dear . . . this is the best . . . and that new black taffeta dress I got for aunt Hattie's funeral six years ago. Well, that's yours too, dear. Isn't that thrilling for you? . . . Of course I'll have to first talk to my husband, Mr. Mann, about it first and see what he has to say . . .

Maid. Yas'sum.

Madame. (Warm.) And you know I wouldn't turn you out anyway, don't you, you old actress, you? Why it's right in daddy's will where we are to give you a home until that day when you lay your old grey and black head on the duckdown pillows and rise no more.

Maid. Yas'sum.

Madame. Now how could I go against daddy's wishes?

Maid. Don' know, ma'am.

Madame. (Smiles.) Good . . . now go back to your kitchen and wait until I call you (pp. 374–75).

Madame's moods change even as she talks about changes in Mamie. She carries herself away on the sentimental vein of the tradition of paternalism, and the maid gives her encouragement to keep soaring on that vision. Mamie's declaration that she does not wish to "upset lil Missy anymo'" is an emotional exaggeration comparable to those seen in Thomas Nelson Page's *In Ole Virginia*, where masters and servants make great lamentations over each other and their possible or real separations. But while changeability and superficial fluffiness may characterize Madame, she still has the fixed attitude of superiority and constant awareness of her power that have characterized

many other less idiotic mistresses. And her own childishness is only
equaled by that which she assigns to her maid. The innocence, the
naivete, the divine simplicity the Madame thinks she sees in Mamie
are quite stereotypical, Blacks and maids in particular being traditionally painted as thus credulous and childlike. Madame rewards
what she sees as Mamie's proper feeling with the traditional conde-
scending gifts of paraphernalia—a two-dollar-a-month raise and a
black taffeta cast-away dress.

Mamie should, stereotypically, jump at her reward and go into her
"Oh, thankee, Missus" act; but since the play is primarily about
change, Mamie at this point undergoes a significant transformation.
When ordered back to the kitchen, she refuses to go:

Maid. (Stands firm.) Well, ma'am . . .
Madame. (Surprised.) What is it, Mamie?
Maid. (Shuffles from one foot to another.) . . . I guess this is as good a
   time as any to tell you . . .
Madame. (Annoyed.) Tell me what, Mamie?
Maid. I'm quittin'.
Madame. (Disbelief.) You're what?
Maid. Quittin'.
Madame. You're not? (To visitor.) Did you hear what she said? (He
   doesn't respond.) You can't be leaving, Mamie?
Maid. I'm so too.
Madame. But you can't.
Maid. Am too.
Madame. But you can't, Mamie, dear.
Maid. Yas I can.
Madame. But what about all these years you've spent with me? With
   us?
Maid. I dunno, ma'am.
Madame. What about my suckling your big flabby breasts?
Maid. They dry now, ma'am.
Madame. . . . and you raised me as one of your own?
Maid. Dat's cause I's never had time fo mah own, ma'am.
Madame. And the love and respect I showed you. (Silence.) And the
   devotion and loyalty and gratitude you have for me. (Silence.)
   What about the will? (Silence.) Daddy said that if you left that it
   would be against his wishes and . . .

Maid. (Loudly.) Yas'sum.
Madame. (Pleads.) Then . . .
Maid. I'm quittin'.
Madame. (Last resort.) What about your raise and . . .
Maid. Tonight's my last night. (She exits.) (pp. 375–376).

The maid has found the courage to shake off what the kitchen has come to mean to her: a tradition of subservience, of bowing and scraping. The catechism through which the mistress puts her is intended to evoke a racial memory of her place in the white house and to play on whatever emotional ties she may feel to that memory, but the maid politely rejects all ties. She recognizes that her breasts have gone dry suckling the white mistress and her ancestors, and that she has given attention to the mistress to the detriment of her own family relationships, both literally and symbolically (perhaps that is why the gentleman turns out to be the way he is?). She apparently recognizes that the love and respect to which the mistress alludes have been tainted by condescension and a less-than-total recognition on the part of the whites of the maid's humanity. Her devotion and loyalty have been forced from her by circumstances, as they are from Ellie and Vi and Mrs. Love. She recognizes, apparently, that the will Madame's father has made is based on an outdated idea of the black woman's place. So far as the powerful white men originally responsible for the racial order in the United States could see, the black woman would always necessarily be dependent on the household of the white woman because few opportunities would be available to the black man that would allow him to support her at home. Witness the position of the gentleman caller; he can only obtain as much as the white man will allow and must gain entry to the white world through the black woman. That invisible white power controls him just as it controls the white woman and the black woman.

Bullins subtitled his play "A Parable." Parables are designed to teach lessons, and Bullins is presenting a lesson: if the revolution is to succeed, those Blacks who have lived in the homes of whites, who have reared their children and who have worn their cast-away clothing, cannot remain tied to them in the sentimental ways that those past relationships would encourage. There must be a freeing of black minds, as Frederick Douglass pointed out, before black bodies can be freed. The important first step to freeing the mind is, then, the severing of those old ties, politely if possible, brutally if necessary. When it becomes apparent to Mamie that her statement of an intention to quit will not satisfy the Madame and, by implication, Mr. Mann, she kills both of them. The bottom rail represented by Mamie, Mildred, and other maids again becomes the top rail.

Mamie kills Mr. Mann offstage, but she drags his body onto the stage in a transcendent reversal of stereotypes.

Maid. (Off, coming closer. Sings.) Now hare come de Judge . . . Hare come de judge . . . yeah . . . Now ev'va body git demself together . . . cause hare come de judge.

Madame. In here, Mamie . . . in here! (Maid enters, dragging Mr. Mann's dead body by the heels.)

Maid. (Stepin Fetchit image.) I'se comin', Missy . . . I'se comin' fast as I can. . . . (She moves remarkably slow.) . . . Feets . . . do yo duty (p. 379).

Mamie announces her entrance with a deadly serious evocation of an old, stereotyping comedy skit, one familiar to the younger part of the play's original audience through the Flip Wilson show or *Hee Haw*: one wherein, amid much minstrel-show, slapstick buffoonery, a judge would pronounce outrageous sentences on the perpetrators of "crimes" which should never have reached adjudication, such as a husband's not turning money over to his wife on a Friday night or his looking at another woman. Mamie gives tragic meaning to a form which, in its usual comic context, has little or no meaning: like Mildred, she turns the "interestin' and amusin'," the hollow, into the substantive. She becomes a real judge who assigns real punishments and really executes them. And at the end of the quoted passage, having transformed the comical judge, Mamie parodies the stereotypical Stepin Fetchit, an emasculated, eyeball-rolling eunuch whom Donald Bogle refers to as the "archetypal coon."[10] In Stepin Fetchit were seen both the black man's hopeful entry into the movie business and the degradation he suffered upon his arrival. Much like black maids who were at the beck and call of their white mistresses, Stepin Fetchit was at the beck and call of white movie-makers and actors. History certainly cannot be denied and Mamie does not attempt to deny it: she confronts it, understands what it means, and moves beyond it. She symbolically overcomes the force which has defined her existence and turned her "offspring" into the perverted gentleman who has called at the Mann house. Since the play is a parable, actions presented represent what *can* be in the future for which Mamie wishes to prepare the way. That future can be a place where black people will define a reality for themselves, not where they will allow their values and selfhood to continue to be shaped by a corrupt white America which has built its stature on the suppression of black people.

But if Mamie can change, and move beyond her history, Madame is still not ready to do so; Madame changes her moods, not her mind. Consider her response when Mamie drags in Mr. Mann's body.

Madame. (Interrogator.) And now, Miss Mamie Lee King, dear, you admit that Mr. Mann is dead?

Maid. Yas'sum.

Madame. . . . you found him dead . . . dead in the john?

Maid. Yas'sum.

Madame. . . . dead from a self-inflicted wound in the throat . . .

Maid. If you say so . . . ma'am.

Madame. . . . from a straight razor!

Maid. Yas'sum. From a straight razor.

Madame. (Distaste.) Well, so much for details. . . . Now let's see what shall we do? . . . hmmm. What do you suggest, Mamie? You always keep a level head in these kinds of emergencies (p. 379).

The Madame, like Anne Fairchild in "Man of All Work," must cling to illusions when all evidence refutes them. Anne wanted to believe Dave was faithful to her and that their good name was intact with the neighbors in spite of what she knew he did with the maids who had been hired and fired so frequently that the neighbors must have—speculated. Madame, whose world is deteriorating around her, cannot consciously confront the possibility that her faithful family retainer is a murderess and that this one instance of violence may be a prelude to more violence. Here desire to cling to the crumbling traditions of the past and to her seemingly frail but destructive image of herself will not allow her to admit that her base of support (and thereby herself) has been rejected, or that Mr. Mann's death signals

her own. She needs to repress her new understanding of the potential violence in Blacks and of the specific violence done by a black
woman within her own home. She would deprive Mamie of the
potential power inherent in the violence by assigning Mr. Mann's
death to himself. She is as absurd as the passerby in the story who,
finding a black man dead along the road with a shotgun blast in his
stomach and his throat slashed, comments on how badly that nigger
must have wanted to commit suicide. If Mr. Mann had indeed
committed suicide (not been forced to by pressure from Blacks or his
own deterioration), perhaps he would be just one broken link in the
chain of power; if his death has more implications, they would
suggest that the entire chain could be broken. The maid's comment
that the razor death is reality if the Madame says so highlights the
madame's need for illusions. If Madame can convince herself that her
husband's death is trivial and does not suggest that the social founda-
tions she depends on are rotting, then she does not yet have to
confront her own fate. Her mental escape, however, does not lead to
a physical one. The maid may seem to ponder what to do about Mr.
Mann's body, but she knows what has happened and that reality
dictates that Madame must also die.

Even as the maid takes a "pump-action shot gun from the rifle
rack" and prepares to kill Madame, the white woman still clings to
her illusions about Blacks. She tells the gentleman: "Do you know
that even when I was just a little girl I never feared for Mamie was
there. She was like the mountains . . . unchanging. Like time . . .
limitless. Always faithful . . . always the source of inspiration. Young
. . . (Paternal.) . . . young man, you can be proud you sprang from her
loins. You can be thankful for having the very salt of the earth . . . the
very blood and marrow of the universe as . . . ." (p. 380), whereupon
Mamie shoots her in the head. Mamie recognizes the impossibility of
even gradual change on Madame's part, and that the only possible
rejection of her and what she represents is a violent one. If Mamie is
indeed like the mountains, faithful and a source of pride, those
virtues shall be used for the advancement of Blacks; too long have
they been in the service of whites.

The gentleman caller could be proud of the sacrifices the Mamies
of the black community have made for young Blacks, but he is too

eager to reap the materialistic benefits of aspiring to what Mr. Mann represents. Those benefits, represented by Mr. Mann's long white beard (which the gentleman grabs and stuffs in his pocket before he is able to help Mamie carry the bodies offstage), are what cause Blacks with middle-class aspirations to become separated from the masses of black Americans; they are the things which cause young black men like the gentleman caller to forget or ignore the whites' long oppression of Blacks in their efforts to grab a bit of the same power and prestige of which white Americans dream. The gentleman caller's stance is ahistorical and therefore acultural. When he picks up Mr. Mann's beard, which, as has been pointed out earlier by Madame, is false, Mamie warns him: "Boy, put down that ole piece of hair . . . it came from between mah granny's legs, anyway. Now I've taken enough of yo silly behind stuff . . . grab his feet like I said" (p. 380). Instead of seeing the falseness of the American Dream, the gentleman caller stuffs the beard into his pocket and clings to what it means to him. In an age of change, he refuses to change. In his refusal, he moves completely into the world of Madame and Mr. Mann, and he suffers their fate. Once he has helped her drag the white bodies offstage, Mamie kills the gentleman caller.

The black revolution of the 1960's had no place for "gentleman" callers, who, because they identified themselves as gentlemen, would not sever connections with the white world. Anyone who, though black in skin color, did not recognize his spiritual blackness, could, like any white, be sacrificed in the interests of unity and nationbuilding; the black revolutionary, Mamie, kills the "Negro" hanger-on, whose attitudes are, in fact, barely a step removed from the "coloured" attitudes of a couple of decades before. The gentleman caller still wants to be integrated into the house of white America, a house which is burning though neither he nor its white inhabitants have detected the flames. Incapable of realizing that he should have anything beyond that which Mr. Mann is willing to allow him, he is incapable of pressing for rights or of violently taking them. His "gentlemanly" silence emphasizes his lack of aggression, his waiting uncomplainingly for what others may consider his due. Only with his demise can the revolution and the play achieve their conclusion.

Offstage, where Mamie has deposited the bodies of Madame and

Mr. Mann and where she has executed the gentleman caller, her transformation is completed. Stage directions let the reader visualize the ultimate change.

> (. . . the lights turn to red and blues. New Black music plays . . . The Maid returns wearing an exotic gown of her own design. Her bandana has been taken off; her *au naturel* hair style complements her strong Black features. She answers the phone.)
>
> *Maid*: (Black and correct.) Hello. Yes, you wish to speak to the madame? Yes, she is speaking. (Pause.) Yes, father . . . the time is now. It is time for Black people to come together. It is time for Black people to rise from their knees and come together in unity, brotherhood and Black spirituality to form a nation that will rise from our enslaved mass and meet the oppressor . . . meet the devil and conquer and destroy him. (Slow curtain as the Queen Mother speaks into the phone passionately.) Yes, we are rising, father. We are forming the foretold Black nation that will survive, conquer and rule under your divine guidance. We Black people are preparing for the future. We are getting ready for the long war ahead of us. DEATH TO THE ENEMIES OF THE BLACK PEOPLE! All praises is due to the Blackman.
>
> Blackout (p. 380).

The ringing phone throughout the play may represent the insistent voice of black America seeking its rights. It cannot reach the Madame because she is not the ultimate source of power and oppression and because acquiescing Blacks like Mamie stand in the way, and the maid cannot respond to it as long as she is in the stereotyped role of the handkerchief-headed black domestic. Her physical change in appearance at the end of the play indicates her total spiritual change. She is now ready to advocate unity among Blacks, a unity which means recognizing the enemies of Blacks, especially when they come with black faces. One critic has called the maid's speech at the end of the play "stark and simplistic,"[11] which may be true, but it makes the thematic intent of the play obvious. The play is designed to contribute to the ongoing struggle of Blacks; the transformation of one black worker who may never have considered herself black is to encourage other such transformations among the audience viewing the play.

Mamie Lee King becomes the model of the revolutionary. If a person so close, so bound, to whites and their heritage of exploitation, suppression, and power can find the courage to resist that influence, then certainly those black people not so closely tied personally to whites but who still suffer the detrimental effects of being black in America can find similar courage. The stance Mamie Lee King has achieved at the end of the play is the culmination of a long process of extrication through which Blacks in general and black maids in particular must go in order to free themselves from the limitations which those outside their culture would place upon them.

NOTES

Preface

1. These are functional definitions for the literary works I treat in this study. Many researchers, however, refer to more specialized divisions among domestics. A large class of black women, especially in the late nineteenth and early twentieth centuries, were washerwomen, and doing laundry was their primary function; cooks stayed in the kitchen, cleaning women cleaned, and nursemaids or child-nurses took care of the children. As technological advances, such as the development of dryers, gas and electric stoves, commercial laundries and bakeries, and processed foods simplified tasks, it was easier to get one servant to perform all the household and childrearing chores. Although one work I treat identifies a nursemaid and another a laundress, I consider primarily those in which mistress/maid relationships take place within a one house–one servant framework.
2. Among the many domestics I interviewed, I found one who had worked for the same family for forty years. I interviewed Mrs. Sarah Brown in Tuscaloosa, Alabama on May 14, 1980.
3. Maids also appear in the following works by black writers: Lorraine Hansberry, *A Raisin in the Sun* (1959); Louis Peterson, *Take A Giant Step* (1953); Mari Evans, *I Am a Black Woman* (1970); Rudolph Fisher, *The Walls of Jericho* (1928); Lorenz Graham, *South Town* (1958); Langston Hughes, *The Ways of White Folks* (1934) and *Not without Laughter* (1930); John Oliver Killens, *The Cotillion* (1972); Jean Toomer, "Blood-Burning Moon" in *Cane* (1923); Paule Marshall, "Reena" (1966); Toni Morrison, *Tarbaby* (1981); Wallace Thurman, *The Blacker the Berry* (1929); and Margaret Walker, *Jubilee* (1966).

Chapter One

1. Alice Childress, *Like One of the Family . . . conversations from a domestic's life* (New York: Independence, 1956), pp. 36, 37. Further references to this source will be parenthesized in the text.

2. Permission granted by Maya Angelou for use of this quotation on the categories into which black women have been placed. Mary Helen Washington offers excellent comments on the stereotypes foisted upon black women in this country in her introduction to *Black-Eyed Susans: Classic Stories by and about Black Women* (New York: Anchor/Doubleday, 1975).

3. Robert Hemenway, *Zora Neale Hurston: A Literary Biography* (Urbana: University of Illinois Press, 1977), p. 325.

4. Alice Childress, letter to the author, Jan. 7, 1980. John A. Williams, in *This Is My Country Too* (New York: New American Library, 1965), pp. 75 and 115, recalls his mother working as a maid as well as his own experiences as a butler in a suburb of Los Angeles. Toni Morrison is another writer who had direct personal experiences with domestic work. As a teenager, she worked for a white family after school. See "Toni Morrison's Black Magic," by Jean Strouse, in *Newsweek*, March 30, 1981, p. 54.

5. Alice Walker, *Meridian* (New York: Harcourt, Brace, Jovanovich, 1976), pp. 107–110.

6. David Katzman, *Seven Days a Week: Women and Domestic Service in Industrializing America* (New York: Oxford University Press, 1978), pp. 6–7, 212.

7. Toni Morrison, *Song of Solomon* (1977; rpt. New York: Signet, 1978), p. 189. Further references to this source will be parenthesized in the text.

8. See Katzman, *Seven Days a Week*, especially Chapters I and II.

9. Elizabeth McTaggart Almquist, *Minorities, Gender, and Work* (Lexington, Mass.: D. C. Heath, 1979), p. 47.

10. Almquist, *Minorities, Gender, and Work*, pp. 47–48.

11. On Southern practice see, for example, Elizabeth Ross Haynes, "Negroes in Domestic Service in the United States," *Journal of Negro History* 8 (Oct. 1923): 413, and Katzman, who comments on the food basket "service pans" in *Seven Days a Week*, pp. 197–198. On the extension of the practice, see Carter G. Woodson, "The Negro Washerwoman, a Vanishing Figure," *Journal of Negro History* 15 (July 1930): 269–277.

12. Ray Marshall, *The Negro Worker* (New York: Random House, 1967), pp. 8–9.

13. Almquist, *Minorities, Gender, and Work*, p. 54.

14. See Katzman, *Seven Days a Week*, especially Chapters I, II, and III.

15. Gerda Lerner, ed. *Black Women in White America: A Documentary History* (New York: Pantheon, 1972), pp. 231–232. Katzman discusses

other union and strike activity in the chapter of *Seven Days a Week* entitled "White Mistress and Black Servant," pp. 184–222.

16. Interviews were taped over a two week period in May, 1980, with women who were working or had worked as domestics.

17. Ella Baker and Marvel Cooke, "The Bronx Slave Market," *Crisis* 42 (Nov. 1935): 330.

18. Katzman, *Seven Days a Week*, p. 188.

19. Characteristics of THE MAID that I outline in this paragraph and in the remainder of this chapter are derived from my analyses of the literary works under consideration and concurring historical data. All domestics may not conform to the patterns: but uniforms, physical and psychological space, forms of compromise, stereotypes, and contradictions between how maids and mistresses act and what they think are the forces which shape the responses of the literary characters I have studied to the environments in which they work as domestics.

20. Uniforms are disappearing with the decrease in the number of women in domestic service. According to Almquist, although black women were only 11 percent of total female work force in 1970, they represented half the private household workers. That percentage had been 36.2 in 1930 and 55.2 in 1950. U.S. Bureau of the Census Statistics.

21. Studs Terkel, *Working: People Talk about What They Do All Day and How They Feel about What They Do* (New York: Pantheon/Random House, 1972), pp. 116–117.

22. Marian Minus, "Girl, Colored," *Crisis* 47 (Sept. 1940): 284.

23. Terkel, *Working*, p. 115.

24. The show appeared on NBC on four nights in 1979 (Jan. 29, Feb. 5, Feb. 12, and Feb. 19). The scene I have described appears in the screen play, but not in the book. Lillian Rogers Parks tells of her mother Maggie's adventures in the White House in *My Thirty Years Backstairs at the White House* (New York: Fleet, 1961). Blaine Edward McKinley provides a revealing study of the nineteenth-century psychology of kitchen architecture as it expressed maid/mistress relationships in *"The Stranger in the Gates": Employer Reactions toward Domestic Servants in America, 1825–1875* (Ann Arbor: University Microfilms, 1974), pp. 241–249.

25. Maggie Holmes lamented about the "milk" and "pound of butter" that her grandmother used to receive instead of money—Terkel, *Working*, p. 113. Many of the women with whom I talked recounted being given food, clothing, and used appliances in addition to or instead of money.

26. Terkel, *Working*, p. 117. One woman I interviewed recalled that she had been indirectly accused of taking a watch. Almost all of the women interviewed had been specifically tested for honesty with money. Mrs.

Mary Dotson, who had been accused of taking the watch, said the testing pattern was so common that, during her thirty years of working as a maid, she got into the habit of asking the white women: "Why you leave this where I got to clean? I don't want your money. My momma taught me not to steal" (Interview, Tuscaloosa, Ala., May 15, 1980). A maid in literature made similarly vivid comments about being tested; the story is related by her daughter: "They planted silver dollars and quarters around the floors, Moma said, to see if she would steal them. One woman planted so many quarters around the floors that Moma left a note describing the places where the quarters lay and said she hadn't dared to move them and that since she couldn't move them, she wasn't able to clean sufficiently." Audrey Lee, "Moma," *Negro Digest* 18 (Feb. 1969): 56. See also Verta Mae Grosnover, *Thursdays and Every Other Sunday Off: A Domestic Rap by Verta Mae* (New York: Doubleday, 1972), pp. 35–36.

27. Terkel, *Working*, p. 116.

Chapter Two

1. David Katzman notes mistresses' responses to "new issue" Blacks in *Seven Days a Week: Women and Domestic Service in Industrializing America* (New York: Oxford University Press, 1978), pp. 192–193.

2. See Toni Morrison, *The Bluest Eye* (1970; rpt. New York: Pocket Books, 1972).

3. Richard Wright, "The Man Who Went to Chicago," in *Eight Men* (New York: Pyramid, 1961), pp. 175–177.

4. Richard Wright, *Native Son* (1940, rpt. New York: Harper and Row, 1966), p. 74. Further references to this source will be parenthesized in the text.

5. Ralph Ellison, *Shadow and Act* (New York: Signet, 1966), p. 173.

6. James Baldwin, "Come Out the Wilderness," in *Going to Meet the Man* (New York: Dell, 1966), pp. 170–197. Claude Brown, *Manchild in the Promised Land* (New York: Signet, 1965), pp. 279–294. Rudolph Fisher, "The City of Refuge," in *Black Writers of America: A Comprehensive Anthology*, ed. Richard Barksdale and Keneth Kinnamon (New York: Macmillan, 1972), pp. 591–598.

7. The story appears on an album by John Kasandra entitled *Color Me Human* (Respect Records, a Division of Stax Records, c. 1969). The tale is related by Ole Mose, a black wise man created by Kasandra. Played on black radio stations in the late 1960's and early 1970's, and again in the spring of 1981, the album was designed to encourage Blacks to recognize

and appreciate their blackness and take the initiative for improving their own conditions. They were especially encouraged to overcome the stumbling block of fear, which, in the description offered by Ole Mose, greatly resembles the characteristic I have described as southernness. I obtained the album from D. L. Holliday of Station WDUR in Durham, N.C., in May 1981.

8. For information on human and animal tricksters in the Afro-American folk tradition, see Lawrence W. Levine, *Black Culture and Black Consciousness: Afro-American Folk Thought from Slavery to Freedom* (New York: Oxford University Press, 1977). Roger D. Abrahams talks about tricksters and badman heroes in black folklore in "Some Varieties of Heroes in America," *Journal of the Folklore Institute* 3 (Dec. 1966): 341–362. For information specifically on Brer Rabbit and his amoral, violent tendencies, see Roger D. Abrahams, "Trickster: the Outrageous Hero" in *Our Living Traditions: An Introduction to American Folklore*, ed. Tristram Potter Coffin (New York: Basic Books, 1968), pp. 170–178. Any of a number of collections of Afro-American folklore will provide tales of the adventures of the slave John. Two good ones are Richard M. Dorson's *American Negro Folktales* (Greenwich, Conn.: Fawcett, 1967) and Zora Neale Hurston's *Mules and Men* (1935; rpt. Bloomington: Indiana University Press, 1978). These sources are also relevant for understanding the tricking activities carried out by Ellie and Vi in Douglas Ward's *Happy Ending* discussed in Chapter VII.

9. Verta Mae Grosnover, *Thursdays and Every Other Sunday Off: A Domestic Rap by Verta Mae* (New York: Doubleday, 1972), p. 40.

10. Interview, Tuscaloosa, Ala., May 14, 1980. "Mrs. Brown's" name has been changed to protect her privacy.

11. Interview, Tuscaloosa, Ala., May 15, 1980. "Mrs. Burton" is also a pseudonym.

12. See "Rabbit and Fox Go Fishing" and "Mr. Rabbit and Mr. Frog Make Mr. Fox and Mr. Bear Their Riding-Horses" in Dorson's *American Negro Folktales*, pp. 91–92 and 87–89 respectively, and "Why Br' Gator's Hide Is So Horny" and "Tar Baby" in Langston Hughes's and Arna Bontemps's *The Book of Negro Folklore* (New York: Dodd, Mead, 1958), pp. 23–30 and 1–2 respectively.

13. See Roger D. Abrahams, *Deep Down in the Jungle: Negro Narrative Folklore from the Streets of Philadelphia* (Chicago: Aldine, 1970), pp. 72–73.

14. For a discussion of Staggolee and the badman heroic tradition into which he fits, plus several toasts which recount his violent exploits, see Abrahams's *Deep Down in the Jungle*.

Chapter Three

1. Jessie W. Parkhurst, "The Role of the Black Mammy in the Plantation Household," *Journal of Negro History* 23 (July 1938): 351, 356, 357. For a discussion primarily of the literary mammy, see the chapter entitled "Dishwater Images" in Jeanne Noble's *Beautiful, Also, Are the Souls of My Black Sisters: A History of the Black Woman in America* (Englewood Cliffs, N.J.: Prentice-Hall, 1978).
2. Parkhurst, "The Role of the Black Mammy," pp. 352–353.
3. The following articles illustrate the kinds of treatment Mammy Jane has received: John M. Reilly, "The Dilemma in Chesnutt's *The Marrow of Tradition*," *Phylon* 32 (Spring 1971): 31–38, and John Wideman, "Charles Waddell Chesnutt: *The Marrow of Tradition*," *American Scholar* 42 (Winter 1972–73): 128–134.
4. William L. Andrews, *The Literary Career of Charles W. Chesnutt* (Baton Rouge: Louisiana State University Press, 1980), p. 201.
5. Andrews, *The Literary Career of Charles W. Chesnutt*, pp. 179, 202.
6. Charles Waddell Chesnutt, *The Marrow of Tradition* (Ann Arbor: University of Michigan Press, 1969), p. 43. Further references to this source will be parenthesized in the text.
7. For superstitions about the evil eye and moles in the neck area, see *The Frank C. Brown Collection of North Carolina Folklore*, Vols. 6 and 7, ed. Newman Ivey White (Durham: Duke University Press, 1961 and 1964), Numbers 5401ff. and 3705. Parkhurst also comments on how black mammies raised their white charges in the superstitions common to black folk culture, "The Role of the Black Mammy," pp. 361–362.
8. Andrews emphasizes that Chesnutt intended the young nurse as a foil to Mammy Jane, to show progress as opposed to stasis. *The Literary Career of Charles W. Chesnutt*, p. 191; see also pp. 197–198, on Mammy Jane's failure to evolve.
9. Andrews discusses the evaluation of tradition and white supremacy which underlies Chesnutt's view of superiority and subservience in the novel on pp. 181–182 of *The Literary Career of Charles W. Chesnutt*.
10. Kristin Hunter, *God Bless the Child* (1964; rpt. New York: Bantam, 1967), pp. 18–19. Further references to this source will be parenthesized in the text.
11. "The 'Black Mammy' taught the children the proper forms of etiquette, of deportment to all of the people of the plantation, the proper forms of address and the proper distances to maintain. . . . In the Old South where much was made of chivalry and where great emphasis was placed upon form, manners in the life of the child meant much. The "Black Mammy' knew just what these manners were—when to speak and when

nót to speak; what was best to say on the proper occasion and what was not; the proper deportment of boy and girl, of young men and young women. . . . A Southerner of the upper class delighted in saying that he was taught his manners by his 'Black Mammy'." Parkhurst, "The Role of the Black Mammy," pp. 362–363.

12. Toni Morrison, *The Bluest Eye* (1970; rpt. New York: Pocket Books, 1972), p. 88. Further references to this source will be parenthesized in the text.

13. Barbara Christian, *Black Women Novelists: The Development of a Tradition, 1892–1976* (Westport, Conn.: Greenwood, 1980), p. 144.

14. Richard Wright, *Black Boy* (New York: Harper and Row, 1966), p. 26.

15. Christian, *Black Women Novelists*, pp. 138–153, and Jacqueline de Weever, "The Inverted World of Toni Morrison's *The Bluest Eye* and *Sula*," *College Language Association Journal* 22 (June 1979): 402–414.

16. Gwendolyn Brooks, *Family Pictures* (Detroit, Michigan: Broadside Press, 1970), p. 9.

Chapter Four

1. David Katzman points out that sexual exploitation of black servants at the hands of white masters was one of the "major abuses" in the South. *Seven Days a Week: Women and Domestic Service in Industrializing America* (New York: Oxford University Press, 1978), especially pp. 216–217. Mothers could offer no protection to their young daughters who went to work for whites, and husbands could be arrested and fined if they dared complain that their wives had been sexually harassed in their domestic work. See also pp. 26–27 in *Seven Days a Week*.

2. Richard Wright, "Man of All Work," in *Eight Men* (New York: Pyramid, 1969), p. 118. Further references to this source will be parenthesized in the text.

3. Grace Halsell, *Soul Sister* (New York: World, 1969), pp. 148–149. Further references to this source will be parenthesized in the text.

4. It is perhaps surprising that Fairchild does not mention that Carl has been alone with the six-year-old Lily all morning.

5. Ella Baker and Marvel Cooke, "The Bronx Slave Market," *Crisis* 42 (Nov. 1935): 330.

6. Robert Hamburger, "A Stranger in the House," *Southern Exposure* 5, (Winter-Spring, 1977): 26–27.

7. Salaries for black domestics around 1950 were closer to five or ten dollars a week; Wright's story was written in the late 1950's.

Chapter Five

1. Ann Petry, *The Street* (1946; rpt. New York: Pyramid, 1961), pp. 108, 110. Further references to this source will be parenthesized in the text.
2. William Melvin Kelley, *dem* (1964; rpt. New York: Collier-Macmillan, 1969), p. 36. Further references to this source will be parenthesized in the text.
3. The belief is one that I heard frequently asserted when I was growing up, but I have not yet found it collected in folklore texts.
4. See "Going to Meet the Man" (1965), *Another Country*, (1962) and *If Beale Street Could Talk* (1974).
5. The joke played on Mitchell rests in part on his being unaware of a common pattern of nicknaming among Blacks. Cooley is named for Calvin Coolidge; Mitchell is unable to make the connection when he meets Calvin and for a long time thereafter. I discuss the effect of his lack of this insider/outsider knowledge upon Mitchell in "'Have You Got the Dog?': Ritual Language of Cultural Recognition in *Invisible Man* and *dem*," scheduled for publication in *Black American Literature Forum*.

Chapter Six

1. Childress's creation of Mildred and her decision to publish serially may have been influenced by Langston Hughes's Jesse B. Simple stories and the fact that they were first so published. Her play, *Just a Little Simple*, is based on Hughes's *Simple Speaks His Mind*.
2. Alice Childress, to the author, letter Jan. 7, 1980.
3. In one conversation, Mildred expresses her desire to be a poet and it is clear from her imaginative presentation of materials that she could become one. For a discussion of this, see Trudier Harris, "'I wish I was a poet': The Character as Artist in Alice Childress' *Like One of the Family*," *Black American Literature Forum*, 14 (Spring 1980): 24–30.
4. Mildred refers to her employers by letters only. Such a device, comparable to that of "changing names to protect privacy," heightens the verisimilitude of the conversations.
5. Alice Childress, *Like One of the Family . . . conversations from a domestic's life* (New York: Independence, 1956), p. 1. Further references to this source will be parenthesized in the text.
6. Carrie Johnson has a similar interview with a prospective employer in Marian Minus's "Girl, Colored," *Crisis* 47 (Sept. 1940): 297. For what can happen beyond the interview, consider the case of Min in Ann Petry's *The Street*: "During the years she had spent doing part-time domestic work she had never raised any objections to the actions of cruelly indifferent employers. She had permitted herself to be saddled

with whole family washes when the agency that had sent her on the job had specified just 'personal pieces.' When the madam added sheets, towels, pillowcases, shirts, bedspreads, curtains—she simply allowed herself to be buried under the great mounds of dirty clothes and it took days to work her way out from under them, getting no extra pay for the extra time involved" (p. 82).

7. The title here brings to mind the tradition that Verta Mae emphasizes in *Thursdays and Every Other Sunday Off*. Live-in domestics in the North found that to be the standard pattern of their existence—Thursdays and every other Sunday off. It was necessary to plan whatever social life one had accordingly.

8. Mildred relates her experience in the language of religious conversion, with which most of her reading audience would have been familiar. Such language would have validated Mildred's experience and intensified the power of it for her audience.

9. Interview, Tuscaloosa, Ala., May 15, 1980. All the names here have been changed.

10. One woman I interviewed, Mrs. Sarah Brown, quit the same job twice— the second time after a particularly frustrating day of being cursed at—her return having been perhaps a testament to how much she needed a job. If the woman had actually tried to touch her, Mrs. Brown said, "I'd a knocked her out." In a short story by Jessie Fauset, published in *Crisis* in 1919, a maid tells a story of another maid who "went after Old Mis' with a knife one day," but that tale is not the one developed in the story. *Crisis* 19 (Dec. 1919): 51–56. See also Robert Hamburger, *A Stranger in the House* (New York: Macmillan, 1978), pp. 58, 60–61.

11. Mrs. Brown stated that the husband of the cursing woman apologized to her. In Audrey Lee's "Moma," a white woman apologizes for cursing Moma out. *Negro Digest* 18 (Feb. 1969): 57.

Chapter Seven

1. John A. Williams's *Sissie* (1963; rpt. Chatham, N.J.: The Chatham Bookseller, 1975) also considers the detrimental effects upon her children of the black woman's work as a maid. Compare Wendell's reminiscences in "Son in the Afternoon," in *The Best Short Stories by Negro Writers*, ed. Langston Hughes (Boston: Little, Brown, 1967), p. 291, to Ralph's in *Sissie*, pp. 245–246: similar reactions are recorded in almost exactly the same language. I chose to focus on Williams's short story, the earlier work, rather than on *Sissie*, because it takes place in the home of the white employer: *Sissie* is less the story of the maid's situation there than it is the reflections of her children about their mother as the strong

matriarchal figure who has warped their lives in many areas. Further references to "Son in the Afternoon" will be parenthesized in the text.

2. The story appeared in 1962 in *The Angry Black* (New York: Lancer). Peter Freese asserts, however, that internal evidence suggests the story takes place in the mid-fifties: "John A. Williams, 'Son in the Afternoon' (1962)," in *The Black American Short Story in the Twentieth Century: A Collection of Critical Essays*, ed. Peter Bruck (Amsterdam: B. R. Grüner, 1977), pp. 146, 154.

3. Freese, "John A. Williams, 'Son in the Afternoon,'" p. 147.

4. Douglas Turner Ward, *Happy Ending and Day of Absence* (New York: Third Press, 1966), pp. 13–14. Further references to this source will be parenthesized in the text.

5. Verta Mae Grosnover defines the servant in this way: "A servant is help, and help is sometimes the maid, who often is the waitress, baby sitter, answering service, cook, chauffeur, psychiatrist, and laundress." *Thursdays and Every Other Sunday Off: A Domestic Rap by Verta Mae* (New York: Doubleday, 1972), p. 146.

6. See a version of the tale in Daryl Dance, *Shuckin' and Jivin': Folklore from Contemporary Black Americans* (Bloomington: Indiana University Press, 1978), pp. 88–89.

7. *Contemporary Black Drama*, ed. Clinton F. Oliver and Stephanie Sills (New York: Scribner's, 1971), p. 321.

8. See Roger Abrahams, *Deep Down in the Jungle: Negro Narrative Folklore from the Streets of Philadelphia* (Chicago: Aldine, 1970) pp. 72–73.

Chapter Eight

1. Barbara Woods, "The Final Supper," in *Ten Times Black: Stories from the Black Experience*, ed. Julian Mayfield (New York: Bantam, 1972), pp. 104–105. Further references to this source will be parenthesized in the text.

2. Particularly in times of unrest, house servants could be suspected of attempting to poison their masters. For representative accounts, see Philip S. Foner, *History of Black Americans: From Africa to the Emergence of the Cotton Kingdom* (Westport, Conn.: Greenwood, 1975), pp. 151, 266–267, 536.

3. Compare the reality of Van Evrie's conquest to the ludicrous fantasies of Mitchell Pierce in *dem*. Van Evrie knows that it is within his power to claim the body of the black woman who works for him, so he does so. His actions are forthright and decisive. By contrast, Mitchell wavers and hesitates, further illustrating that he is not a part of the tradition of conquering white men that he wishes himself to be.

4. Inconsistencies between Christian theory and Christians' practice during slavery have been well documented. A particularly vivid and humorous fictional example can be found in William Wells Brown's *Clotel; or, the President's Daughter* (New York: Collier-Macmillan, 1969), pp. 103–105.

5. Ted Shine, *Contribution*, in *Black Drama: An Anthology*, ed. William Brasmer and Dominick Consolo (Columbus, Ohio: Charles E. Merrill, 1970), p. 375. Further references to this source will be parenthesized in the text.

6. Alice Walker, *In Love and Trouble: Stories of Black Women* (New York: Harcourt, Brace, Jovanovich, 1973), pp. 60–80.

7. Two women in Margaret Walker's *Jubilee* (Boston: Houghton Mifflin, 1966), pp. 67, 98–104, are hanged because they are suspected of having poisoned their master's food.

8. Shine delights in such name play: his Katy works for a Mrs. Comfort.

9. Ed Bullins, *The Gentleman Caller*, in *Contemporary Black Drama*, ed. Clinton F. Oliver and Stephanie Sills (New York: Scribner's, 1971), p. 371. Further references to this source will be parenthesized in the text.

10. Donald Bogle, *Toms, Coons, Mulattoes, Mammies, and Bucks: An Interpretative History of Blacks in American Films* (New York: Viking, 1973), p. 40.

11. Oliver and Sills, *Contemporary Black Drama*, p. 369.

SELECTED BIBLIOGRAPHY

Abrahams, Roger D. *Deep Down in the Jungle: Negro Narrative Folklore from the Streets of Philadelphia.* Chicago: Aldine, 1970.
——————. "Some Varieties of Heroes in America." *Journal of the Folklore Institute* 3 (Dec. 1966): 341–362.
Almquist, Elizabeth McTaggart. *Minorities, Gender, and Work.* Lexington, Mass.: D. C. Heath, 1979.
Andrews, William L. *The Literary Career of Charles W. Chesnutt.* Baton Rouge: Louisiana State University Press, 1980.
Angelou, Maya. *I Know Why the Caged Bird Sings.* New York: Bantam, 1970.
Baker, Ella, and Cooke, Marvel. "The Bronx Slave Market." *Crisis* 42 (Nov. 1935): 330–331, 340.
Bakerman, Jane. "The Seams Can't Show: An Interview with Toni Morrison." *Black American Literature Forum* 12 (Summer 1978): 56–60.
Baldwin, James. *Going to Meet the Man.* New York: Dell, 1966.
Barksdale, Richard, and Kinnamon, Keneth, eds. *Black Writers of America: A Comprehensive Anthology.* New York: Macmillan, 1972.
Bell, Roseann P., Parker, Bettye J., and Guy-Sheftall, Beverly. *Sturdy Black Bridges: Visions of Black Women in Literature.* New York: Doubleday, 1979.
Bethel, Elizabeth Rauh. "From Vanguard to Backwater: The Nineteenth Century Origins of Contemporary Negro Women's Domestic Service." Paper read at the annual meeting of the Southern Sociological Society, April 2–4, 1981, in Louisville, Ky.
Bischoff, Joan. "The Novels of Toni Morrison: Studies in Thwarted Sensitivity." *Studies in Black Literature* 6 (Fall 1975): 21–23.
Bogle, Donald. *Toms, Coons, Mulattoes, Mammies, and Bucks: An Interpretative History of Blacks in American Films.* New York: Viking, 1973.
Brooks, Gwendolyn. *Family Pictures.* Detroit, Michigan: Broadside, 1970.
Brown, Claude. *Manchild in the Promised Land.* New York: Signet, 1965.
Brown, William Wells. *Clotel; or, the President's Daughter.* 1853; rpt. New York: Collier-Macmillan, 1969.

Chesnutt, Charles Waddell. *The Marrow of Tradition*. 1901; rpt. Ann Arbor: University of Michigan Press, 1970.

Childress, Alice. *Like One of the Family . . . conversations from a domestic's life*. New York: Independence, 1956.

Christian, Barbara. *Black Women Novelists: The Development of a Tradition, 1892–1976*. Westport, Conn.: Greenwood, 1980.

Coffin, Tristram Potter, ed. *Our Living Traditions: An Introduction to American Folklore*. New York: Basic Books, 1968.

Coles, Robert, and Coles, Jane Hallowell. *Women of Crisis: Lives of Struggle and Hope*. New York: Delacorte Press/Seymour Lawrence, 1978.

Dance, Daryl. *Shuckin' and Jivin': Folklore from Contemporary Black Americans*. Bloomington: Indiana University Press, 1978.

de Weever, Jacqueline. "The Inverted World of Toni Morrison's *The Bluest Eye* and *Sula*." *College Language Association Journal* 22 (June 1979): 402–414.

Dollard, John. *Caste and Class in a Southern Town*. 1937; rpt. New York: Doubleday, 1957.

Dorson, Richard M. *American Negro Folktales*. Greenwich, Conn.: Fawcett, 1967.

DuBois, W. E. B. *The Philadelphia Negro: A Social Study, Together with a Special Report on Domestic Service by Isabel Eaton*. 1899; rpt. New York: Benjamin Blom, 1967.

Ellison, Ralph. *Invisible Man*. New York: Vintage, 1972.

—————. *Shadow and Act*. New York: Signet, 1966.

Evans, Mari. *I Am a Black Woman*. New York: William Morrow, 1970.

Fauset, Jessie. "Mary Elizabeth." *Crisis* 19 (Dec. 1919): 51–56.

Foner, Philip S. *History of Black Americans: From Africa to the Emergence of the Cotton Kingdom*. Westport, Conn.: Greenwood, 1975.

Freese, Peter. "John A. Williams: 'Son in the Afternoon' (1962)." In *The Black American Short Story in the Twentieth Century: A Collection of Critical Essays*, ed. Peter Bruck. Amsterdam: Grüner, 1977, pp. 141–155.

Gayle, Addison. *The Way of the New World: The Black Novel in America*. New York: Doubleday, 1976.

Graham, Lorenz. *South Town*. 1958; rpt. New York: Signet, 1966.

Grosnover, Verta Mae. *Thursdays and Every Other Sunday Off: A Domestic Rap by Verta Mae*. New York: Doubleday, 1972.

Halsell, Grace. *Soul Sister*. New York: World, 1969.

Hamburger, Robert. "A Stranger in the House." *Southern Exposure* 5 (Winter-Spring 1977): 22–31.

—————. *A Stranger in the House*. New York: Macmillan, 1978.

Harris, Trudier. "'I wish I was a poet': The Character as Artist in Alice

Childress' *Like One of the Family.*" *Black American Literature Forum* 14 (Spring 1980): 24–30.

Haynes, Elizabeth Ross. "Negroes in Domestic Service in the United States." *Journal of Negro History* 8 (Oct. 1923): 384–442.

Hemenway, Robert. *Zora Neale Hurston: A Literary Biography.* Urbana: University of Illinois Press, 1977.

Hughes, Langston. *The Ways of White Folks.* 1933; rpt. New York: Vintage, 1971.

——————. *Not without Laughter.* New York: Knopf, 1930.

—————— and Bontemps, Arna. *The Book of Negro Folklore.* New York: Dodd, Mead, 1958.

Hunter, Kristin. *God Bless the Child.* 1964; rpt. New York: Bantam, 1967.

Hurston, Zora Neale. *Mules and Men.* 1935; rpt. Bloomington: Indiana University Press, 1978.

Ivy, James W. "Ann Petry Talks About First Novel." *Crisis* 53 (Feb. 1948): 48–49.

——————. "Mrs. Petry's Harlem." *Crisis* 53 (May 1946): 154–155.

Katzman, David. *Seven Days a Week: Women and Domestic Service in Industrializing America.* New York: Oxford University Press, 1978.

Kelley, William Melvin. *dem.* 1964; rpt. New York: Collier-Macmillan, 1969.

Klotman, Phyllis R. "Dick-and-Jane and the Shirley Temple Sensibility in *The Bluest Eye.*" *Black American Literature Forum* 13 (Winter 1979): 123–125.

Ladner, Joyce A. *Tomorrow's Tomorrow: The Black Woman.* New York: Doubleday, 1971.

Lattin, Vernon E. "Ann Petry and the American Dream." *Black American Literature Forum* 12 (Summer 1978): 69–72.

Lee, Audrey. "Moma." *Negro Digest* 18 (Feb. 1969): 53–65.

Lerner, Gerda, ed. *Black Women in White America: A Documentary History.* New York: Pantheon, 1972.

Levine, Lawrence W. *Black Culture and Black Consciousness: Afro-American Folk Thought from Slavery to Freedom.* New York: Oxford University Press, 1977.

Marshall, Paule. "Reena." In Mary Helen Washington, ed. *Black-Eyed Susans: Classic Stories by and about Black Women.* New York: Anchor/Doubleday, 1975.

Marshall, Ray, *The Negro Worker.* New York: Random House, 1967.

McKinley, Blaine Edward. *"The Stranger in the Gates": Employer Reactions toward Domestic Servants in America, 1825–1875.* Ann Arbor: University Microfilms, 1974.

Minus, Marian. "Girl, Colored." *Crisis* 47 (Sept. 1940): 284, 297, 301.

Morrison, Toni. *Song of Solomon*. 1977; rpt. New York: Signet, 1978.
──────. *Tarbaby*. New York: Knopf, 1981.
──────. *The Bluest Eye*. 1970; rpt. New York: Pocket Books, 1972.
Noble, Jeanne. *Beautiful, Also, Are the Souls of My Black Sisters*. Englewood Cliffs, N.J.: Prentice-Hall, 1978.
O'Brien, John, ed. *Interviews with Black Writers*. New York: Liveright, 1973.
Ogunyemi, Chikwenye Okonjo. "Order and Disorder in Toni Morrison's *The Bluest Eye*." *Critique: Studies in Modern Fiction* 19 (1977): 112–120.
Oliver, Clinton F., and Sills, Stephanie, eds. *Contemporary Black Drama*. New York: Scribner's, 1971.
Ottley, Roi, and Weatherby, William J., eds. *The Negro in New York: An Informal Social History, 1626–1940*. New York: Praeger, 1969.
Parkhurst, Jessie W. "The Role of the Black Mammy in the Plantation Household." *Journal of Negro History* 23 (July 1938): 349–369.
Parks, Lillian Rogers. *My Thirty Years Backstairs at the White House*. New York: Fleet, 1961.
Petry, Ann. *The Street*. 1946; rpt. New York: Pyramid, 1961.
Reilly, John M. "The Dilemma in Chesnutt's *The Marrow of Tradition*." *Phylon* 32 (Spring 1971): 31–38.
Shine, Ted. *Contribution*. In *Black Drama: An Anthology*, ed. William Brasmer and Dominick Consolo. Columbus, Ohio: Charles E. Merrill, 1970.
Silberman, Charles E. *Criminal Violence, Criminal Justice*. New York: Random House, 1978.
Small, Robert C., Jr. "*South Town*: A Junior Novel of Prejudice." *Negro American Literature Forum* 4 (Winter 1970): 136–141.
Spaulding, Henry D. *Encyclopedia of Black Folklore and Humor*. Middle Village, N.Y.: Jonathan David, 1972.
Strouse, Jean. "Toni Morrison's Black Magic." *Newsweek*, March 30, 1981, pp. 52–57.
Terkel, Studs. *Working: People Talk about What They Do All Day and How They Feel about What They Do*. New York: Pantheon/Random House, 1972.
Walcott, Ronald. "The Early Fiction of John A. Williams." *College Language Association Journal* 16 (Dec. 1972): 198–213.
Walker, Alice. *Meridian*. New York: Harcourt, Brace, Jovanovich 1976.
──────. *In Love and Trouble: Stories of Black Women*. New York: Harcourt, Brace, Jovanovich, 1973.
Walker, Margaret. *Jubilee*. Boston: Houghton Mifflin, 1966.
Ward, Douglas Turner. *Happy Ending and Day of Absence*. New York: The Third Press, 1966.

White, Newman Ivey. *The Frank C. Brown Collection of North Carolina Folklore*, vols. 6 and 7. Durham: Duke University Press, 1961 and 1964.

Wideman, John. "Charles Waddell Chesnutt: *The Marrow of Tradition*." *American Scholar* 42 (Winter 1972–73): 128–134.

Williams, John A. "Son in the Afternoon." In *The Best Short Stories by Negro Writers*, ed. Langston Hughes. Boston: Little, Brown, 1967.

——————. *Sissie*. 1963; rpt. Chatham, N.J.: The Chatham Bookseller, 1975.

——————. *This is My Country Too*. New York: New American Library, 1965.

Woods, Barbara. "The Final Supper." In *Ten Times Black: Stories from the Black Experience*, ed. Julian Mayfield. New York: Bantam, 1972.

Woodson, Carter G. "The Negro Washerwoman, A Vanishing Figure." *Journal of Negro History* 15 (July 1930): 269–277.

Wright, Richard. *Black Boy*. New York: Harper and Row, 1966.

——————. *Eight Men*. New York: Pyramid, 1969.

——————. *Native Son*. New York: Harper and Row, 1966.

——————. *Uncle Tom's Children*. New York: Harper and Row, 1937.

Wright, Sarah E., Lincoln, Abbey, Childress, Alice, and Marshall, Paule. "The Negro Woman in American Literature." *Freedomways* 6 (Winter 1966): 8–25.

INDEX

Almquist, Elizabeth McTaggart, 8–9
American Dream, 17, 92, 113, 168, 177; pursuit of by maids, 17
Amorality, 31, 32; as trait in trickster maids, 34, 149
Andrews, William L., 37
Angelou, Maya, 4, 18

Backstairs at the White House, 15, 50; and "service pans," 18
Baldwin, James, 14, 28, 86, 96, 104
Baltimore Afro-American, 111, 112
Baraka, Amiri, 142
Big Boy: as character in "Big Boy Leaves Home" (Wright), 76
Bigger Thomas, 25, 26–28, 76; as character in *Native Son*, 25, 26; compared to maids, 26–28
Black Women in White America (Lerner), 10
"Blood-Burning Moon" (Toomer), 103
Bluest Eye, The (Morrison), 15, 17, 18, 25, 36, 59–69, 137; analysis of mammy character in, 59–69; plot and characters of, 59
Bogle, Donald, 174
Brer Rabbit, 24, 29, 116, 130, 143, 144, 149, 150, 153, 154, 164; behavior as model for maids, 33–34; characteristics of, 32; militancy of, 32. *See also* Tricksters
"Bronx Slave Market, The" (Baker and Cooke), 11, 84
Brooks, Gwendolyn, 68
Brown, Claude, 28
Bullins, Ed, 34, 125, 135, 154, 155, 156, 160, 168; *The Gentleman Caller*, 168–179

Carmichael, Stokeley, 129
Cast-aways, 112, 117, 172, 173. *See also* Hand-me-downs; "Service pans"

Ceremonies in Dark Old Men (Elder), 152
Chesnutt, Charles Waddell, 25, 36; *The Marrow of Tradition*, 36–45
Childress, Alice, 3, 5, 14, 19, 33, 111; *Like One of the Family*, 111–133
Christian, Barbara, 68
Christianity, 31, 67–68, 191 n.4; rejection of by maids, 148, 156, 159, 165
"City of Refuge, The" (Fisher), 28
"Come Out the Wilderness" (Baldwin), 28
Compromise, 24: forms of, 16–17, 62, 63; necessity for in white woman's house, 14. *See also* Role-playing; Mask-wearing
Contribution (Shine), 34, 154, 156; analysis of militant maid in, 160–168
Cultural identity, 25, 27, 113, 132; loss of, as form of compromise, 17, 23, 64, 67. *See also* Domestic workers; Racial identity
Custom: influence on maids in the South, 9, 20

dem (Kelley), 15, 31, 87, 100; analysis of maid in, 100–109; characters and plot of, 100
de Weever, Jacqueline, 68
Dick and Jane: story as model for maid's family, 59–60, 68
Domestic work: as only work available to black women, 5, 6, 8; by the day, 112; competition for, 11; development in the United States, 8–9; difficulty of finding in the North, 11; done by black writers, 5; how obtained, 11; live-in, 47, 88; transportation to, 14–15
Domestic workers: college education in relation to, 6–7; college girls as, 5; definition of, xi, 181 n.1, 183 n.19; influence of immigration upon, 8; im-

199